The Life and Times of
The Last Kid
Picked

REFERENCES

ABOUT THE AUTHOR

An award-winning lyricist, popular writer, and sought-after speaker, Claire Cloninger is one of the country's foremost Christian communicators. She is a five-time Gospel Music Association Dove Award winner whose Christian songs have been widely recorded by such artists as Amy Grant, Sandi Patti, Wayne Watson, and B. J. Thomas. She has written more than two dozen musicals for church choir including *My Utmost for His Highest, Experiencing God,* and *Welcome to Our World.*

Claire's inspirational books include *E-Mail from God for Teens, More E-Mail from God for Teens, A Place Called Simplicity, Simple Joys, When the Glass Slipper Doesn't Fit,* and *Postcards from Heaven.*

Claire holds a B. A. and an M. A. in Education from the University of Southwestern Louisiana in Lafayette, where she was named Outstanding Alumna in 1991. Her teaching skills are put to good use in her national ministry as an inspirational speaker and retreat leader.

Claire and her husband, Robert, an artist, reside in a log home on the banks of a river in Alabama. They are active members of Christ Anglican Church, where he is Chairman of the Evangelism Committee and she serves on the Parish Prayer Team. They are the parents of two grown sons and grandparents of two granddaughters and one grandson.

Additional copies of this book
and other titles in the *E-mail from God* series
are available from your local bookstore.

E-mail from God for Teens
More E-mail from God for Teens
E-mail from God for Men
E-mail from God for Kids
E-mail from God for Teens screensaver

RIVER
OAK
PUBLISHING

The Life and Times of
The Last Kid Picked

David Benjamin

 Random House New York

Grateful acknowledgment is made to Irving Music, Inc., for permission to reprint
an excerpt from "Ballad of Paladin," words and music by Johnny Western,
Richard Boone and Sam Rolfe. Copyright © Irving Music, Inc. (BMI).
International copyright secured. All rights reserved. Reprinted by permission of
Irving Music, Inc.

Library of Congress Cataloging-in-Publication Data is available.

Random House website address: www.atrandom.com

Printed in the United States of America on acid-free paper

9 8 7 6 5 4 3 2

FIRST EDITION

Book design by Joseph Rutt

FOR HOTLIPS

AUTHOR'S NOTE

Tomah is a real place.

The people in this story, like Koscal, Overacker, Feeney, Buster the dog and my (somewhat improved) sister, Peg, are real people. However, I've changed names and identities liberally, and most of the people with these aliases will have a hard time figuring out who they are in the story.

The events in this story really happened. However, I learned story-telling from my main grandfather, Papa, who understood that any story worth sharing usually turns out better if you don't spin it out exactly how it happened, or necessarily in the right order. Better to let it flow from your memory, backwards and forwards, at its own pace and by its own accord.

CONTENTS

A Perfect Day

Not counting barehand softball at recess, and backyard Wiffleball, my first formal baseball game (nine guys on a side, everybody using a mitt, no electrical tape on the ball) was at a father-and-son picnic for the St. Mary's School "servers" (the diocese's preferred term for altar boys). I stood out from the crowd because I was the kid without the father. In the Fifties, in Wisconsin, especially among Catholics, divorce was something that appeared mainly in movies condemned by the Legion of Decency and, occasionally, on *The Edge of Night*—a daytime drama that came on at 3:30 in the afternoon, causing my grandmother to turn off the stove, abandon her rugsweeper and unravel in front of the Motorola. There were, in fact, children of divorce in Tomah other than my brother and sister and me, but they were all Protestants. These included the Bleeker kids over on Jackson Street and the Pankows, who lived out by the Seven-Up bottling plant on Highway 12. All of us, otherwise indistinguishable in color and odor from nondivorced kids, were universally sighed over as unruly and ill-fated because our mothers—who worked (usually as cocktail waitresses)—had frequent conversation with a range of men that flouted the community's threshold of seemliness.

The best way to spot one of us broken-homers was to organize some parent-intensive event like a father-son picnic, where my fatherlessness made me stick out like a stork in the smorgasbord. Still, by late fifth grade, when the servers' game occurred, at a roadside park over in Sparta, I was pretty well adapted to my stigma. Dad's customary absence wasn't the thing that struck me as odd that day. But something was strange, and I couldn't put my finger on it. I don't guess I caught on 'til about thirty years later.

The game, because it involved all the St. Mary's servers, included every grade from fifth through eighth. This in itself was weird. Normally, kids didn't cross grade lines in sports. Fifth played with fifth, sixth with sixth and so forth. However, every summer, with school out, games got organized by neighborhood rather than by grade, and age guidelines were waived. The fathers-servers game was a similar exception. I was a little scared of the eighth graders, but this was normal. Since time immemorial, eighth graders have been one of nature's most terrifying phenomena. Dinosaurs, when they roamed the earth, steered clear of eighth graders.

It wasn't surprising, either, that I was the most incompetent player on the field that day. I lived in mortal terror of the dread "hardball." Right up to the day before the servers' picnic, I had never owned any baseball stuff. The news that the featured event of the servers' picnic would be a baseball game plunged me into an abyss of consternation, confusion, fear and diarrhea. Not only had I never played hardball, I was not equipped to do so.

I had no glove.

I spent a day begging my mother to buy me a glove; she spent the same day reminding me that we were broke, that she had about $8 to tide us over 'til the end of the month, and this was only the 10th. Subsequently, I prowled the stores downtown, Burris's Dime Store and the Ben Franklin, the Tomah Hardware, the Coast-to-Coast and S&H Hardware, hunting for a baseball glove that could possibly fit into a budget of no money at all. The best I could find was a sort of baseball mitt caricature—a webless, rigid oven mitt vaguely reminiscent of the glove I'd seen worn by Dan Dailey in a movie bio of Dizzy Dean and the 1934 Gashouse Gang. I found this artifact at

Steele's Rexall Drug Store, on a shelf with barrettes, notepads, clip-on sunglasses, rubber change purses, swimming goggles, plastic rain scarves and a dead spider. The price was 99 cents.

Less than a buck for a baseball glove! This was almost free. Up Superior Avenue at the Coast-to-Coast, Wilson gloves and MacGregors were going for almost $10. Of course, the gloves at the Coast-to-Coast actually folded in the middle. This one, after I'd managed to work my left hand inside it, displayed roughly the same flexibility as a plaster cast. I could make it bend slightly, but the effort required both hands, straining from both inside and outside. Using this mitt in an actual game would be like wandering the outfield with a dinner plate strapped to my hand.

Still, 99 cents!

I could oil it down, soak it overnight, soften it up, make it work. Sure.

The thing was, the money. Mom had made it clear; her well was dry. My personal treasury consisted of a nickel and two pennies, which left me no choice but to negotiate with Bill, my little brother, and my mean, stingy, anal-retentive sister, Peg. Peg saved money. At any given moment, she was richer than Mom. She had the dough, but that was the point, wasn't it? She had the dough because she never let go of it. Nobody knew where she kept it. If we'd known where she kept it, she wouldn't have had it. Bill and I were thieves.

First things first. I sold Bill a mummified horny toad I'd once bought as a pet at the dime store, but which died, probably of starvation, six months later because I had no idea what a horny toad eats. Bill didn't really want the dead horny toad, but he was small and stupid and I convinced him that it was a rare conversation piece that would make him the envy of the third grade.

Bill's contribution left me 83 cents short, with no resort but to grovel at Peg's feet.

"Eighty-three cents? God! What for?"

"A baseball glove. C'mon, Peg, please."

"What do you need a baseball glove for?"

"There's a game at the servers' picnic tomorrow."

"So, don't go."

"I gotta go."

"Why?"

"I'm a server."

"Barely. You haven't even memorized your Latin yet."

"Yes I have. *Kyrie eleison, kyrie eleison, kyrie—*"

"Yeah, right. Do the *Agnus Dei.*"

"I'm not up to that yet."

"Well, I don't have 83 cents."

"Yes, you do."

"No, I don't."

"Do, too."

"What if I did?"

"Well, I just wanna borrow it. I need a glove."

"Doesn't Papa have that old baseball glove in the garage? Can't you use that?"

"It's not a fielder's glove. That's a catcher's mitt."

"So? A baseball glove is a baseball glove. Be a catcher."

"I can't be a catcher."

"Why not?"

I paused. The obvious course here was to swallow my pride.

"Well, I can't catch."

Peg, a cold-blooded logician besides being anal, was always a step ahead of me.

"Well, if you can't catch a baseball, what do you need any kind of glove for?"

I paused again, groping for answers.

"If I don't have a glove, how'm I ever gonna learn?"

Peg leapt right ahead of me.

"The game is tomorrow, isn't it? How much you gonna learn overnight?"

As usual, grace and good intentions had no power over Peg. All I had left was begging.

"C'mon, Peg. Pleeeese."

"No."

Twelve "pleases," twelve "nos." Finally:

"What if . . ."

"What if what?"

"Awright, lend me the money, and I'll do the dishes for ya. All week."

"All week? No. Two months."

"Two *months*? That's forever!"

"Take it or leave it."

"Come on, Peg. Three weeks."

Once I had steered her into negotiations, I knew I had the money. We settled on five weeks' worth of Peg's dishes. Each of us three kids had dish duty two nights a week, leaving Sunday uncovered, a problem we never solved. Dirty dishes just piled up like driftwood on Sunday and left the Monday dishwasher with the Augean kitchen sink.

After buying the glove, however, it was worse than I thought. I tried several types of oil on it, plus a lot of Mom's Vaseline, and succeeded only in making it slimy. After soaking overnight, the glove was still stiffer than my horny toad—which Bill eventually coated with airplane glue and set on fire, magnificently. He was dumb, but blessed with a streak of morbid creativity.

On the bus ride to Sparta, I kept my oven mitt tucked beneath my shirt as the other servers, ignoring me, tossed a ball among the seats. Their gloves were supple shells of swarthy leather, webbed, knotted, deep-pocketed and embossed with immortal signatures . . . Johnny Logan, Eddie Mathews, Joe Adcock, Red Schoendienst. The other kids flicked a glove, and it swallowed a passing baseball like a hawk snuffing a sparrow. I sank into a deepening shame over my wretched Rexall glove. When we arrived, I trailed the ecstatic mob and stopped long enough to toss the glove under the bus. Except for Vaseline goo on my shirt, there was no sign I had ever owned a baseball glove.

I decided I didn't have to play that day. I could watch. I'd ask Dad for a real baseball glove for my next birthday. Dad wasn't much for showing up, but he always went ape on birthdays.

Unfortunately, I had not considered the Father Seubert factor. Father Seubert was the new assistant pastor. He was young, good-looking, vivacious and, above all (a shocking departure from his Dickensian predecessor, Father Rourke), infinitely compassionate. Noting my glovelessness, Father Seubert simply ordered Winchell, a kid from my grade on the opposing team, to lend me his glove. And out I went, into the Valley of Death—commonly known as right field.

My first chance with the borrowed glove went swimmingly. The batter hit a grounder past our second baseman. The ball rolled to me and nestled into my pocket. I took it out and threw it toward first base, behind the runner, who promptly took second. A few kids and several fathers shouted some sort of criticism but I had no idea what they were getting at. I was new to this.

Eventually, some balls came to me in the air. I held up my borrowed glove, waved at them as they went by, and then gave chase. I was a quick runner and an earnest thrower, so only one of these flyballs resulted in a home run. The others stopped at second or third. I was disappointed not to catch any balls, especially with Winchell's splendid glove. But I hadn't expected to catch any balls. It was just one of those things that you hope for. After each inning that I missed a flyball, Father Seubert patted my back and said, "Nice try."

I got to bat four times. These were my first efforts to hit a hardball, which I couldn't help thinking might unexpectedly veer off the pitcher's hand and smash into my face, inflicting brain damage so severe that I would end up at the Tomah V.A. Hospital in one of those rooms way up on the top floors with the bars over the windows, from which an occasional bloodcurdling scream would echo across the quadrangle. In anticipation of this youth-wrecking calamity, I winced and leaned backwards every time the ball bored in on home plate. Then I swung. Lending impressive weight to the blind squirrel theory, I managed one foul ball in my twelve swings.

Whiffing four times is a dispiriting experience, but one that I shared—I realized much later in life—with Rocky Colavito, Reggie Jackson, Dave Kingman, Mark McGwire. It happens to the greats as well as to the incompetents. Besides, I hadn't anticipated hitting a ball any more than I'd expected to catch one.

But there was something odd about this game, something unlike all the games in all the kid sports I had played in my whole life up until that day. As the game went on, as my fielding errors and strike-outs accumulated, I noticed that the chorus of derision that greeted my every effort grew louder and harsher. Coming from my peers, this was S.O.P. I was used to ridicule. Kids are mean. They go for the throat. Besides, it was only fair. I was the worst player on the field. I deserved to get yelled at.

But some of those voices were pretty deep.

After the last out, I was standing by the backstop. Kids were hanging around the field, some of them being jostled paternally by their dads. An adult peeled off from the group and shambled hugely toward me. There was seriousness in his stride. When he reached me, he bent down, blocking the sun with a face so large it came to me in VistaVision. He had that male smell that the men in town seemed to wear like a uniform—tobacco, sweat, Old Spice and Brylcreem.

He leaned close, breathing in my eyes. I had no idea whose father he was, probably Gunderson or Overacker, two of my numerous nemeses. He knew my name, though. He said it.

"Yeah?" I replied.

"You lost the game," he said.

He pointed at my nose.

"You."

He went on.

"You stunk."

Point taken. I kept quiet. This was his moment and I would have been rude to spoil it. Was he finished?

Not quite.

"They shouldn't've let you play."

As he walked away, a bounce of closure in his step, I had an unusual reaction. I was used to kids telling me I stunk. On the playground at St. Mary's, it was a veritable mantra, usually accompanied by a kick, or a whack upside my head, or a noogie. This dad person had delivered the standard verbal abuse and hadn't laid a finger on me. Yet there were tears welling in my eyes.

Typically, the game was forgotten in the next ten minutes, as several dads fired up barbecue grills and started slinging burgers. So, it wasn't 'til later that I finally sensed—without being able to express it—something different about that day, and about that dad with his finger in my face.

Kids and grownups, when I was a kid, went their separate ways. They lived together in close proximity, even shared the same rest rooms and ate at the same table—but we were segregated. Grownups were prone to drinking too much, to smoking like chimneys, even to lust and violence. They knew these flaws in their character and they knew they weren't healthy for kids. So they kept their distance. Grownups stuck to clear roles. Kids were bossed by moms, cuddled by grandparents, joshed by old folks, tolerated by store people, chased off the grass by the neighborhood grouch, lectured, goaded and measured by teachers, patronized by priests and more or less mystified by sexually mature adult males—whose moods, habits, milieu and language made us vaguely ambivalent about the prospect of growing up and becoming one of them.

In a small town, men who finished high school and didn't go away someplace else did a few things real fast—got laid, got a job, got married, had kids, joined the bowling league down at Vlasek's. Everything else slowed to a crawl. Money. Promotions. Opportunity. Hours. Days. Months. Life. Kids grew up in Tomah in the shadow of grown men who were largely underemployed, undereducated, unfulfilled, bored and vaguely aware that they were missing out on something fairly important. There was a touch of menace in these men, a tendency to explode unexpectedly. The prudent kid steered just clear enough to duck.

Kids knew our own deficiencies, too, and we were often reminded by parents. We were careless, sloppy, loud, irksome, quarrelsome, selfish and filthy. We whined. We pouted. We got underfoot. We got into things we shouldn't get into. We spilled stuff. We broke things, including ourselves. We interrupted important conversations.

On the whole, kids probably appreciated segregation more than grownups. As long as they left us alone, without offering deviant interpretations of their outbursts and excesses, we had a clear choice. We could be like them, or we could shoot for better.

While we observed, and ducked, our sole caveat was not to horn in on grownups' business—a convenient arrangement because we couldn't care less what they were about. We had our games. We formed our teams. We made rules as we went along. The perfect day, which could only occur in summer when teachers and clerics had no claim on us, was easily defined. Mom would push me out the door at eight in the morning and wouldn't look to see me again until fourteen hours later, when other mothers were leaning out the screen door calling their kids, and I needed a little real food, and my feet needed washing before putting me to bed. Sometime during the day, I might have cadged lunch from my grandmother Annie and I might have bought candy or pop or baseball cards from Mose or Betty at Woodruff's Store, but everyone else I saw all that perfect day was just another kid.

After I had succumbed to nature and grown up, I found myself often pausing by Little League fields. One day, in California, in an emerald youth baseball complex, complete with galvanized backstops, dugouts and bat racks and bleachers, sprinkler systems and even a batting cage, I counted twenty-two very small boys, perhaps eight years old, practicing baseball. I counted coaches, adult males just like those I'd grown up avoiding—smelling of Old Spice and white-lipped with some nameless frustration. There were ten coaches, all of whom would shout in chorus at each eight-year-old batter, hounding him with encouragement, insights, pointers, pressure. The other kids, unlike kids I'd grown up with, had no comment. They watched in silence—clearly grateful to be, for the moment, beyond scrutiny.

Watching this familiar ritual, I remembered the dad who came up to me after the father-son servers' game thirty years before and told me I stunk. I remembered the hurt he had inflicted, but I remembered something that—in a way—redeemed that son of a bitch. He had violated the segregation of kids and grownups to deliver an insult to a child, but then he had crossed back over the line, never to acknowledge me again. He had shown no interest in my improvement. He gave me no advice, offered me no consolation, volunteered no coaching. He muttered his piece, then tossed me back into the trial and error of bungling boyhood, to study hardball on my own and find a way, if possible, to make it fun even if I could never do it well—which is how things turned out.

All summer long, way back then, all I had to do for a perfect day was leave the house in the morning and find an idle kid. But for today's new improved kids, the only perfect day they could possibly conceive would be to go four-for-four with five RBI, no errors, two stolen bases and maybe a nice one-bounce assist at home plate. Otherwise, they fail.

Besides playing ball, when I was a kid, I read—including way too many of those Clair Bee/John R. Tunis sports epics. The books tended to be about some kid athlete of enormous talent, prodigious skill and unearthly humility succeeding spectacularly—often while bleeding—and bringing down upon himself the well-deserved adulation of his contemporaries and a legion of proud elders. My sports saga, on the other hand, was a story in which—although I never stopped playing and occasionally discerned some improvement in certain areas (mostly by dint of sheer repetition)—I was almost never notably successful. Nor did I ever seriously anticipate success. I went out and played every day because that's what kids did—go out and play. Success—applause, victory laps, league batting titles—didn't concern me because I was doing kid stuff. Grownups, who had more dignity then, ignored what I did most of the time unless it got me in trouble and—probably because grownups ignored it—I had fun.

I think this was the rule. Even the kids I played with who were exceptional athletes never eventually amounted to much—as athletes. They grew up and did something else and succeeded or failed regardless of how well they played baseball, or two-line soccer, or pom-pom pollaway when they were twelve.

Lately, I think it terribly important to remember clearly about sport the way it was—once—for almost every kid on earth, in games that were incompetent and playful, badly lit, ill-equipped, oft-delayed and experimental—with outcomes that were frequently disputed, often uncertain and instantly forgotten.

Well, yeah, it mattered who won, every game—but only until we chose up again and started over.

PART I

"Jesus Christ, kid! Go outside."

There was no "natural world" in Tomah, or anywhere nearby. Kids knew about nature, theoretically. But we tended to locate it elsewhere. For the literates among us, it resided at the Tomah Public Library, in yellow-backed issues of *National Geographic*. For the rest, nature's closest outpost was "Up North," a mythic realm whose frontier began well beyond the distance a kid could ride his bike on any given summer day. We knew nature wasn't local because it had animals we never saw in Tomah. Moose and wolves and grizzlies. Gila monsters and warthogs and duckbilled platypuses.

Kids looked around Tomah and we saw . . .

. . . Chicago.

We saw bars and stores and two-story bank buildings. We saw beer cans in the gutter and cats in the garbage. We saw asphalt, Florsheim shoes, TV antennas and stifling civilization.

The woods, swamps and fields that seduced us and then spit us out again at dusk—scratched, bitten, exhausted and fearful of the dark—these weren't nature. All this stuff was just "outside."

"Jesus Christ, kid!" someone would holler. "Go outside."

Forced outside, we worked outward gradually, checking the ballfields, trying out the playgrounds, the parks, the lake. Eventually, naturally, a kid would venture farther and farther, into bogs and cloverfields, up trees, over hills, down holes and into culverts, into the unknown.

Nobody ever wondered where we had gone. We were outside, where we belonged. Sometimes, we ventured afield in virtual throngs. Once, four of us—my cousins Danny and Bobby, my moron brother, Bill, and I—discovered a perfect swimming hole, its bottom lined with freshwater clams, and the only hitch to get there was that we had to pedal like maniacs through a pack of Baskerville-class farm hounds. More often, we entered the wilderness in pairs. I put up with Koscal, for instance, because he had a nose for snakes. Snakes were the ultimate quarry. Sometimes, we even teamed with grownups, but only when there was real blood-hunting involved, because Dad owned all the guns.

But, if no one else was interested, I would go out alone day after summer day, searching the canopy for movement, lifting wet rocks or standing knee-deep in cold muck, staring into the water, harassed by bugs, hunting for tadpoles, wary of snappers. I had no plan. None of us did. Kids just lit out for the woods, because the woods were there for lighting out.

Kids roamed but we never "hiked." Kids lived on the seats of our Schwinns and J.C. Higginses but we never went "biking." We clambered up the vertical crags of Mill Bluff but we never in our lives went "rock climbing." The farther we stretched the edges of town, the more mystery, the more fun, the more peril was possible—although the available perils rarely amounted to more than wood ticks, yellowjackets, green apples, hostile turtles and the occasional psychotic squirrel.

Koscal

Feeney was the kid who tagged Koscal a "Polack."

In every classroom in every schoolhouse, everywhere, there has always been a social director. Actually two of them, one for girls, one for boys. But since boys ignore girls, and vice versa, each pupil in each class only deals with one of these petty tyrants. Feeney was ours. His job, which no one gave him—somehow, it was his destiny—was to administer the pecking order among boys. Although Feeney wielded more power than any kid in our class, his place was neither high nor exalted. He willingly installed a small coterie of alpha males above him—the tall, the strong, the handsome and sleek, a prosperous, confident and fashionable few—so that, by serving them, he enlarged himself. Feeney was small—a ferret among lions. The rest of us, the unchosen, Feeney labeled, graded, dismissed and derided. He never laid a glove on me or anyone among the culls and outcasts; that would have been risky. Some among us—a kid named Gladstone, one of the Kamperschroer brothers, certainly Koscal—had the bulk and agility, if provoked, to crush Feeney like a loose cockroach. But Feeney, who did his damage with tongue and tone, delegated the occasional strong-arm work to the alphas. Feeney was the first bureaucrat I'd ever met;

the first kid of my acquaintance who understood the ethics of adult-hood, in which one's ability to push to the front of a crowd—or, preferably, to persuade someone bigger to do the pushing on your behalf—trumps talent, ability, knowledge and character. Feeney proved the efficacy of the executive mind every Monday at recess, during the weekly choose-ups for softball or soccer or football. Despite his half-pint size and dubious skills at every sport, he was the first chosen after the most gifted jocks and coveted teammates had been divvied up. He contributed nothing to the athletic endeavor, but he had insinuated himself among the elite and he had assidu-ously distanced himself from the unclean, unnoticed and unloved.

I never figured out how Feeney got this job; nor was it sensible to wonder. Feeney was already a fact of life, established and im-mutable, passing judgment and juggling black balls, the day I showed up. He disliked me on sight. He liked Koscal even less. On Koscal's first day, Feeney called him "Polack." Thereafter, everyone called Koscal "Polack." This was supposed to humble Koscal. Trou-ble was, nothing humbled Koscal.

Besides, "Polack" was a poor excuse for an ethnic slur. In those days, "Polack" didn't carry the same sting it developed later when Polish-Americans discovered the benefits of political correctness. In those days, "Polack" was just a synonym for "Pole," slightly more satisfying on the palate because of that nice sharp plosive at the end. My main grandfather, whom we called Papa, had a fondness for eth-nic insults, but only if they were fun to say—"Polack," "Hunyok," "Mulyok," "plow jockey." In his Saturday badinage among the mer-chants and shopkeepers on Superior Avenue, he called people "Po-lack" and "Hunyok" affectionately and interchangeably, without regard to national origin. "Plow jockey" was his only term of genu-ine disparagement, which Papa applied exclusively to slow drivers who got in his way on Superior Avenue. This habit left me with the lasting impression that farmers are the world's worst drivers. Papa never said "plow jockey" outside his car, however, because a farmer might overhear. If Papa sensed that any of his mild sobriquets might be hurtful, he held his tongue. He was a man without malice.

When Feeney called Koscal "Polack," it sounded different from Papa's formulation. It sounded mean in Feeney's mouth, which was Feeney's point. Most of us got the point. Koscal, if he got it, gave no indication. He was numb to insults.

Of course, I deplored Koscal. Everybody deplored Koscal. Deploring Koscal was as auto-muscular as breathing and farting. If we'd been asked to explain our universal contempt for Koscal, we would have probably said, "Well, 'cause he's just such a *jerk!*"

Koscal's defining quality, for which we had no word, was *chutzpah.* Where others trod softly, Koscal barged. Where others spoke barely above a whisper, Koscal crowed. Where others shrank self-consciously into the background, Koscal thrust out his chest—the better to display the hand-me-down bolo tie he just got for his birthday. Koscal had a lot to be self-conscious about, and he wasn't self-conscious. Koscal was poor, he was Polish, he was raggedy and soiled. His hair was shaggy, black and unkempt. He ate strange, fragrant homemade lunches from greasy paper bags. He had an unseemly number of siblings, even for an ethnic Catholic. His family, every time they showed up *en masse* at Mass, were shockingly uncool. They laughed, they sang, they hugged and bellowed and generally had more fun than immigrant paupers were even supposed to think about having. Perhaps worst of all, Koscal had no sibling shame. He seemed to like his brothers and sisters. This was a gross violation of the unspoken law among kids that it was acceptable to have siblings as long as you didn't flaunt the fact. Koscal not only violated this rule; he seemed not to realize that it existed. He *talked* about his brothers and sisters. Out loud. He greeted them in the hallways at St. Mary's. He sought them out at lunchtime and carried on with them, flagrantly, even when they tried to avoid him. Which they often did. Not all the Koscals were as brazen and outgoing as he was. Some of them understood society and tried to conform. He screwed things up for them.

Koscal screwed things up for everybody. With nuns and teachers, for instance, kids were supposed to be respectful. We had rituals to observe, greetings to recite. But Koscal didn't just go through the motions. He performed the rituals with *joie de vivre*. He didn't mumble his mandatory greetings; he orated them. The rest of us, seeing Sister Terence turn a corner and penguin toward us, would all mutter, "G'mn, S't'r T'rnce." Behind us, suddenly, Koscal would erupt, bugling his salutation loud enough to wake up roosters in Vernon County.

"Hey! Sister Terence! G'morning! What a nice day, huh?"

"It certainly is, Mr. Koscal," Sister Terence would say, glowing. And then she'd turn to everyone else, her voice dripping with disappointment for our un-Koscalian absence of enthusiasm.

Her "Good morning, children" came out as more an indictment than a hello.

"Koscal, you prick!"

"Wha'd I do?"

Poor kids weren't supposed to be loud. Kids with obvious ethnic names didn't shout and challenge people. They cringed and apologized. Poor kids didn't laugh and toss insults back at their insulters. They kept a low profile. I kept a low profile. But Koscal screwed it up, made life miserable for all the rest of the outcasts in class. He kept barging in among Feeney's inner circle of jocks and snobs—Kiegel, Fin, Gunderson, Overacker—and kept getting kicked out. He always emerged unfazed and dove right back in, as though his perpetual exclusion was some sort of mistake.

Even more annoying, Koscal had talent. His grades teetered perpetually on the cusp of catastrophe, which redounded to Koscal's credit. Poor kids and farmers weren't supposed to be brains. But Koscal did several extracurricular things appallingly well. For instance, he could sing. Worse than this, he liked singing, right out in front, among a classful of kids for whom any sort of public performance was the equivalent of dropping your pants, lifting your shirt and doing a pirouette on the playground—at lunch hour. Koscal not only sang. He pulled it off, in style, then smiled and bowed and carried on as if this singing crap was something to be proud of. He even did encores. Not that anybody asked for one.

One Christmas season, Sister Claveria was trying fecklessly to get us to sing the world's hardest carol, "O Holy Night," in four-part harmony. In the midst of our bleating and squawking, she heard one angelic tenor hitting all the right notes and cruising through the impossible passages—you know, where it goes, *"O night/divine!/ O night, when Christ was born . . ."* The annoying perfect voice was— who else?—Koscal. That son of a bitch. Nuns love to show up the whole class with one shining example of how splendid they all could be if only they weren't a reeking heap of harelipped cretins. Here was one of those triumphant moments for Sister Claveria. She stood Koscal up in front of everyone and directed him to sing "O Holy Night," all the way through, a cappella, emphasizing, with a few melismatic flourishes and reverent gestures, the parts that made your eyeballs bleed. Thereafter, given false hope by Koscal's virtuosity, Sister Claveria redoubled her efforts, every day, torturously, to squeeze from us a musical Christmas miracle. We could all handle "Joy to the World," and we could sing the bobtails out of "Jingle Bells." We never got a chance. And did Koscal have any clue? Did he shuffle and blush and curry our sympathy for his exposure and all the added pain his virtuosity imposed on us? Koscal? Not Koscal. Koscal swelled. He smirked his way through every eight-octave verse. He strutted and fretted his hour upon the stage like a Shakespearean ham. We all wanted to kill him, cut him up and send his body parts to all his innumerable brothers and sisters who lived on the wrong side of the tracks, down by the Seven-Up bottling plant.

Koscal was even more annoying on the playground. Poor kids, farmers, pariahs and outcasts had a certain style at recess. We played the games because the nuns would interfere if they saw some of us loitering motionlessly on the fringe. But even as we played, we held back, in exaggerated attitudes of submission. Koscal, of course, accepted none of this. He didn't have to, because he was good. He could hit, he could run. He caught every pass that got close to him—although it was often intended for someone else. He could throw the ball a mile and kick it through a wall. Koscal was a jock. He should have been the pride of the outcast class; we should have loved him, and taken him as our hero. This is what reject kids do in the movies, when one of their kind turns out to be the second coming of DiMaggio. The Koscal character leads the lepers from the ghetto, and they carry him on their shoulders through cheering crowds of penitent aristocrats. In real life, every Koscal touchdown, home run, goal or basket mortified us. It made our lives worse, because Feeney and the jocks couldn't take out their resentment on Koscal. He could stand his ground and actually beat some of them up. He was a problem they couldn't solve. They didn't mess with Koscal, except with insults that had no effect. Instead, the rest of us, the suffering classes, stand-ins for Koscal, got picked on, sniped at, pounded and pestered. And Koscal didn't even notice. The son of a bitch was clueless.

I hated Koscal. This, of course, was self-hate. While shunning him, I was drawn to him. We had a lot in common. We were penniless and messy. Our knees were patched and our shoes were brown. We distinguished ourselves in unpopular skills; Koscal could sing, I could spell. We were permanently excluded from Feeney's elite. While the thoroughbreds lived rigid lives of grade school conformity and macho bonding, Koscal and I were free. Because our every word or deed was greeted with derision, we could do or say anything that occurred to us. Koscal understood this strange liberty better than I. His annoying insouciance was simply the freedom of an unselfconscious boyhood. He shouted, he laughed, he roamed where he wanted, he got dirty and wet and he snuck into places where he shouldn't have gone. He could be curious about unfashionable things, like animals and chemistry and woodburning and playing the marimba. Amidst the contempt of his stifling peers, Koscal enjoyed life.

Inevitably, while studiously deploring him and all his antics, I gradually, grudgingly befriended the unbefriendable Koscal.

I justified this social dead end as my Christian duty. Among all the kids in my class at St. Mary's, I was the one who found meaning in our catechism lessons and took Jesus literally, as a real guy, who went around Palestine buddying up with ragamuffins, hugging spastics, coddling panhandlers and feeding multitudes. He didn't mind thieves, he treated whores like ladies, and some of his best friends were Jews. If Jesus could forgive Pontius Pilate for sending him off to his crucifixion, I could make friends with Koscal.

Fat Vinny was an even bigger reclamation project. Fat Vinny, who was one grade above mine, and therefore technically none of my responsibility, was so detested by everyone in school that his presence on the playground incited periodic riots. After participating once in an anti–Fat Vinny demonstration, throwing sticks and rocks at him as he retreated toward school, cordoned off by his bodyguards—Fat Vinny was the only kid I ever knew who paid other kids to protect him from spontaneous assault by mobs of disgusted schoolmates—I was overcome with shame and remorse. Would Jesus have pitched pebbles at Fat Vinny and chanted, "Fat fat Vinny's full of greasy grimy gopher guts, greasy grimy gopher guts, greasy grimy gopher guts," over and over, in bad harmony with the apostles, 'til he was hoarse? This was a question that needed no answer.

A few weeks later, I approached Fat Vinny in an aisle at the Red Owl store. He didn't recognize me as one of his tormentors. He had too many enemies to actually pick faces out of the ugly mob. So I had to introduce myself before I apologized, and then had to remind him of the particular riot for which I was sorry. Fat Vinny, intuiting that in me he had found a live one, forgave me on the spot and agreed to let me help him in his various downtown hustles. Fat Vinny was a twelve-year-old entrepreneur. He had the franchise on shoveling snow in front of most of the twenty or thirty bars in downtown Tomah, and the exclusive rights to distribute advertising flyers for the Coast-to-Coast Store, S&Q Hardware, both drugstores, and sundry other retail outlets. In getting to know Fat Vinny over the next year, I learned the main reason why other kids hated him so passionately. He was—in kid terms—rich. Because he had so many schemes working all the time, he always had pocket money that came in bills, not coins. In those days, the average kid's allowance topped off at fifty cents a week. The only known income source beyond that was a paper route, which earned your average

kid about three bucks a week, maybe—except Freddy Foss, a worka-
holic geek who earned twice as much as anybody else, because he
had 120 customers on his *La Crosse Tribune* route, which ran literally from one end of the town to the other, and took three or four
hours a day, except for collecting—which was literally a full-time
job three days a week. Freddy Foss sacrificed his childhood to the
La Crosse Tribune.

Another reason to hate Fat Vinny was that he was a piker. If
he could find a sucker to help him do his chores on Superior Avenue, he'd let the sucker do all the work, collect five bucks from the
bartender at the Hofbrau or old man Sorenson at the Tomah Hardware, and then Fat Vinny would turn around and give his helper—
often me—a quarter. Fat Vinny knew a quarter was a fortune to a
kid in those days. But even I figured out eventually that a fifty-fifty
split on five bucks was more than two bits.

Still, the main reason kids hated Fat Vinny—kids who didn't even
go to the same school, kids who'd never met him, never talked to
him, rarely even set eyes on Fat Vinny—was that Fat Vinny was the
worst kind of fat. He was fat in that sloppy, droopy, voluptuous way
that forty-year-old men are fat. Fat Vinny was adult-fat, and he was
adult-ugly. Fat Vinny's ugly was sneery and vulgar and degenerate.
You could see in Fat Vinny, at age twelve, the seeds of a sleazy adulthood, full of spilled booze, petty crime, mean swindles and trailer
park sex with underage girls. Kids sensed in Fat Vinny the worst
possibilities of their own future, and they recoiled. Once, walking
home from school with Fat Vinny, I stopped to watch a few minutes of a baseball game at the public school playground. Some kid I
didn't know was pitching to another kid I didn't know. The pitcher
looked our way.

"Shit," he announced suddenly to every kid on both teams, who
responded by looking our way, "it's that tub of shit Fat Vinny."

Fat Vinny, who was inured to his infamy, didn't flinch or acknowledge the pitcher. He just stood there while the pitcher bent
over, found a large smooth rock at his feet, straightened and flung
the rock, with all his strength, at Fat Vinny. The rock missed Fat

Vinny, but not by much. The kid had a good arm. The rock hit me in the forehead, staggering me backwards and almost knocking me unconscious. I hadn't ducked because I hadn't expected such violence to explode from so normal a scene. Indeed, the pitcher, having cast his stone, returned to the game, and none of the players on the field paid us any more notice. I walked home dizzy, with an enormous lump on my face. What I had forgotten, in my eagerness to befriend Fat Vinny and restore him to the good graces of humankind, was that I was the only one with so pure a heart. Everyone else still hated Fat Vinny.

It didn't occur to me at the time, but after Mom and Dad examined the whopping lump on my head, neither mentioned—or even entertained—the idea of seeking redress from the parents of the pitcher. The incident occurred on the Miller School playground, but Mom never thought of storming off to the principal's office. Above all, neither Mom nor Dad questioned my choice of Fat Vinny as a sidekick. They never asked (although my meddling sister, Peg, did so regularly), "What are you doing hanging around with that pig-faced punk anyway?" To ask the question would have crossed the line between two irreconcilable worlds.

One reality grownups and kids understood, implicitly, was that kids couldn't entirely manage life on their own, but parents weren't really welcome, or inclined, to help out. The solution was sidekicks. Without at least one sidekick, my life might quickly deteriorate into one of those grim European novels about sensitive boys who write maudlin poems and slash their wrists. For a kid like me, defined by Feeney as an undesirable, any quest for sidekicks necessarily followed the path of least resistance. Pity was my guiding light. I befriended Koscal and Fat Vinny because nobody else would ever think to volunteer. Koscal and Fat Vinny, in turn, hung out with me. With Koscal, I turned over rocks to see what might be slithering underneath. With Fat Vinny, most days after school, I had a vanilla Coke (Vinny preferred cherry) at the soda fountain at Steele's Rexall.

In a more grownup-intensive world—which no kid wanted—

the intervention of parental disapproval might have spared me the fellowship of Koscal. He was, after all, a Polack from the flats, and his grades were a travesty. He goofed around constantly, shot off his mouth too much and dressed like an *Our Gang* urchin—only dirtier. Fat Vinny—who could have given Peter Lorre a case of the willies—was even less acceptable. But kid companionship (unless you were hanging around the pool hall with Indians) was not an issue for grownups unless the cops showed up at the door. Only after kids hit puberty—which threw sex, booze and Chevrolets into the hopper—did grownups show the least interest in a kid's sidekicks. Ideally, parents didn't even know your friends' names.

Koscal? Koscal who?

Kids are instinctively feral. Unleash them from school and church and home, as every kid was invariably set loose every summer in the Little-League-less Fifties, and kids will hunt down whatever wild game crawls in their territory.

The summer hunt is an ecstasy of freedom. Suddenly, in the last days of May, after a useless morning in class, school ends. The doors open and kids stumble, blinking, into the sun. We hear our first robin sing. We see our first forsythias. We breathe chalkless, nunless, heathen air. We break into a run, to get home, not to do anything there—just to show up at a time of day when we should be stuck in school, gazing wistfully out the window at blue skies and budding birches. On the way, the hunt begins. We tear off every dandelion we see and invade the kitchen, handing Mom a fistful of milk-drippy weeds. She replies with a grilled-cheese sandwich and a "Get out."

This "Get out" applied to the whole summer.

I knew of kids, rich kids, who went somewhere in the summer, on vacation, with their families. They would return in the fall and present mind-boggling show-and-tell slide shows of Yellowstone Park or Mackinac Island. Until they petered out in October, these spectacles would upstage and mock my own show-and-tells, which usually featured either dehydrated insects or clippings from *The Saturday Evening Post*. But these peripatetic kids were freaks of affluence. In the Fifties, vacation was mostly a synonym for summer, for dads to pull less overtime and do more fishing, for moms to make lemonade and sit on the sun porch bonding with the Avon lady, or peeling tomatoes for canning. Summer was for detachment. Families drifted apart blissfully. Kids had no hours. We had no plans. We had no summer jobs. We had no meetings. We barely had lunch. We had no goals or expectations. We had no coaches, no guidance, no batting order, no lineup cards. We batted but we had no batting averages. We kicked, and counted no goals. We fought, we fell, we crashed, we bled, we twisted and strangled and throttled ourselves. We almost drowned, in unfiltered water. Set loose without instructions, we melted into the neighborhood, populated the playgrounds and sandlots, pilfered the orchards and puked green apples. We slunk into the woods and we hunted.

Summer by summer, I hunted and captured virtually everything that slithered and crept and hummed and stung. Butterflies, bumblebees, beetles and locusts. Milk snakes, salamanders, sparrows and crawdads. Angleworms, lightning bugs and June bugs.

One summer, the June bugs went apeshit and turned into a plague. As night fell, they rose in millions from their shallow burrows and thronged the streetlights. For a week, every streetlight on Superior Avenue was obscured by clouds of sex-crazed June bugs. It rained June bugs. As they collided in midair and lost their gyros, they plunged, in crackling spirals to the pavement, or into the hair of passersby. Their victims were often tipsy ladies in cocktail dresses emerging from the Buckhorn Bar into a hailstorm of whizzing, spike-legged, juice-leaking bugs. Screams punctuated the humid nights. As each night wore on, injured, confused, exhausted, orgasmic June bugs would accumulate beneath each light, building a creeping, buzzing pyramid that was knee-deep and six feet around. They blocked the sidewalk and streamed along the gutters. You walked gingerly but crushed hundreds, feeling them snap and spread beneath your soles. Each morning, the living bugs were gone, leaving behind a pile of curl-legged mahogany corpses and a sidewalk treacherous with bugjuice. On Superior Avenue, where we lived, it was bug nirvana for a week. In a normal summer, I would catch the occasional June bug, and pop it into a jam jar, watching with fading interest until it died in captivity, unrequited in its ten-day dance with lust and death. That summer, I went out to the streetlights with a shovel and filled cartons with June bugs. I was filthy-rich with June bugs. I was an insect tycoon. I had no use for them. I caught them because I was a kid, born to hunt, and this June, these bugs turned me into Frank "Bring 'Em Back Alive" Buck. And then they died—down to the last dried-up husk—in my cartons, after rustling and clabbering over each other eerily for a week on my porch, twenty feet above Monowau Street.

One Koscal summer, I ended up with a washtub full of turtles on the porch. It was a weird porch, a teetering appendage of planks, tin and timbers bolted to the back of a brick commercial building. Downstairs was the S&Q Hardware. Upstairs, in apartments that were periodically condemned by the building inspector and just as periodically deemed fit for human habitation after our landlady enacted a few grudging repairs, were us—in the back apartment—and the Randalls up front. The Randalls were full-blooded Winnebagos, in a bygone time when Winnebagos were still Indians and not vacation vehicles for golden-agers. The good thing about the porch was that you could throw stuff off of it, right onto Monowau Street down below. If you lofted a rotten orange, for instance—with the right arc—it would hit a passing car's windshield like a bomb from a diving Stuka, splattering twenty feet. By the time the driver jumped from the car and looked for the kid who tossed the orange, we'd be charging down the front steps of the building and popping out, innocently, onto Superior Avenue, half a block from the scene of the mischief.

But the best thing we ever dropped off the porch was twenty gallons of dead tadpoles. The tadpoles had come from Koscal's swamp behind the Ranger Station on Highway 12. Only Koscal and I knew about the swamp.

As swamps go, this one had just about everything a kid could desire. It was hidden in a glade, a wet sprawl in an oddly unswampy terrain. Looking back, I suspect it probably got started when the Milwaukee Road, which owned most of the land back there, had needed some fill. So they rolled in a backhoe and a bulldozer, scraped away a few hundred cubic yards of topsoil and dug a small pit about four feet deep. Groundwater, probably from a thin creek nearby, had turned the pit into a weed-rimmed waist-deep swimming hole. The surrounding shallows, pimpled with cattail hummocks, were only wet about half the summer, drying up by late August. The high ground of the swamp included a rockpile, where the railroad had dumped a few loads of discarded concrete and asphalt, apparently for the felicitous purpose of breeding garter snakes. Beyond the rockpile, closer to the Milwaukee Road frog shops, there was a network of shallow mud holes. The mud holes, above the water table, filled to overflowing every spring with snowmelt. By mid-July, they had shrunk to separate puddles no more than eight feet broad and a few inches deep. The puddles in July wriggled constantly with millions and millions of desperate tadpoles.

The tadpoles had hatched perhaps a month before, when the puddles were one big shallow pond, with plenty of room to swim. But each day, the sun nibbled at the edges and evaporated the water. The tadpoles crowded closer and closer, stirring the mud and clouding the water. They rested there blind, floating in brown soup, steeping in the summer heat, mindless of their suspense. Which would come first? Death or legs?

Koscal and I, one day, unaware of the tadpoles, ventured barefoot into one of the big brown pools. Suddenly, around our feet, the tadpoles exploded in panic. The chocolate surface boiled. We leapt away, surprised. But we hurried back, because there was no feeling like this. It was cold, it was warm. It was frenzied and it was soothing. It was a whirlpool of slippery, tickly fingers on our naked skin. The tadpoles swirled and bumped and bubbled and fled, harmless, panicky, sensuous. No experience, in my life, ever compared to the feeling of a thousand frenzied tadpoles trapped in lukewarm water, caressing my ankles and splashing my calves while mud squoze spermacetically between my toes.

"Holy shit, Koscal," I said.

"Wow," said Koscal.

We tested every puddle. Each was the same, a warm spring that burst with squiggling violence at the touch of a toe. We wandered delirious from pond to pond.

"Yeah," said Koscal, "but what are we gonna *do* with 'em?"

We were, remember, hunters. It was against our nature to leave anything well enough alone. These were not merely tadpoles; they were quarry. We had to bag them.

So, the next day, we returned with buckets. We made several trips, each with two heavy-laden pails balanced on our handlebars, wobbling nearly two miles from Koscal's swamp to my apartment. We shlepped the buckets up the rickety steps into our swaying porch and dumped, into a twenty-gallon galvanized washtub, about eight thousand displaced tadpoles.

Then what?

Nothing.

Like white hunters in Tanganyika, Koscal and I had no interest, and no purpose, save the trophy. We had our tadpoles. We had more tadpoles, more easily, than any kids in the history of tadpoles. We stood atop the tadpole world. If anybody wanted proof of our dominion, they need only negotiate the deadly steps up to the condemned porch and stick a hand into the fetid washtub, where an amphibian volcano would suddenly burst. And if a grownup had asked the inevitable, ridiculous adult question, "What are you going to do with all those tadpoles?" I had an answer. A kid with captured creatures can always resort to the science experiment dodge.

"Metamorphosis," I'd say. "All these tadpoles are gonna turn into frogs. They'll slowly grow little legs, and their mouths will change, and they'll turn color, and their tails will fall off and they'll start to hop around—"

"They'll die first."

"No, I'm feeding 'em."

"Feeding them? What?"

"Leftovers! See?"

Kids always fed leftovers to animals. It didn't matter which animals. Whatever food survived supper went straight to the prison cafeteria. The bottom of my washtub, if you stuck your hand down there, was a gooey layer of liquefied bread crumbs, desiccated wax beans and carrots, and tadpole shit. A few gray hunks of hamburger floated on the greasy surface of the water.

"See?"

None of my tadpoles grew legs. All eight thousand died. When I sensed their fate, I lost interest in metamorphosis. The washtub simply slipped from my universe. Koscal and I paid it no attention for two weeks, and only then because my mother finally noticed.

Mom preferred not to notice many things that happened around that drafty and dim-lit apartment above the S&Q Hardware. She didn't like the place, and neither did we. Whenever Papa came to pick us up, he tended to look around the place and shudder involuntarily. Once, when I managed to talk a couple of kids in my class, Fuchs and Lagerbloom, into coming upstairs—a black and narrow ascent into the unknown—they stopped stock-still in the doorway, glassy-eyed and frightened, as though they'd taken a wrong turn in the Big City and wandered into the slums. The building was a two-story, turn-of-the-century brick box without insulation. In our apartment, the ceilings were high, and they hoarded heat four feet above our heads. The windows were tall single-panes with thirty years of grime caked on the outside, creating inside an endless dusk. We had no storm windows. In the winter, you could stand a cup of water on any window sill and make ice in an hour. Our only heat was a stamped-steel oil-burning stove, shaped like a homemade warhead, parked in the middle of the sprawling living room. Turned on full blast, it roared like a jet and you'd burn your fingers if you touched it. But we couldn't afford to turn it up overnight. On mornings in the dead of winter, two rooms away from the heater, Bill and I would creep reluctantly from beneath a pile of blankets and place bare feet on floors that were as cold as the hockey surface at Boston Garden. There was frost on the inside of the windows. Our breath puffed around our heads in white billows. We grabbed clothes, scurried to the stove, turned it up and hugged it coaxingly as it foomed, sputtered and clanked to life. Bill or I would hit the john first, because we didn't need to warm our butts before peeing, as Peg did. The toilet seat was a crescent of ice. We warmed our clothes on the heater before dressing. If we left them too long, the heater would burn into the material its personal signature of stripes and cross-hatches. I was responsible for keeping the heater fueled, which required that I carry a five-gallon oil can out onto the swaying porch, usually in my stocking feet, and stand in ice and filthy snow, the wind sweeping under my shirt, while fuel oil trickled tauntingly slow from the big drum beside the porch rail. Then I carried the can, now weighing about forty pounds, back inside, where I had to try to pour the fuel through a two-inch hole in the back of the heater, without spilling any oil on the door and as little as possible on myself. All winter, a faint pyromaniac aroma of gasoline followed me everywhere.

We lived in this walkup dungeon because, for Mom, it was the least of three evils, the first being Dad, who had lost control of his temper one too many times when I was about eight. Mom had fled back home, to the enormous house of T.J., my "other" grandfather. Mom had grown up in the giant farmhouse under her father's thumb, where she had mounted a personal revolution and shaken her dainty fist at tyranny. When she finally came back home, Peg, Bill and I trailing terrified behind her, T.J. had greeted his prodigal daughter with scorn. T.J. was not a magnanimous or forgiving man.

As our days of terror in the lair of T.J. added up one after another, and T.J. took every opportunity to remind Mom of her filial treason, her satanic marriage to a Lutheran satyr, her indelible stain of mortal sin, her reputation throughout Monroe County, western Wisconsin and parts of Minnesota as a harlot and a voluptuary, and her utter failure as wife and mother of three degenerate mongrels, it dawned on us that Mom was less an actual mother—in the recognized sense of the concept—than a big sister. Cowering in T.J.'s remorseless thrall, she was one of us kids—older but just as clueless, equally powerless.

She made efforts to stand up and fight back, but it all came down to whining and halfhearted bickering. Mom versus T.J. conveyed the impression of a poodle taking on a mountain lion. All she could really do was yap at the beast and steer clear of his claws. Eventually, in every argument, T.J. would rise up and crush Mom with the reminder that she was a charity case, mooching on the second floor and groveling for crusts and scraps at the master's table.

In all her life, Mom had licked T.J. only once, by taking up with Dad and turning teen love into a scorched-earth crusade. Mom flaunted Dad under T.J.'s nose. T.J. fumed. Mom refused T.J.'s every demand to cut her sinful bonds with that (statutorily) damned Protestant boy. T.J. banned Dad. Mom carried on in secret. The war escalated. T.J. threatened the wrath of God. Mom burned her bridges. Forcing both families into a Montague-Capulet parody on the altar of St. Mary's, Mom defiantly committed the rest of her life to a spoiled adolescent boy whose future prospects rested almost exclusively on a foundation of good looks, high school popularity and raging hormones. The spoils of Mom's victory were a restless husband too young for his responsibilities, a cold-water bungalow the size of a chicken coop and three baby-boom mozniks she could barely afford to feed.

The irony in Mom's private revolution was that she was, at heart, T.J.'s proudest pupil. She was a devout rule-follower and a knee-jerk Catholic. She had broken the rules of the Church to marry an infidel, and she broke them again to leave him and file for divorce. But between those two mortal sins, she never missed Mass. She launched a whole new civil war—this time with Dad—by sending us, at crippling expense, to the Catholic school. And she kept her catechism as her guiding light. The rigid faith of her family had long since ordained Mom's style of operation. She questioned almost nothing and followed directions, instructions and recipes with maddening exactitude. She didn't add ingredients. She didn't venture

shortcuts. She never deviated a jot from the revealed word of Christ
Jesus, Betty Crocker or any of the other unassailable authorities who
trod, imperiously, the narrow path between her ears.

Every time, for the sake of her sanity—or for our sakes—Mom
got up the nerve to escape the bonds that held her down—T.J., or
Dad, or eventually Tomah itself—she had no rules. It was an experiment. She had no idea what she was getting into, nor did we, as
we dragged along behind her. Getting used to that frightening
apartment above the S&Q Hardware was a triumph of adaptability.
Eventually, Peg staked out an island of obstinate neatness amidst the
disorder that Bill and I cultivated, as we ranged through the place
like yearling steers. Mom fled the subterranean gloom that en-
veloped the apartment constantly, even on sunny days in mid-
summer, by going to work. She disappeared from late afternoon 'til
the wee hours of the morning to work at the Carlton. The place became ours. It took on a sort of Addams Family homeyness. But
there were places in the apartment where even Mom feared to
tread, mainly the porch. She thought—with good reason—that the
damned rickety contraption might lose its grip on the brick building
at any moment and collapse into a hideous pile of shattered timbers,
disemboweled cardboard cartons, spilled fuel oil and David's critters. She ventured out there, gingerly, only to hang laundry. In the
summer, pinning up clean clothes, it bothered her when the porch—
besides its numerous other faults—tended to smell like a slaughter-
house offal wagon.

"David, what's in that tub out there?"

"Uh, tadpoles."

"Why do they smell so bad? I can't hang laundry out there anymore."

"Well, I haven't changed the water in a while."

This was an embellishment. I had never changed the water.

"Are they alive?"

"What?"

"The tadpoles."

"Um . . ."

"Are they dead?"

"Well . . ."

"They're dead, aren't they?"

"I'n'no."

"My God, David. Get rid of them."

"Awjeezma!"

"Today!"

"David, you're a pig."

"Shut up, Peg!"

The responsibility of disposing of eight thousand dead tadpoles, who had been percolating quietly in the August heat for upwards of a week, had not entirely eluded my conscience. I knew I'd end up facing it by and by, if only to free up the washtub for whatever critters Koscal and I snared next. I just wasn't eager for the undertaking. My tadpoles were not merely deceased. They were deep into death. Most had metamorphosed, from recognizable tadpoles into inert blobs of putrescent gray jelly. The mixture of tadpole rot, mosquito larvae and last month's unconsumed leftovers had established our washtub unofficially as Tomah's foremost public health threat. Over several summers of exploring swamps and delving into dumps in search of fort-building materials, I had pretty much inured myself to sticking my hand into just about anything. But I was squeamish about the washtub.

But how to get rid of it? From time to time, I would approach the putrid tub, strategizing. It weighed perhaps seventy pounds, too heavy to carry down the steps. I couldn't pump it out into, say, the kitchen sink or toilet, because I had a) no pump and b) no knowledge of, or curiosity about, hydraulics. I was a scientist, not an engineer. Besides, Mom would never allow eight thousand dead tadpoles to flow through her plumbing. I could bail the tub, bucket by bucket, an arduous prospect that would require at least a dozen trips, up and down our perilous staircase, to pour the offal into the S&Q parking lot. Or I could just bide my time. Eventually, I reasoned, the water would evaporate, rendering the tadpoles into a portable scum that could simply be left downstairs, washtub and all, for the garbageman. Alas, this approach would require the family to endure the odor of the tub until winter froze it over sometime in November. And the stink would return with spring.

It was my pestiferous brother, Bill, whose scruples never interfered with his ingenuity, who divined the solution.

"We could dump it," he said.

The sheer, brazen magnitude of this proposal at first bewildered me. What did he mean?

"Dump it?"

Bill nodded toward the porch rail, a gap-toothed picket row, forty inches high, that overhung the Monowau Street sidewalk.

"Over the rail," said Bill, suppressing a grin of diabolical glee.

"Awjeez, Bill!"

Over our several years at 1022½ Superior Avenue, Bill and I dropped, slung, launched or poured perhaps five hundred pounds of fruits and vegetables, dairy products, food scraps, waste fluids, toys, missiles and athletic items over the rail, covering a 270-degree arc that extended forty yards outward and covered all the turf from Monowau Street to the sidewall of Jaffe's emporium. But these had all been small payloads. Rarely had either of us ever attempted to fly an object heavier than two pounds or bigger than a cantaloupe. Bill was proposing a quantum leap in firepower. For a moment, struck by Bill's audacity and the stench of the washtub, my mind reeled.

Of course, I could not long deny Bill's logic. In one stroke, without doing a lick of work, I would be rid of a problem that had stymied me for weeks. Even better, Bill and I would be pulling the biggest drop in porch history. We had no idea what it would look like, but we knew it would be breathtaking.

It was.

For one of us, lifting the tub to the top of the rail—only spilling a few quarts of gooey water on ourselves—would have been unmanageable. Together, we accomplished the lift deftly. The stinking washtub balanced for a moment as we changed our grip.

"Now," I said.

On "three," we tipped the tub. For several seconds, this was gradual—until the weight of the water achieved its own momentum. As we stared downward, clinging by our fingertips to keep the tub itself from dropping, a vast gray sheet of toxic water and dead tadpoles plummeted toward the sidewalk. We hadn't bothered to check for possible passersby before we tipped the tub. A lady in a white summer dress had heard us clunking and grunting above her, and she had paused for a moment, looking up. As soon as she saw the tub tilting toward her and felt the first drops of the torrent, she broke into a run, uttering God's name in vain.

The water hit the sidewalk with a juicy, gratifying splat, and spewed itself halfway across Monowau. It spread swiftly, darkening the pavement and flooding the gutter. From above, we could spot countless little black lumps and specks, the dead tadpoles who hadn't yet decayed into nebulous blots of scum. Looking down at what we had wrought, Bill and I felt like bombardiers on a Flying Fortress, gazing through the bombsight as the pattern of our explosions begins to mushroom from the roof of a German munitions factory.

"Holy shit," said Bill.

The smell hit us then, like the breath of a thousand outhouses. Our eyes watered and our stomachs leapt.

"Awjeez!"

Simultaneously, the dispatcher from the Tomah Cab Company, whose office faced our porch across the street, who watched us day and night for potential damage to his cabs and disruptions to his daily routine, burst from his doorway and bellowed at the sight and aroma of eight thousand dead tadpoles crashing to the street in a wave of flying slime.

"JESUS CHRIST!"

Bill and I dropped the tub and took off.

We hit Superior Avenue in twelve seconds flat, almost knocking over the lady we had almost knocked over. The back of her dress was dotted with wet gray flecks. The cab dispatcher was rounding the corner of Monowau and Superior Avenue, shouting for the police, as Bill and I ducked into Burris's Dime Store and zigzagged through the aisles of notions, picture frames, lipsticks and sticker books. We popped out the back door and headed down the alley, away from home.

"Wow!" Bill raved. "Did you see that! Wow!"

"Whoosh!" I said.

We made ourselves scarce for the next twelve hours. By then, the cab dispatcher's shift had ended. The police had lost interest in what amounted to a ten-second prank. When we got home, Mom was at work, serving drinks and dinner at the Carlton Supper Club. When she got home, probably unaware of the great Monowau Street tadpole holocaust, we were sleeping angelically. By the next day, every tadpole had shriveled in the sun and disappeared. The sidewalk was dry. Only the smell remained, to shock pedestrians and force them across the street for the next two weeks.

The washtub went from tadpoles to turtles, who were far more durable. But the best turtle of that summer never reached the washtub on our porch.

In mid-August, school was barely two weeks from starting up. Koscal's swamp was shriveling fast. The tadpole pools were arid ovals of cracked mud. Our "swimming" hole was unswimmably shallow and choked with algae. The focus of our attention shifted to the cattail marsh between the swimming hole and the woods beyond. The marsh was a checkerboard of grassy humps, below which a hundred pockets of stagnant water resisted the sun. Some of the pockets had already evaporated into a glutinous muck, but others were still nearly knee-deep with black water. Koscal and I, prowling the woods, had caught a few wood turtles, and we suspected more turtles, as well as leopard frogs, could be found hiding in the brackish holes among the cattails. We slogged from pool to pool, alert for movement, feeling among the roots and into the goosh.

One afternoon, while Koscal poked a stick into the rockpile hoping to rouse a rattlesnake, I came upon a promising water hole in the heart of the cattails. I thrust my right hand in, halfway to the elbow, and felt something smooth. I reached deeper. The surface was hard, with ridges and palpable seams. Eureka. It was a turtle. It had to be. A big one. The adrenaline was just surging through my valves when I felt a swift movement in the water beneath and a shooting pain that engulfed my index finger.

"Aaaagh!" I screamed.

I yanked my hand from the water, but it wouldn't come out. Whatever had bitten my finger wasn't letting go. It pulled my hand deeper into the oily pit.

"Koscal!"

I pulled as hard as I could. The creature gave way grudgingly, until, finally, my thumb surfaced. Just behind it came the base of my index finger and attached to it were a pair of black jaws and one black beady lifeless eyeball.

"Aaaaaaaaagh! Kosca-a-a-al!"

Far away, a sound, like Koscal asking a polite question in class.

"KOSCA-A-A-A-A-AL!"

The thing holding my finger flexed its muscles. Down went my hand into the clammy depths. The thing began working its jaws, determined to gnaw my finger from its roots and eat it.

"Jesus Christ! Kosca-al!"

Suddenly, Koscal was present, hovering over my shoulder.

"Whaddya got?" he asked eagerly.

My pulse was racing, my face was flushed, my other hand trembled. And yet, my voice was steady with the analytical reserve of the scientist. "A snapper! A snapper! I think it's a goddamn snapper! Jesus Christ, Koscal! He won't let go."

"Well, they don't, y'know," said Koscal. "They'll grab ahold of a duck and they'll pull it under, and just hold on 'til it drowns."

I was a little insulted that Koscal would patronize me with such common knowledge.

"I'm not a goddamn *duck*, Koscal!"

I yanked. The snapper yanked back.

"This'll be easy," said Koscal.

"Easy?!"

Annoyingly, Koscal was right. We had the snapping turtle outnumbered two to one, and my finger was occupying the snapper's only weapon—his viselike mouth. Koscal calculated the position of the turtle's tail, reached into the water and presto, lifted the beast from its hole. It hung upside down, glaring murderously at both of us, pinwheeling its legs and firmly attached to me.

"Whoo!" said Koscal. "He's a beaut."

The snapper stretched three feet from nose to tail-tip, its shell the diameter of a medium pizza. Its head was as big, and as hard, as a croquet ball. Algae streaked its ebony carapace and leeches bivouacked in the hollows around its legs. Held by its tail, the snapper was helpless and yet, it bristled with more danger than I had ever been so close to.

I felt a weird rush of pride, at being intimately joined to the most fearsome creature I had ever seen. Still, I stayed worried.

"Oh, shit, Koscal. He's gonna chew my finger off."

"Nah," said Koscal, holding the snapper with both hands, his scrawny arms straining. "We got him now. He can't do nothin'."

"Oh yeah? Why does it feel like he's got *me*?"

"Don't worry. We'll get 'im off."

"How?"

Koscal offered no advice, just led me out of the swamp, past the Ranger Station, across Highway 12 and down the block to his house. Twice, we had to stop for Koscal to rest his arms. During these breaks, I had to sit on the ground, beside the snapper, watching my blood congeal around the monster's mandibles.

"I think," said Koscal, "we should name him Snappy."

Koscal's family had two different houses in the couple of years I hung out with him. The second was normal. But when Koscal and I caught Snappy, Koscal was still living in the first. Koscal's house was one of those places where a family ends up when the breadwinner loses a good job at the plastic factory and has to take anything he can get until something better comes along, like cooking short-order at the Chicken-in-a-Basket out on the highway halfway to Sparta. Koscal's house was a fern-green shingle-sided sloop sinking into a rank weed-grown lot next to an LP gas tank. I remember the interior of the house as a jungle of unfinished pine planks, wet laundry, soiled siblings scrabbling hither and thither, and a lot of secondhand, perpetually damp (God knew what with) sofas. The house's drafty and leaky attic had been turned into a large communal bunkhouse for kids, largely through the hasty construction of a staircase—out of scrap lumber and bent nails—that was steeper than the roof pitch of a French cathedral. The best part of the house was the garage, where no one but Koscal and I ever ventured. It was a ruin, half open to the sky. Scattered in moldy disarray were a dozen tenants' accumulation of auto parts, seat-sprung beach chairs, bicycle frames, rain-bonded *National Geographic*s, hip-deep litter and, in one eternally dripping corner, a ten-inch stalagmite growing out of the floor.

The redeeming feature of Koscal's house was the kitchen, where Koscal's mom, exotically beautiful and inexplicably serene, ran heaven's assembly lines, confecting aromatic miracles out of flour and sugar and great greasy black cast iron cauldrons. Koscal's mother created pastries from another world. She made buns and fried cakes, and heavy breads and baklava. There was always something new, sending out gusts of temptation from her cavernous lair, in which the only light was the glow of gas flame and the smile of Koscal's mom.

She didn't smile when she saw us on the doorstep with Snappy. We were breaking a basic kid-mom taboo. In summer, with the exception of brief and taciturn mealtimes, moms didn't expect to see ablebodied male children during daylight. Nonetheless, here we were, the sun high in the August sky, standing on the brink of the tabernacle.

Another kid-mom rule was what might be called the Eddie Haskell Dispensation. Not being liable for the depredations committed by a son's best friend and boon companion, a mom could overlook the friend's personality flaws and criminal tendencies. By rule, a mom would always treat the friend much better than her own son. Nonetheless, Koscal's mom drew her line in the sand at the sight of her son's sidekick standing in the doorway with a prehistoric predator clamped to his finger and dripping swamp.

"Huh uh!" said Koscal's mom. "Don't move one inch closer. Get that disgusting thing out of here."

"But, Ma," said Koscal, "it won't let go."

"Especially not in here! Go!"

We went, out into the yard, which Koscal was supposed to mow weekly. The grass came up almost to our knees.

"What are we gonna do?" I said.

"Make him let go," replied Koscal.

"Yeah? How?"

This commenced a series of grisly experiments, testing the tenacity of your typical North American snapping turtle. Suffice to say that various poking devices—knives, needles, darts, hairpins—had no discernible effect whatsoever. We might just as well have been jabbing a Brazil nut. Whacking Snappy—with hammer, tongs, Louisville Slugger, etc.—was a reiteration of the Brazil nut effect. An open flame, either from a Zippo lighter or a propane torch, was similarly ineffectual. I ordered Koscal to desist at the point that Snappy's burning flesh began to smell like a smoldering peat bog.

I sat on Koscal's flattened grass, hunched over Snappy, my elbow bent uncomfortably. Snappy displayed no emotion. He had calmed to the point of ennui, and only sporadically churned his legs in an effort to drag me bodily to the nearest bog, where he could hold me underwater until my flesh marinated to an edible consistency.

"Maybe a distraction would work," said Koscal, clinically.

"What, a girl snapper?" I said.

"Or a boy," said Koscal. "We really don't know what Snappy is."

"How do you tell?" I said.

"Look under his tail."

"*You* look under his tail!"

"For what?"

"It was your idea, Koscal."

"Well, I'm not lookin' under his tail."

" 'Cause you don't know what the hell you're lookin' for."

Koscal, losing ground, switched topics.

"We could try food," he said.

"You mean, like, show him somethin' t' eat?"

"Yeah."

We both liked this idea. Koscal headed to the house, leaving me to commune with Snappy. Koscal's first distraction was a saltine.

"A cracker? Snappers don't eat crackers!"

I was right. Koscal waved the saltine at Snappy, but didn't get a glance.

"Well, what do *you* suggest?"

"How about a duck?"

"Yeah, sure."

"They like ducks."

"Where'm I gonna get a duck?"

"A fish then."

"A fish! Yeah!"

Koscal ran off. He came back with a fish, a dressed bluegill from the family fridge—frozen.

"It's frozen, Koscal!"

"So?"

"Jesus! He can't smell a frozen fish!"

"It's the only fish we got—" Suddenly, a light bulb over Koscal's head. "Wait!"

He was gone about five minutes, returning with a freshly opened can of sardines, in mustard sauce.

I approved of this, but wasn't sure about the mustard sauce. We decided to try sardines both ways. While I dangled a mustard-drenched sardine a millimeter from Snappy's nostrils, Koscal swabbed another sardine through the grass until the sauce was all wiped away. We alternated our sardines for ten minutes. Snappy didn't flinch. He had no interest in canned fish.

Koscal made several further forays into the kitchen, for cookies, dog biscuits, leftover pork steak, raw liver, even one of his mother's feathery and delectable rosettes—which I ate after Snappy declined. I also snarfed the sardines and shared the cookies with Koscal.

An hour had passed. Snappy and I were one.

"I'm gonna have to go back," said Koscal.

"Where?"

"The swamp."

I understood. Snappy had set up housekeeping in the cattails because of the frogs. It was a cushy life for a snapping turtle, just lying in a puddle, in the middle of a frog neighborhood, waiting for a meal to kick by.

"Don't just get one," I said. "Get two or three. Nice lively ones."

Koscal departed without another word. I sat in the grass, looking at Snappy, trying to think like a reptile. What would make him let go? What motivates a turtle? I sank down, trying to lock on to Snappy's eyes. I worked my way into the grass, until I was lying down, face-to-face, inches away. I stared. I studied. I pondered.

"Why not just let go?" I asked Snappy. "I'm too big to eat. You're prob'ly too tired to eat me anyway. Wouldn't you rather just go back in the water? What about your friends? You got any friends? They might be lookin' for ya. And why a finger? There's not much meat on a finger. Especially a kid's finger. We're gonna get a frog. Wouldja like a frog? A nice fat frog! A lot tastier than a finger. Especially a skinny old dirty kid's finger! Hey!"

It finally occurred to me. If he liked fingers, maybe he'd go for a *fresh* finger! And if I could get him to jump at a new finger, he'd have to let go. All I would have to do then is get the other finger out of the way before he grabbed it. Tempt him with finger No. 2 to get him off finger No. 1.

Genius.

I edged closer to Snappy. For a moment I considered my left-hand finger options. I decided not to risk the index finger because I depended on it too much. The thumb was out of the question. Finally I fisted up my hand and stuck out the pinkie.

"Take a look," I said to Snappy. "A fresh finger!"

I moved into Snappy's face, flourished the naked pinkie and then moved my hands close together. I displayed my juicy left pinkie in front of the trapped finger, just under where Snappy's chin would have been if snapping turtles had chins.

I said, "Come on, Snappy! Fresh finger! Go for that finger. See if you're quick enough. I bet you're not, you turtle son of a bitch! You can't do it, you chickenshit reptile!"

I think it was the taunting that finally did it. I think Snappy's pride was hurt. Whatever the reason, Snappy finally snapped.

Trouble was, he didn't go for the pinkie. He didn't care about fingers anymore. His eye was on a bigger prize.

Before I could react, move, even think, Snappy struck. Hissing and lunging, his mouth suddenly agape—I swear I saw fangs!—Snappy went straight for my nose. He didn't have to go far. It was right in front of him. My eyes crossed as I stared in horror at Snappy's enormous pink maw.

Snappy's jaws snapped shut and pain engulfed me. I shrieked, more in surprise than in fear, and recoiled violently. Flesh tore! Blood gushed! Legends of the giant kid-eating snappers of Council Creek flashed in my mind. I could hear Snappy scurrying along the grass after me, clicking his jaws. I rolled and crawled to escape before Snappy could pounce on me and rip my heart from my chest in one colossal chomp.

"Oh my goodness." Koscal's mom was standing above me. I had bumped into her legs. For a moment, the world spun on its axis. I stared at Koscal's mom's shoes until the whirling stopped. I looked back in terror, at Snappy, who was humping lazily through the sticky grass, away from us, looking for a pond. I touched my nose with my once more operative right index finger. I looked at my finger. Nose blood blended with finger blood.

Koscal's mom smiled. "That's a nasty nip," she said. "But that was a clever trick. You got him to let go. I'll get a band-aid."

Koscal got back, frogless, while his mom was patching up my nose. The turtle bite was barely deep enough to bleed. It healed in two days. That night, we put Snappy in a washtub in the yard, but he was gone the next morning, back to the swamp. I still picture him crawling across Highway 12, dodging semis and pausing on the white line to snack on a little roadkill possum.

About a year later, prowling the mudbars on the Lemonweir River, I caught another snapper. By then, I'd made the acquaintance

of Acey and Meredith, a couple of aspiring hillbillies who lived
about forty minutes' bike ride out into the country. I took the turtle
to Acey and Meredith because they were virtual professionals at
snapper hunting. They would roam the creekside in back of their
barnyard with a pitchfork, watching for snappers to raise their heads
out of the mud. In one thrust, Acey or Meredith would pierce the
snapper's leathery neck and yank the whole turtle up from the creek,
hanging by its angry head.

Butchering a snapping turtle, as I learned from watching Acey
and Meredith, was an overnight job. They'd set the turtle on a chopping block. Acey would stick a rake in the snapper's mouth and pull
'til the neck was stretched. Meredith would drop the ax blade just
behind the turtle's skull, clipping off the head without sacrificing
any neck meat.

The snapper would be strung up in a tree, to bleed out all night.
In the morning, Meredith would deftly cut away the carapace and
slice all the cartilage that held the shell onto the snapper's back. A
naked turtle inside its shell, all its limbs and organs exposed, is like
looking at a flesh-tinted X-ray. I was surprised by the beauty of the
thing. I was even more surprised when Meredith, twelve hours after
decapitating the snapper, cut out its heart and watched it beat
steadily on the chopping block.

"Son of a bitch'll probably still be alive when we're eatin' 'im,"
said Acey.

Eating the turtle took another day. Snapper meat is so tough it
has to be parboiled overnight—Acey and Meredith's mom did
that—before it can be delicately sautéed, with onions and a few
spices, into a dish that makes fried chicken taste, by comparison, like
catfood.

Mom moved us to Madison just a few weeks later. The snapper I
ate was the last one I ever caught. Snappy, the one who almost ate
me, is probably still out there, twice as big, lying in wait, killing
frogs, and lying to his grandchildren about the finger that got away.

Gun Penance

Small-town Wisconsin in the Fifties and early Sixties was the heart of America's gun culture. Guns were everywhere. Somewhere in every house, there was at least one matter-of-fact firearm lying sheathed on a pantry shelf or leaning naked in the broom closet next to the Hoover. We were ready, if necessary, to repel the Reds from Russia or the red wolves from Jackson County—whichever came first. But nobody ever seemed to seriously regard guns as weapons. Lethal force seemed to apply mainly to the guns we saw in the movies. When Cagney or Cooper took gun in hand, the gun was a star. When Dad loaded his rifle and took it out in the country, it was a tool, like a needle-nosed pliers, or a plunger.

My grandfather kept his shootin' iron, an old pump-action .22 with a loose stock and a crooked gunsight, in the bathroom closet. Now and then, after taking a leak and before flushing, I'd poke into the closet to examine the rifle—which hadn't been fired, or even loaded, for at least twenty years and never would be again. True to its unstinting dormancy, Papa's gun didn't seem any scarier to me than an air rifle or a toy six-shooter, because I knew its firepower was as spent as Papa's youth. Still, I knew that once, long ago, this was the family squirrel rifle and the first line of household defense. The old .22 enhanced my admiration of Papa's frontier perspicacity;

I pictured him shrugging off the flaws of his weaponry, venturing into the woods and felling his rodent quarry with the steady hand and unerring eye of Davy Crockett, king of the wild frontier.

Pistols were another matter entirely. I never saw a handgun around the house—or anywhere—except strapped to a cop or brandished by Richard Boone and James Arness on CBS. Handguns were for hunting people, not game, and—although shooting someone might be the obvious best way to put everyone out of their misery—most folks thought it a pattern not prudently encouraged in a town where every third storefront on Superior Avenue was a bar. Our local gun culture's general disapproval of handguns imposed problems for the aspiring mass murderers in our midst.

For instance, there was the time (long before the current fad for schoolyard massacres) a sorely aggrieved recent graduate took it in his head to assassinate a local high school principal. When he burst through the school doors and charged down the corridors brandishing a bear rifle, there weren't any heroes who leapt forward to disarm him. Nonetheless, people definitely knew he was on the scene, and they had a good idea what he was up to. So, by the time the boy had put a bullet or two into the principal and came back out into the hallway wild-eyed and itchy-fingered, that huge unconcealable rifle had done its good deed for the day. There wasn't anybody left in the building for the kid to shoot.

And then, there was Earl—who dwelt down Pearl Street from my grandmother Annie's house. When he failed in his business and blew his head off, he had to resort to a 12-gauge shotgun. He killed himself, age forty-nine, in his garage, which was on the curbless little back street we called The Alley. Earl's garage had a dirt floor that—in all the times I went in there—was never really dry. Earl, I learned from the grapevine, had propped the stock of the 12-gauge on the damp old dirt floor and tucked the barrel under his chin. In that position he couldn't reach the trigger. So he took off his right shoe and used his big toe to fire the gun.

That bothered me. It was bad enough picturing Earl—a nice neighbor who went Up North fishing some weekends and gave away enormous muskellunge when he came home and even once showed all the kids on the block this impossible prehistoric fish called a sturgeon—lying dead with the top of his head blown all over the ceiling. Mostly, I didn't like the idea that he was in that dank oil-smelling garage with one shoe off and one shoe on. I thought Earl deserved a little more dignity. If he'd had a handgun, he could've kept his shoes on.

The reason every household had a gun—actually, several rifles—was that, come the season, every ablebodied breadwinner in Monroe County had to get his deer. The season began around Thanksgiving and ran into the beginning of snow. Everyone hoped for early snow, because—they said—it made your deer easier to track. Actually, I figured out by and by that this advantage tended to be offset by the fact that walking in the woods in a foot of snow is easier for a well-fed autumn deer than it is for an overweight Midwestern male who'd spent most of his spare time for the past eleven months sitting still and relating intimately to the Beer That Made Milwaukee Famous. The snow also meant colder weather, which tended to increase medicinal drinking among deer hunters, dramatically reducing their range and compromising their marksmanship.

After the season, the main thing men asked each other for a few weeks was "Did you get your deer?" It was always phrased this way, as though every male resident of Wisconsin (plus a few hardy truck stop waitresses) had a deer out there someplace with his name tattooed on its ear, and if he didn't go out and "get" it, he had squandered his birthright. No deer hunter ever used verbs like "shoot" or "kill." You *got* your deer, much the way you'd get your hay in before the snow flew. Deer season was the year's last harvest.

Those days, the state said you were only allowed one deer, if you could find one and shoot straight enough to hit a vital organ. Some guys went out ten straight years and never saw a deer. Sometimes, the deer walked right into your sights. Papa told me about the time my uncle Harry—who competed with my uncle Winnie for the title of Monroe County's Funniest Uncle—went out to get his deer and he'd barely stepped into the woods when this curious six-point buck stuck his head through a bush, apparently wondering what all the racket was. Uncle Harry, a scrawny elf who was known to thrash about and chuckle indiscriminately, was never known for his stealth. When the buck saw Harry gaping in surprise and hastily trying to jam a shell into the chamber of his single-shot thirty-aught-six, the buck ducked back out of the bush. This was followed, as quickly and wildly as possible, by Harry blasting at the bush.

A moment later, as Harry was about to plunge through the thorns to see if he'd hit the deer, the buck—six-point rack, pricked-up ears, curious gaze—stuck his head back through the bush. Harry staggered back. The deer staggered back. Harry chambered another round and fired at the bush.

Harry waited, watching the bush warily. Sure enough, the buck—obviously stupider than your average whitetail—appeared again, looking around, spotting Harry again and vanishing hastily. Harry fired again.

Harry waited. The buck, at last, did not reappear. Harry was not sanguine that he'd bagged his deer. Despite his service under Black Jack Pershing in the AEF (followed by a legendary period of carousing in postwar Gay Paree), Harry had never been mistaken for Alvin York. Obviously, his first two shots hadn't even scared the damn deer. The third had probably just sent it hightailing over the ridge. Nonetheless, he lowered a shoulder and struggled through the undergrowth in hopes of finding a blood trail to follow. Once through the brush, he found, lying in a neat row, three dead six-point bucks.

Not only did Harry have to gut three deer and drag them half a mile through the woods, the fine he had to pay for shooting three bucks in a one-deer hunting season was enough to buy a year's worth of T-bone steak—which (Papa added) is a damn sight tastier than the 150 pounds of stringy venison Harry ended up with.

Sometime before I was old enough to go out after my own virgin deer, I saw Bambi's mother killed at the Erwin Theater. This should have deterred me, but I was a precocious realist. I figured the spell of Disney would wear off, and I'd end up out in the woods, dressed in orange with a number on my back, stalking dewy-eyed ruminants amongst the rest of the barbarians. In fact, I never did. Instead, I moved to Madison, a hunting-free oasis in the midst of the endless killing fields. Hence, my hunting adventures consisted entirely of squirrels, which made a lot more sense to me anyway, because squirrels were easier to find and they tasted better. They also inspired one of my profoundest moments of theological insight. Squirrel-hunting brought me closer to God.

Besides deer, squirrels and rabbits were the main thing people hunted around Tomah. We had a lake, a few swamps and—not far away—a whole network of cranberry bogs, which drew plenty of ducks and geese to the vicinity. But I never noticed much duck-hunting up our way, probably because people just weren't affluent enough for ducks. I've always sensed something disturbingly bourgeois about duck-hunting. You couldn't just grab your rifle on a Saturday morning, after chores, and head out into the fields to pot a few mallards. Duck-hunting required a lot of preparation and a load of paraphernalia—waders and decoys, camouflage and blinds, boats and dogs and complicated paperwork filed with the Wisconsin Conservation Department. There was also some detail about "duck stamps" that I never quite figured out. Then you had to get up at 3:00 A.M., to go out in subfreezing cold, and stand stock-still, in the pitch dark, in ice water. And for all that aggravation and hypothermia, you could spend the whole day staring up at nothing but blue sky, and even if you found yourself in the middle of the world's biggest flock of pintails, you had to stop your carnage after two or three ducks.

And then there was the feather-plucking.

All this self-abuse made duck-hunting a little like fly-fishing—more of an executive pastime than a way to put meat on the table without having to go to the grocery store.

Squirrels were a vastly preferable form of game. They were

nearby, on dry land, abundant, nobody counted how many you shot, and easier to skin than taking off a pair of kid gloves.

Squirrel-hunting—especially if I had my dad's trusty scope-mounted .22 rifle—wasn't exactly fair to squirrels. They weren't armed, and they usually didn't have any plans to kill and eat me. But squirrel-hunting wasn't easy, either.

The squirrels of the Wisconsin woods weren't the cute, pudgy, pushy, Chip 'n' Dale panhandlers that citydwellers encounter in Union Square or the Boston Public Garden. Our squirrels were wiry and wary, hated by farmers (for poaching their corn), hunted by men with guns and—worst of all—stalked by martens. They foraged with an eye over their shoulder and a hollow tree always within scrambling distance. When you surprised one halfway up a tree, he'd be on the other side of the trunk before you clicked off the safety. If you rounded the tree, the squirrel would also round the tree. You could hear his claws skittering on the bark, but you'd never see him again that month. If you were lucky, you'd eventually spot the hole, thirty feet high, where he had crawled in and made himself unavailable for consumption.

Dad and I probably spent more time squirrel-hunting than just about anything we did together when I was a kid. This wasn't necessarily because of our mutual desire to bond. However, because there was a gun involved—and people then thought twice about putting a firearm in the hands of a twelve-year-old—I wasn't allowed to hunt unless Dad went along. Besides, it was his gun. The main reason why I got into the woods with Dad pretty regular, though, was that squirrels didn't require that Dad get up early in the morning. They'd be out there, rooting around in the woods and fields, pretty much from dawn to dusk. So, Dad could arise at a civilized 11:00 A.M., have a hearty breakfast, four or five cigarettes and a cold beer, and get me out into the October woods with a good four hours of daylight left.

My pestilent little brother, Bill, would come along but he wasn't old enough to carry a gun. He did the jobs that a beagle would have done, if we'd had access to a beagle. When we spotted a squirrel over yonder, we'd send Bill circling around the area to flush the game in our direction. He was also handy for toting stuff—food if we'd brought any, dead squirrels if we'd shot any—and he'd be the one to go around behind a tree if a squirrel was clinging to the far trunk. Bill wasn't as dependable at these jobs as our imaginary beagle would have been, but we had to bring him along because nobody wanted him home, whining, pouting and kicking chair legs all afternoon because he wasn't allowed to go hunting with Dad.

Every time we got in the car and went off after squirrel, Dad would tend to head in a new direction. Up toward the ridge. Out toward Mather, or Oakdale, or over by Camp McCoy. I never asked him what inspired his choice of hunting grounds, although now I know. The simple fact was that any one of a thousand wooded groves, with a fair stand of oak and a cornfield nearby, was likely to shelter as many squirrels as any other, and these squirrels would be just as cunning and elusive as all the others. Dad went in a direction he hadn't gone in a while just for the pleasure of each new woods's unfamiliarity. He didn't even follow the cornfield rule all the time. Now and then, he'd drive up to Camp McCoy, the military base, where the U.S. Army didn't grow any corn. I suppose he did this for the change of scene. Besides, there were plenty of pinecones, a popular squirrel food, up that way—although McCoy tended to harbor red squirrels, which were inedible.

Once Dad shot a red squirrel among the pines at McCoy. I went to pick up the squirrel.

"Leave it," he said.

"Why?" I was amazed.

"It's a red squirrel. Can't eat 'em."

"Oh."

I waited for more information, but in the woods—even more than in the parlor—Dad wasn't prone to dispensing unsolicited background data. So I finally nudged the dialogue.

"Well, if you can't eat 'em, why'd you shoot 'im?"

"They're pests."

"Pests." I chewed the word conclusively, but had no idea what I meant.

What made red squirrels pests, while gray squirrels and fox squirrels were good citizens?

I didn't press the point with Dad, because we were hunting again. But my curiosity kept me wondering. Eventually, from the library and from old-timers, I found out red squirrels are the gangsters of squirreldom. When red squirrels inhabit a woods, they don't tolerate any other squirrels on their turf. The grays and foxes get squeezed out, and the whole neighborhood becomes a wasteland for squirrel hunters.

Dad's execution of that red squirrel troubled me, nevertheless. Whatever the red squirrel's offenses, this was the woods, not the town. People made the rules and defined the pests in town, but I didn't figure our jurisdiction extended into the woods. If the red squirrel was a pest, he wasn't a pest we should be dealing with; he was the responsibility of the other woodland creatures, and if they were putting up with the annoying little son of a bitch, then we two-leggers had no business horning in.

Didn't say that to Dad, though. Nor did I hold it against him. I was in no position to cast the first stone. I had committed a few gun sins of my own. We all do.

I'm not sure what sort of woodsman Dad was, because he was never exactly full of advice. He pretty much expected you to pay attention to what he did and you'd figure out how to conduct yourself. His only deviation from this reticence was to drill me pretty heavily on how to handle the gun properly, including keeping the safety engaged in any circumstances where I might accidentally shoot my father in the ass. Getting extensive verbal instruction like that, from Dad, was always a novelty. I enjoyed it, but it scared me a little.

Teaching, after all, wasn't Dad's job. Kids and grownups operated under a pretty strict division of labor. Different grownups played different roles in kids' lives and they didn't muscle into one another's territory. This meant that parents, preoccupied with working, cooking, cleaning the house, driving the car, paying bills, fighting, smoking cigarettes, drinking and dragging kids to church on Sunday, didn't interfere with school stuff. The school, for its part, took over completely for parents from eight o'clock Mass to 3:30 P.M. every weekday during the school year. Parents never contradicted teachers and never argued with principals. School possessed a mystic authority so powerful that parents hesitated to teach anything. Teaching was for teachers. As a result, when kids squeezed any sort of knowledge from nonteacher grownups, we usually accomplished this by watching. I watched Papa build a hundred things, but I never learned enough metalworking or carpentry—or any of Papa's wondrous manual skills—to build anything nearly as good myself, because Papa never explained what he was doing. He just went ahead and did it. And I never asked.

Besides, it didn't really pay to ask. Once, while Annie was darning one of Papa's socks, I asked her how she did that.

She said, "Well, watch."

There were a couple of exceptions to the nonteaching rule. The first of these was chores. Grownups could go on for hours telling us just exactly how to wash or dry dishes properly, sweep the garage, mow the lawn, yank the weeds, peel the spuds, wash the windows without leaving streaks or make sure the snow is cleared all the way down to the sidewalk so the mailman doesn't hit an ice patch and split his head open on the steps.

The other exception involved stuff grownups liked to do that wasn't hard to teach. Besides Dad showing me how not to shoot him in the ass with his own .22, this category included bowling (with Dad), blueberry-picking (with Annie and Papa), fishing (with Dad) and betting the harness races every Fourth of July at the Monroe County Fairgrounds (with Papa). Dad's bowling instructions, for example, were masterpieces of economy. Lesson No. 1, just before Peg or Bill or I staggered toward the foul line under the weight of a fourteen-pound ball, was:

"Remember. Keep your wrist straight."

Lesson No. 2, right after the gutter ball, was:

"Were you listening?"

"Uh. Yeah."

"Wha'd I tell ya?"

"Uh. Keep my wrist straight."

"Didja?"

"Uh, guess not."

"And you saw what happened?"

"Yeah."

"Hmh."

Dad's hunting lessons, besides the use of the safety button and the pointlessness of shooting at squirrel nests (they were always empty), were almost as brief. After our first expedition, the thing Dad said most often in the woods was "Sh!"

When Dad told me to shut up, I shut up—not really out of fear, or even respect. It was habit. I was accustomed to shutting up. So was Bill. So was every kid I knew. Shutting up was what kids did. No adult in his or her right mind would ever entertain the mad thought of telling a kid to express himself, unless the adult in question was some sort of shrink (something we'd heard of, but no one had ever seen), or a cop trying to get a confession.

Besides, when you were hunting, shutting up was good policy. First time out hunting with Dad, whenever that was, before I was allowed a gun, I thought hunting involved a lot of skulking and stalking, even a little bit of chasing and shooting on the run, as if we were armed lions of the veldt dragging down a Cape buffalo in full gallop. After a fifteen-minute stroll through the rustling brush and crackling leaves, far enough that we couldn't see the road or the car parked on the shoulder, I found that hunting is mainly standing still and listening—which doesn't mean that you're going to find any squirrels. What happens, though—squirrels or no squirrels—is that you realize that even a little island of a woods, with fields all around, and a road a hundred yards back that way, and a farm close enough you could shoot a hole in the chicken coop, is riotous with activity. When we stopped moving, everything else—after a decent interval—started back up again. Peeps, squawks, chatters, footfalls on leaves, trees creaking in the wind. We'd listen as the noises built up, hoping for a squirrel sound. I learned that you hunted with the sides of your head, with your ears and the corners of your eyes. Nothing ever happened right out front; it was always off to the side—shadows, flutters and flickers.

I stopped carrying a gun before I was sixteen, but I've never lost the habit of going into the woods and standing still. One of my favorite forest surprises is chickadees and titmice. They're restless birds, tiny and ephemeral. They pass low among the leaves more like a fog than a flock. You never notice them coming. Suddenly, they're all around you, a scolding flurry of peep-peep-peep-peep, as they scurry up and down skinny branches pecking imaginary bugs from the bark, like little girls having a tea party with empty cups. They're brazen, fearless of any other creature because they are too quick and too clever to be prey to anything but the hysterical pace of their own pulse. Years later, I would go out into the New England woods and stand, waiting with a camera and a telephoto lens. Eventually, they'd come, chickadees, bushtits, titmice. I'd plant myself in a well-lit spot, sunlight shafting through the branches. I stalked the tiny birds, waiting for a moment in the light, focusing quickly, tensing my shutter finger . . . gone! I chased them, but they measured my pace and moved a little faster—still peeping, foraging, devouring their invisible meals, teasing me, eluding my viewfinder and sifting off into the dappled distance, silence in their wake. In a dozen trips to the woods, in a hundred exposures, I was lucky to get one printable chickadee.

I shot one once, with Dad's .22. The little songbird had perched on a limb, twenty yards off, resting to digest his latest huge meal of air and make-believe. By then, edgy, I hadn't seen a squirrel in two hours hunting. Dad and Bill were in another part of the forest. I was alone with my gun and a tired tufted titmouse. I pointed the rifle and sighted. The safety was off. The bird was a ball of fluff in my crosshairs, preening a wingpit. I curled my finger on the trigger and paused, steadying the gun.

A titmouse is a living nervous tic. In a tenth of a second it can change from seeming repose to lightning—a flash of wavy flight and a trembling twig. The only thing more sudden, more elusive, in all the woods, is a bullet.

I watched a few seconds, delaying my shot, expecting the bird to take off—oops—zip—gone! But he held his fatal perch, puffing his feathers to fill them with warmth. I think I hoped for his escape, just as I squeezed. The gun cracked sharply, once. Magnified through the sight, I saw the titmouse explode fluffily.

I walked over, picked him up, felt the warmth and softness of a body I had shot almost in two. The bird's deadness wasn't as troubling to me—I'd done in a number of squirrels—as its utter waste. You killed a fish or a rabbit, and you had some use for it.

For the first time ever, I appreciated the frightening force in Dad's scope-mounted .22. Until then, it had always seemed a wondrous device that opened the portals of adventure and made possible my equality with the athletic genius of nature. I knew I might possibly shoot myself with it, but I was scrupulous about gun safety and harbored no serious anxieties in that respect. The frightening thing that day, as I laid the dead titmouse in the leaves and quickly fled the scene of the crime, was that the gun had seduced me.

Tucked in my arm, warm from my body, the gun had been dormant all day. With this gun, I knew, I was able to see more closely, to move more stealthily, to shoot more keenly, to vanquish all things as far as my eyes could see. But only if I used it, only if I shot something. Left unfired, it was dead weight; it was unfulfilled. Lying in the crook of my arm, its awesome potential untapped, the gun was the snake in the Garden, whispering that there was more to life than strolling among the leaves, gazing at the birds, nibbling the occasional wintergreen berry. I could shatter the calm of the forest, kill those birds, show them who's boss, express myself.

As I fled the dead titmouse, hoping Dad wouldn't come across the tiny corpse and ask me about it, I understood how guns alter people. Guns want to be used. Guns want.

A lyric, possibly the most oft-repeated song among boys my age (with the possible exception of No. 1 on the Camp-Out Hit Parade, "One Hundred Bottles of Beer on the Wall"), came to me as I resumed the squirrel hunt. The song, which stuck in my head for hours, was more than just the theme of a TV Western. It was the ineffable Code by which we all survived one another's depredations. All kids lived by the Code. (When I say "kid," I mean, of course, "boy." A "girl" was a girl, and never a "kid." A school-age boy was always referred to as a "kid," as in "Hey! Kid! Is that a dog, or are you walkin' your mother?" Boys never called boys "boys.")

The Code existed without a name or a rationale. It made each one of us an existential archetype, a solitary Comanche scout cantering into the Void. No kid I knew had words for the Code. The closest any kid ever came to articulating it happened when I was in tenth grade. The kid's name was Bruce.

One day on the school bus, Bruce grew quiet. After knowing me for a month or so, he had decided he could trust me. Careful not to let anyone else see what he was doing, Bruce took out his wallet— your typical kid wallet. It was imitation leather, shiny and brown, with a snap-close change pouch. All its plastic windows were rubbed dull and disintegrating from the heat, sweat and pressure of imprisonment inside the hip pocket of a pair of hyperactive Levi's. It had a secret compartment. From that compartment, protected by a zipper and a flap, Bruce extracted several rectangles of typing paper, cut to the size of a business card. Reverently, without a word, as a bond to our new friendship, as a sign of our common cause, Bruce offered me his card. He had drawn and lettered each card, identically, meticulously, in No. 2 pencil. It read:

HAVE GUN
WILL TRAVEL
WIRE PALADIN

In the center of the card was Bruce's cunning, painstaking depiction of a chess knight.

The only item missing from the card's classic formula was the last line: "San Francisco," which, of course, deviated from Bruce's current address on Simpson Street. The deletion was necessary. Bruce had never been to San Francisco. No one had. To suggest it would have violated the Code.

In offering me his hand-fashioned calling card, Bruce had expressed the philosophy and mythology, the lonesome ethos, that ruled the life of every kid.

"Have gun, will travel."

For grownups, *Have Gun, Will Travel* was a TV show on Saturday night, in between *Wanted: Dead or Alive* and *Gunsmoke*. For kids in Tomah, that series of three Westerns on Channel 8 on Saturday was holier than the Stations of the Cross. *Have Gun, Will Travel* was our Apostles' Creed. Every kid knew the look and contents of that card, which Richard Boone, starring as Paladin, flashed in every show. We didn't know that "paladin" was a synonym for "knight," nor did most of us grasp the symbolic interplay of word and image. None of us perceived any irony in the fact that we had no guns and most of us needed permission to "travel" across Jackson Street. What we knew was that every one of us was a Paladin in our soul. We lived in the apparent comfort of home and hearth, as Paladin lived in the opulence of Frisco's fanciest hotel. But at a moment's notice, each one of us might be cast (metaphorically) into the wilderness, thrown from our horse, disarmed and bleeding from a bullet in our thigh, drinking only the water we could suck from a barrel cactus, shaking a fist at the circling vultures and hunted by villains so murderous that no ordinary lawman dared stand up to them. Only Paladin . . .

> *"Have gun, will travel,"*
> *Reads the card of a man . . .*

Every kid knew every word to the theme song. Every kid I ever knew was "a knight without armor in a savage land."

When Bruce—who by then was a sixteen-year-old junior in high school—handed me his Paladin card, without comment, without smirking, I understood. Any kid would have understood. Bruce would stand by me and I would stand by him, because without each other, we were Paladin, Paladin, "far, far from home."

Eventually, of course, Bruce passed from my life, largely through the intrusion of a girlfriend named Nutsy. But Bruce's passage was true to the Code, which stated that no one is ever really true to anyone else. All we ever really had was what kept Paladin alive, prime-time season after prime-time season: his guts, his wits, his horse and his six-shooter.

After the titmouse murder, I stuck to squirrels, but even then, there were gun sins. The worst was when I found a squirrel on the ground, looking for acorns among the leaves. The squirrel was so preoccupied that she hadn't heard my footsteps. I'd come surprisingly close, so near that the telescopic gunsight was superfluous. Actually, I was too close. I aimed hastily, concerned that the squirrel would turn and see me looming hugely over her. I fired too quickly. The bullet, instead of hitting her head or heart, killing her instantly, was a gut shot.

The squirrel lurched violently, thrashed in the leaves for a moment, seemingly trying to dig her way out of sight. Perhaps I should have shot again, to end her pain, but I had learned that too many shots into a creature so small would mangle the meat. So I froze, as the squirrel, her hind legs paralyzed, blood spurting from the hole in her side, trembled and crawled three feet among the brown leaves, bound nowhere, dying, her eyes enormous, her mouth opening and closing mechanically. She died from shock and blood loss, in perhaps forty-five seconds—not long for the death of an unwary rodent, but too long for a twelve-year-old boy to watch without a pang of shame.

I recovered, of course, as I did from the *Bambi* murder, and went on hunting. But I strove to be a more careful, more deadly aim. And I knew that somehow, somewhere, my penance would fall due.

Usually, woodland squirrels didn't let themselves get caught on the ground. They traveled the forest from branch to branch,

only descending briefly to collect their goodies, sheltered by bushes among the dead leaves, and always with a tree close by. Like us, they listened, but their ears were keener. This meant that your most likely shot at a squirrel was to spot him high in the trees, while he was traveling, where he felt safer and a tad less vigilant.

The day of my penance was gray and balmy, with one of those autumn overcasts that keep the cold air from settling down and creeping into my grandmother's bones. Despite the mild weather, Annie had made me take along a jacket. She insisted the woods would be chilly. They weren't, and I'd left the jacket in the car. As I hunted, comfortable, I was wearing a good flannel shirt and a pair of new OshKosh overalls about two sizes too big with rolled-up cuffs. It was a rule of thumb, those days, to buy kids' clothes with plenty of growing room.

As usual, after about a half-hour, I went one way, and Dad led Bill another way. This was prudent hunting policy because Dad could always get Bill to shut up and pay attention; I couldn't. We stayed within hailing range, but only now and then, across a clearing or along a snaking corridor of trees, could I see Dad moving silently in the distance. I crept twenty or thirty yards at a time, watching the ground and the trees alternately. I would stop for two or three minutes, listen, notice things—lichen patterns on tree trunks, mushrooms just emerging from the humus, a mourning cloak floating among dull yellow leaves. Then I'd change locations. I hunted an hour without any sign of prey.

Typically, the squirrel surprised me, closer than I expected. He was almost straight up from me, eighty feet high on a dead black walnut branch, almost concealed by a spray of mottled leaves. He'd seen me first and he'd launched into one of those maniacal chattering jags that squirrels use either to warn other squirrels or—my guess—simply to issue a kind of "Come and get me, motherfucker!" message to the landlubber way down there. I doubted that squirrels treat hawks and martens with similar insolence.

Impertinent or not, the squirrel was an easy target, if I hit him clean. He was sure of himself, because he was obviously close to a

hole, where he could quickly retreat if I missed, or if I merely winged him. I'd shot squirrels before, only to watch them limp into a hole and perish there, out of reach, wasted victuals.

I backed up to a tree to steady myself, clicked off the safety, shouldered the gun and found the squirrel in my sights. All I could see, through the leaves, was his busy, noisy mouth and the spastic twitching of his angry tail. I centered my crosshairs where the squirrel's chest would be. Gently, I squeezed. The gun fired, and three seconds of pandemonium suddenly broke out in the black walnut tree.

The squirrel's perch seemed to leap beneath him. He jerked forward, about to flee, then reversed his field, twisting toward the tree trunk, but too late. Suddenly, the dead branch plummeted toward the forest floor. The squirrel, for another second, clung by a single claw to the brittle stump, and then followed the severed branch downward.

Until both branch and squirrel hit the ground, I didn't know my shot had missed, cutting off the branch but leaving the squirrel unharmed. The squirrel landed in an already advanced state of rodent frenzy. His only thought—if squirrels think—was that he was on the ground, face-to-face, disoriented and defenseless, with a heavily armed predator. The squirrel froze for a split second, legs splayed, trembling from twitching nose to shuddering tail. He was six feet away from me. I could have stepped forward and squished him. Of course, that never occurred to me. Nor did I have the wits to shoot him while he was sitting still. I just stood there, surprised by everything.

This turns out to be the story of my life.

The squirrel needed two things: a) cover and b) a tree to climb. His tiny black eyes twirled in their sockets until he saw the answer to his prayers—if squirrels pray. There was a tunnel! Leading upwards!

In an explosion of whirling feet and flying leaves, he burst across a treacherous expanse of exposed ground and dove for sanctuary, clawing his way desperately up toward safety.

Up my leg. Inside my overalls.

I will not suggest that, at that precise moment, I saw God's hand in the creation of the universe. Suffice to say that, in retrospect—and I shared this insight later, during religion class, with Father Seubert (who humored me)—I understood the subtle interconnectedness, the sentient foresight that certainly some power beyond human comprehension had invested in the infinite diversity of nature. Later, as I was healing, I realized that tree bark—rough, drab and thoroughly devoid of grace or glamour—was one of some Supreme Being's profoundest inspirations. For if trees had no bark, if they were covered, like so many of God's other creatures, only in tender flesh and sparse hair and the occasional birthmark, they would be— every time a squirrel started climbing one—screaming, dancing, pounding frantically at their own tortured extremities and bleeding so profusely that they would all be shortly dead, eventually causing the extinction of their symbiotic tormentors, the infernal knife- footed squirrels.

As I screamed and whacked at myself, the squirrel, his panic in- creasing as he discovered that his escape tunnel was a dead end, ran bloody circles around my thigh. When I hit him, he would shove desperately upward, poking and clawing toward my gonads. My shrieking intensified.

"Ah! Ah! A-a-ah! A-A-A-AH!"

Somewhere, far away, I heard Dad call. I didn't answer. I was busy, beating my leg into hamburger. Blood was soaking through my overalls. Finally, I trapped the squirrel, my hands around his neck. I felt his teeth in my thigh. I let go. The squirrel took another lap around my thigh.

For twenty seconds, thirty seconds, four hours—something—I bounded and jitted and shook and whaled away. The squirrel, doing his part, climbed and climbed, circled and circled, creating a beaten track on my skin. Neither of us were getting anywhere.

It was purely by accident that I stumbled into a fallen log and toppled over on my back, my legs suddenly pointing at the sky.

Somewhere in my pants, the squirrel noticed this drastic reversal of orientation. Instinct clicked in his idiot brain.

Up! He had to go up!

Before I could regain my feet, he had made an excruciating U-turn in the soft tissue behind my knee and he had launched himself—up!—toward my sneaker. He popped out of my overalls like a cartoon banana.

For a moment, he paused, clinging to my sole, staring bug-eyed and clueless at my human kisser. I thought I was a goner. He had me down, a hunter, helpless. He could scurry over my body and rip my eyes out of my face before I was able to fight him off. He could make me pay for centuries of terror and slaughter.

Of course, he didn't do anything of the sort, because—I figured out later—it isn't part of God's plan for squirrels to wreak vengeance on the food chain. The squirrel—just as Dad's hurried footsteps could be heard pounding toward us—leapt magnificently from my foot, hit the ground running and disappeared up the black walnut tree. For about two yards up the trunk, there were tiny, cute, red footprints.

PART II

"We gonna go fishing?"

I can't resist TV fishing. Whenever I'm surfing the cable and I click onto one of those fishing shows on TNN or ESPN2, just as a redneck bass pro yanks a nine-pound largemouth from the drink, I freeze in wonder.

TV fishermen drive boats that cost more than a month in Paris. They have whisper-silent outboards, quadraphonic sonar, Shakespeare reels and artificial lures that look like a collaboration between Rube Goldberg and Pablo Picasso. TV fishing consists entirely of those choice moments when TV fishermen catch monster fish, hold them up (staggering beneath the weight) for the camera and then— Oh my God! No!—let them go.

In real fishing, you never let them go. You run a stringer through their gills, plant the stringer in the mud, and let them die. Later, you eat them.

All my fishing was real, and most of it came before I was fifteen. It was solitary, unsanitary, monotonous and all my fish were runts. And every day, I couldn't wait to get out there.

On a good fishing day, I'd be walking down Pearl, toward the lake, as the sun was only a gray glimmer on the fringe of the sky. I'd cross the weedy lawn behind the Lakeside Motel through an orange mob of Indian paintbrush, my sneakers soaked through with dew. On the lake, an inch of fog hugged the water against the dawn and the breeze. Grateful mosquitoes swarmed to me for a last snack before the heat drove them into the reeds. Pumpkinseeds, sunfish and perch, most with mouths too small to fit my hook, stirred the surface, making evanescent trails of hungry bubbles. A mallard or two, cranky at my intrusion, shuffled from the shoreweeds and plopped into the water, paddling sleepily out of range. One rare day, the far shore was a white floe of trumpeter swans, protesting the dawn like truckers in traffic. Once, I stumbled back and fell, awestruck as a great blue heron unfolded six feet away, spread its centaur wings and rose dripping from the water into the mist, like a Japanese ghost story.

On a day like that, the driftwood never snagged my tackle, the nightcrawlers were faithful to the hook, the wind fashioned an open spot among the water weeds, the rock bass were ravenous and the bullheads were jealous. As I fished, I could look both ways down the meandering shore, where pines and weeds gave way to piled concrete slabs lapped by algae-gummy water, and there was no one in sight but me, small, soggy, dead serious and mute—except for the occasional word of sympathy to a doomed bluegill.

The Incompleat Angler

I took to fishing like a trout to mercury.

One day, about seven years old, I was a yard-dwelling kid whose knowledge of the wide and varied environs of Tomah stretched only as far as the Keeton compound on one side of my grandmother Annie's house and Tillie Fredericks's vast garden complex on the other side, with one exception: I was a regular visitor among the eight Weiner children and their toy-strewn half-acre, located over yonder, one house beyond May Street. And I played twilight games—stoop tag and red rover and hide-'n'-go-seek down across the alley in the Draak yard. But none of these places were far to go, and I rarely crossed Pearl Street, which ran right in front of Annie's house and served as the portal to Lake Street, Butts Avenue, the fairgrounds and the universe.

Next day, everything changed. Galaxies unfolded. Coaxed from the nest by Dad, I became a vagabond fisherman, barely passing a warm day without a visit to Lake Tomah—dammed by Franklin Delano Roosevelt and fed by the Lemonweir River. My angling gear never improved far beyond rudiments, first a cane pole, later a whole Zebco push-button spin-cast ensemble, plus a slimy fist of worms in a Campbell's can. After that, the Keetons, Weiners, Draaks, they could come along to the lake, or stay behind. Didn't matter. I had places to go, bluegills to outwit, bellies to slit and guts to grab, and miles to reel before I slept.

There is nothing like fishing to express the fullness of being a kid. It is steeped in filth, good rich earthy organic goo—worm dung and fish slime and entrails between your fingers. It has machismo, the hooking of the wild, struggling quarry, the yanking and landing, the subduing of the thing with bare hands, the bloody retrieval of the lethal barb, sometimes torn from the very viscera of the flopping bug-eyed critter when the "goddamn stupid fish swallowed the hook, goddammit"—and the fish themselves, masculine to the throes of death, squirting fish shit all over your hands, bristling with teeth and spikes, lashing desperately at their captor, writhing and puncturing, especially the frog-slippery, hypodermic bullhead. But also, in fishing, there is the ineffable female side, the delicate craft of tying hook to silken line, and weaving the worm, fingers slick, onto the hook, and the guile of searching the impassive water's surface for pockets of hungry, furtive life beneath, and the itchy patience of watching, waiting, teasing the nibble-nibble suitor 'til, roused beyond prudence, it opens wide, gobbles whole and snags itself on the irresistible.

There was freedom in fishing, beyond any other kid activity. You left home and yard and family, and crossed into a remnant of wilderness. Fishing had no social element that wasn't entirely voluntary. You could fish with others, but once immersed in the quest, society boiled down to you and the pole and the fish. There might be conversation, but it was talk so small and sporadic that it was tuneless bugbuzz. No dialogue of any depth or importance ever occurred during real fishing. Fishing had no clock; the fish were always there, although their timetable for biting and not biting was capricious and impenetrable; the lake had no closing time. And when you went home, no one asked where you'd been, or wondered why you were gone so long to return so late. Fishing explained itself. You stood for all to regard, soiled and pungent and carrying a stringerful of provender. You couldn't be punished for too much fishing.

Best, I think, was fishing's mystery. Only rarely could you look through the viscous veil of a lake's surface and see the fish you sought. And then, you never caught the fish you saw. Visible fish were either wary or disdainful; no way to tell which. Could you read a bass's mind? Does a bass have a mind? The fish you caught, if you caught any, were the others, the invisible fish, cruising and snuffling in the dark depths. But how? How could a kid, this clunky, land-lubbing sack of ribs and thumbs, capture a fish—a silver glimmer of now-you-see-it lightning, possessed of some divine power to turn water into air, and breathe in the drowning pool? Why would this shimmering thing sacrifice its life to a nightcrawler, a crude bamboo pole and a half-formed biped? How could anyone catch a fish?

Every fish I ever landed, all my life, renewed my wonderment. It suggested, through its gasping liplessness, that depths unseeable could offer up countless jewels of wriggling beauty, that feats un-imaginable were inexplicably attainable. A boy who could catch a perch could walk on the moon, or cure cancer . . .

My dad gave me fishing. The idea seemed to come over him all of a sudden, on a Friday, in the late spring, too soon for my birthday. He tracked me down after school.

Dad didn't tell me where we were going that day. He just piled me into the Ford—we were, more or less, a Ford family—and drove over by the high school, not far from where the Fuchses lived. In the Fifties, businesses were still like metastases; they popped up ran-domly, all through a town, unexpected growths that drew their sus-tenance from the neighborhood, then subtly spread their influence outward, osmotically, throughout the town. So, in what was part house and part business, on a tree-lined street two blocks from the Conoco station, a man named Olson had started a sporting goods shop. It took up what should have been a living room, a dining room, possibly a master bedroom. Hard to say, because the space was so densely filled with lures and poles and reels and bobbers and hooks and sinkers, plus guns, shells, gloves, balls, bows and arrows. Just outside the door was an elephant's foot umbrella stand and in it was a bouquet of cane poles, bamboo rods segmenting up to lengths of eight feet, ten feet, twelve feet, straight as a die 'til they curved wearily toward their skinny tips, each pole lacquered dark and shiny against the rain and sun. We weren't even inside the shop. Dad said, "Pick one out."

Until that moment, he hadn't said we were buying anything, much less buying something for *me*. Dad had said barely a word on the short drive over. Suddenly, this trip was for me. Me! To buy something. Not just something; this great, graceful whip of jungle-wood!

I kept my mouth shut, the better not to shatter Dad's mood of generosity and bring him to his senses. I touched one, timidly. Dad, benevolently impatient, seized the pole I had touched, freed it from the cluster, put it into my hands. I wrapped my fingers around it, almost in self-defense.

"See how it feels. Heft it a little."

I hefted it a little, timidly, not quite sure how one hefted a cane pole. Dad stood back, regarding my experiment with the irony that, in all his life, never ceased to animate his features.

"Um," I said.

"Well?"

"Yeah," I said.

"How's it feel?"

"Um, good."

"That the one you want?"

This was the clincher. He was going to buy me one of these beautiful, gigantic magic wands. Holy smokes!

"Um," I said.

"Try another one."

I did. There was no difference, except, of course, trying another one, knowing that one of these—guaranteed—was going to be mine, personally, forever. I gripped it manfully, stroked it erotically, whipped its tip around in the sky like Lash LaRue preparing to flick off the black hat of a bushwhacking owlhoot.

Dad lost interest. "I'll be inside," he said.

With that, I made a hasty choice—a ten-footer, gold-brown with maple-dark ridges. I tried to bring it inside and figured out why the cane poles were outside the door. Finally, suddenly terrified that someone else would come along a moment later and claim my personal private bamboo rod, I left it against the door frame, separate from the other, the unchosen, the inferior poles. I followed Dad inside, into Olson's treasure trove. It was dim in there, its atmosphere imposed by oak floors that were almost black with a hundred generations of wax. There were windows, but blocked by shelves and piled with display cards of fishing lures and sunglasses and mosquito repellent. The walls were a riot of racks—rod racks, rifle racks, racquet racks. The abundance was dizzying. Olson was there, motionless and genial on a stool behind a cluttered counter. He and Dad talked like adults talked, in that easy familiarity that struck my ears as a sort of jazz chorus, tightly structured but improvisational, a language to be studied and mastered and carried into life like a guild card or a passport. While Dad small-talked, he moved expertly among an infinity of trays on counters, each tray sectioned into rows and squares, each square bearing a tiny label, each tray filled with the mystic implements of fishing. Hooks, single ones to invade mouths as small as minnows and sticklebacks, as big as northerns and muskies. Treble hooks for catching monsters, whales and giant morays. Sinkers you had to bite, sinkers with rubber inserts so you didn't have to bite them. Corks and bobbers in a thousand sizes, but almost all of them half-red, half-white. Swivels and leaders and teardrops and poppers and pinkies and doll flies, wet flies and treble-hooked spoons with delicious names like "daredevil" and "basskiller."

I poked into squares, touched the barbed lures gingerly, dazzled myself with the intricate bulbous complications of a bass plug, reveled in exotica while Dad—all business—picked out what I needed, nothing more. A dozen hooks, a plastic box of pellet sinkers (the biting kind), a spool of black nylon line strong enough to lift a cinder block, three bobbers, a stringer and a cheap tin tackle box to hold it all.

Olson charged fifty cents for the pole, more than that for the tackle box, much less for everything else. Dad got out of there for about a buck and a half, my admission price to the world beyond Pearl.

> *. . . A soldier of fortune*
> *Is the man called*
> *Paladin . . .*

My dad's day job was painting—houses, garages, cars, interiors and exteriors. Our tiny house down on The Alley was stacked with wallpaper sample albums. Dad roared off to work, whenever the urge moved him, wearing splattered white coveralls that suggested a frenzied ambush by Jackson Pollock. His most pampered tool was the compressed air pump he used for spray painting. Dad was a pioneer of spray painting, avoiding rollers and brushes whenever possible because they were slow and, I think, he hated the tedium of smearing one color endlessly, back and forth, up and down, dab-dab-dab on the rough spots and curvy moldings, and counting hours 'til it was over and he could head for the Carlton, or the Tee Pee, the Crow Bar or Kelly's up in Oakdale, where he was the foremost bartender of his day.

In Tomah, every bar in town, if the door was open as you passed by, hit you with the jaded ambience of all the beer that had been spilled, splashed, tossed and belched there in the past eon and couldn't be mopped up, waxed over or purged from the murky air. Stale beer was the smell of walking down Superior Avenue. It was the spoor of adulthood. It was dirty jokes and hoarse laughter and empty threats bellowed point-blank over two short bottles of Old Style. It was Lucky Strikes in the cigarette machines, Beer Nuts on the bar and jukebox bathos from Patsy Cline. It was GIs on leave from McCoy and desperate divorced women in bright red low-cut dresses. It was the sinner's incense, the aroma of desire. I slowed down whenever I passed a bar, just to sniff the innuendo.

My dad was luminary in this Stygian demimonde, an ace barkeep in a beer town. Everybody knew Dad's name. Dad was social and sarcastic, an ironist among the literal and the feebled, a young strong handsome guy in command of everything he surveyed. His hands were a blur. His wit was an icepick. His smile was Robert Mitchum's. I'd sit on a barstool near him, nursing a tall ginger ale (saving my maraschino 'til the glass was drained)—staying quiet so as not to be noticed, challenged and sent home to bed—watching him mix Manhattans, draw Pabsts, shake martinis, pour grasshoppers, humor barflies and flirt with every woman in town. Dad would also drink some, just to keep folks company—'til past 2:00 A.M., every night but bowling night.

Trouble was . . .

The offshoot of all the late nights and hangovers—plus a real fondness for sleep—meant that Dad, most days, was a reluctant fisherman. From the day Dad took me over to Olson's store, going on forever, he would resolve for my sake to rise before dawn, to reach the fish before the sun killed their mysterious appetites. He would promise to get up. He would vow. He would set the alarm. In the black-dark morn next day, while I bounced from bed and dressed hurriedly in heavy duds to fend the predawn chill, I'd bump things, brush Dad's bed, gauge the depth of Dad's snore, estimate the grip of his oblivion. The alarm would sound, only to be silenced by a reflex that wakened only Dad's arm. Five minutes. Ten. Tick tick.

Sighing, timorous, "Dad?"

Zilch.

Small hands rustling a large shoulder, as I ducked the stale exhaust from his mouth.

"Hey, Dad. It's after six."

Visceral noises.

"We gonna go fishing?"

A growl, a refusal, a threat.

Persistence. "Dad?"

"What, *god*dam't?"

I'd retreat then, frightened, wait, remember the fish, silvery, elusive, seductive, find courage and attack again, nudge him harder.

"Dad?"

"Wha?"

"It's gettin' late, Dad."

"Jeez *Christ!*"

This is how the ritual began, dragging on for another hour or more, until I failed and gave up on that day's fishing; or until grumbling, lumbering, softening, remembering my hopefulness, he'd detach from the bed, emerge from sleep and—after a breakfast on the road that I didn't want to eat because the fish, *the fish!* were waiting—we'd reach the sated, sleepy fish by nine or ten, under a withering sun, and hope that, among the fish, there were a few risers as slow as Dad.

Dad loved fishing, too. This was obvious when I finally coaxed him from the spell of sleep and the hangover's hold. He knew good fishing holes, cared for his tackle, handled his rod like Henry Aaron at bat and played his strikes with nimble ferocity. And, once awake, he never begrudged me my efforts to limit him to three miserable hours of sleep and ruin his rightful recovery from Friday night.

He'd take me, sometimes, to a spot on Lake Tomah called the Point, but not in daylight. We went to the Point as night was falling, because this was the hour when the crappies bit. They struck suddenly, a ten-inch explosion of black and silver, running and twisting in the dusk, tossing droplets from Dad's taut line like sparks from a brainstorm. Fishing for crappies at twilight, Dad would fit a transparent teardrop float on his line, and space his bait, a pinkie or a dead minnow or a chunk of worm, a foot or so from the float. He'd cast this temptation into the lake what seemed like a mile, until it disappeared into the dark. He'd reel fast, jerking the line, retrieving the teardrop, but alert, vigilant, expectant. Dad somehow knew when the crappies were hungry. He had a psychic connection to crappies, who, like him, woke slowly in the morning and cringed in sunlight, but felt their juices flow and appetite clawing at their ribs as night fell and spots of false light formed a jagged necklace around the lake. Dad rarely went three straight casts without a hit. A splash would sound invisibly across the black ripples, the line would sing, the drag would buzz for a second. And then Dad would be leaning against the rod, the rod curving toward the water, and the struggling crappie, fighting the deadly surface, would zigzag toward shore.

Dad never offered a word of instruction about catching crappies. It was probably something personal, like his vendetta against red squirrels. But he broke the usual code of silence long enough to teach me how to catch the other fish. He wanted me to learn about fishing. Fishing took him back to being a kid, it took him away from being a grownup and deep into the heart of fatherhood.

On my very first day out with Dad, after the trip to Olson's store, after Dad taught me how to tie my line to the tip of my cane pole, tie the hook, clasp the sinker and set the bobber, we fished in the morning—not early, but early enough—down at the lake. We'd go to a spot below the dam, a basin of muddy water, ten feet deep, where the fish always gathered in remarkable variety—perch, bluegill, sunfish, bullhead, rock bass, white bass, even the occasional fearsome maneating poisonfleshed prehistoric dogfish.

He taught me the ritual of twisting a worm into small loops, fixing each loop by plunging the hook through the worm's body, ignoring the writhing of the sacrifice with each fresh puncture, and making sure the last loop fit inside the barb—or else the worm would wriggle partly free and trail in the water for a fish to devour without risking death.

Nothing left to do but swing my line into the water. With a cane pole, this was simple. The line was as long as the pole. The bobber was a pendulum which swung out above the water. You let it drop when it reached full extension. It settled there, held in place by bait and sinker, perhaps fifteen feet from shore. Nothing left to do but wait, 'til a fish rose to the worm. When one did—and my first day was a good day—the bobber spoke, in bobberspeak. Dad interpreted, teaching me the language.

. . . When it bounces up and down, steady like that, with the waves, it's just the waves. Don't get excited. Hold on. There. You see? It's bouncing a little, but not steady. You got a nibble. But wait. He hasn't taken it yet. [Fish are always "he."] Get ready. Now, you see, it's moving. Not just up and down, but a little sideways. He's taking it. He's got it in his mouth. But wait. He might be too small to get his mouth around the hook. He's still just nibbling.

Then!

Shloop!

Suddenly, the whole bobber, a wondrous red-and-white plunge, came to life.

"He's got it!" said Dad, as excited as I ever heard his voice. "Pull!"

I pulled, desperately, violently, prodigiously!

Out of the water, in an eye-ripping streak, came bobber, sinker, hook, line and a spray of green water. No fish. No worm. Hook and line, like a tangle of barbed wire homing in on an electromagnet, flew straight at me, slapped my face soggily, buried a barb in my forearm and wrapped me in nylon.

"A little too hard," said Dad, the irony back in his voice.

But the fish were *there*!

We went again. This time, the fish was less cautious. He found the new worm, bounced the bobber once, glommed my worm and then beelined for Davy Jones's locker. And this time, Dad instructing, me listening, I tightened the line sharply once, and let up for a split second, setting the hook in the fish's lip. Then . . .

"Now, pull."

I felt desperate resistance as the fish's every muscle reacted. The line and the bamboo telegraphed sensation into my fingers. A twist, a hard shiver, a desperate flutter and a lashing tail, clawing for purchase in the frictionless water as I pulled, pulled. The fish, helpless on my hook, broke the surface with a soft gulp and swung to me, twisting and resisting and chewing the implacable hook.

"Bluegill," said Dad.

He was a fat, broad, epic bluegill, as big as a dessert plate, his scales an iridescent green, changing colors in the sun, his belly mottled orange and white, the blue tag on his gill the color of lapis. I caught him flying toward me, let him slip off my hand, stared at him dangling, struggling on my line, alive, yanked from the soul of the earth through rivers of protoplasm and jungles of seaweed. Dad interceded, grabbed the bluegill before it could shake itself off the hook, or escape by shredding its jaw. He showed me how to remove the hook and how to stringer the fish. The bluegill battled through it all, flapping and gasping. Stringered, back in the water, its gills working, restoring oxygen to its shocked tissues, the fish lived on, feathering its fins, testing its tether, alive, doomed.

All told that day, I caught ten fish, sharpening my bamboo finesse with each strike. Somewhere, there's a photo that Dad took when we got home—me and my mess of bluegills, sunfish, bullheads, all dead by then.

Every word Dad said that day was education, nothing more, nothing superfluous. Fishing is not a talkative sport. But even when not fishing, we were not talkative, me and Dad. He gave me fishing out of a love he never articulated. This was hardly unique. I never knew a kid, in those days, whose dad went around saying "I love you" and mush like that. Maybe it was Midwestern reticence or masculine repression. Maybe it was just a sensible reluctance to express the obvious. In my world, dads by definition—even the total incompetents and the frightening thugs—loved their kids, and there were no agnostics to the faith. Anger, jokes, pedagogy, my first precious lessons in sarcasm—for these matters Dad had words. But love went unspoken. Dad loved me through gestures, through lessons and gifts. I never thought myself deprived of his love, even a year later, when Mom finally lost patience with Dad's arrested adolescence and moved us out, making Dad only an occasional visitor to the rest of my life. All I had to do, to remember Dad's love, wherever I was, wherever he might be, was look at a fish.

Nevertheless, because Dad remained hopelessly unreliable in the morning, I swiftly developed my own fishing routine, every day for weeks in the summer, trekking down to the lake and lingering 'til noon, then shlepping back home with a stringer so heavy with fish I could barely carry it—which meant an afternoon elbow-deep in slime, scaling bluegills, skinning bullheads, lopping heads, piling up fishguts in a fly-mad pile on the picnic table in Annie's yard, under the ancient shadebush. By giving me fishing and then bailing out on me, Dad set me free. But he also circumscribed my childhood. I became a provider, one foot—shod in a Ked and damp from the lake—in the grownup world.

Fishing sketched the personalities of my different summers. One year, I was a lone fisher, strolling in first morning light to the lake edge, to a few dependable spots that teemed with yellow perch and strawberry bass. One morning, I saw my first loon, raving by the shore in a veil of fog. I'd fish 'til almost noon, filling a stringer. I'd head back in time for Annie's faithful lunch, with Papa, my grandfather, who walked home at twelve sharp from the Milwaukee Road frog shops. By two o'clock, my fish were cleaned and wrapped, a few to serve for supper, the rest piling up in the freezer. The day was but begun. The Tomah Public Library opened at two. I knew no pleasure then finer than finishing with fish and switching to books. I would cross the Monroe Street hill in the middle of town, where all the schools and the Catholic church overlooked the main street. I'd dump a half dozen books, devoured overnight and emptied of delight, on the circulation desk, and hurry to the stacks for new discoveries. The library was like fishing, but without the muck and suffocation.

Another summer, brother Bill and I, a contentious pair, formed a prickly foursome with our cousins, Danny and Bobby, who had moved over the winter to Tomah. They hailed from exotic Necedah, rattlesnake capital of Wisconsin and the home of a woman who—she insisted—had had visions of the Virgin Mary just outside her privy. Thousands of Catholics flocked every year to Necedah to stake out the holy outhouse and petition the Virgin for leukemia cures. Meanwhile, back in Tomah, Danny and Bobby, Bill and I were straddling the concrete wall that slanted down from the bridge below the dam and reeling in bullheads from the languid Lemonweir. It was the summer of the bullheads. Somehow, all the mother bullheads in Lake Tomah had spawned the bumperest crop of baby bullheads in piscine history. None were more than six inches long. And they were ravenous. They struck our worms almost before they hit the surface of the water. We jettisoned corks and bobbers, fished with hooks, naked lines and any bait we found in the fridge—beefsteak, pork fat, pimentos. The little bullheads ate it all, hooked themselves, and came flying from the Lemonweir at a rate of a hundred an hour, until our arms were weary and our hands bloody from bullhead spikes. For a week or so, we fished for infant bullheads and never threw any of them back into the creek. We kept them all, let them die in our creels and took them home for food. Well, food was our intention. But bullheads, whose skin must be stripped, take a long time to clean. If we had dutifully dressed all of our little bullheads, we would have lost time preferably spent riding our bikes, playing baseball, swimming and examining each other's bodies from head to toe for wood ticks burrowing at our veins and capillaries. The bullheads we'd caught and killed went to waste for a while, and then we began throwing them back into the Lemonweir, whereat they would lunge for the next hook they saw. We began to catch them over and over, counting the hookmarks in their iron jaws, recognizing their faces.

That summer, too, a heat wave struck, lingering for weeks, turning the waters of Lake Tomah into a warm bath. The fish retreated deep into the middle of the lake, out of our reach, while the water lilies near shore, nourished by the sun and fed by their own rot, spread riotously. In August, a boat full of municipal employees counter-attacked the water lilies, dumping herbicides into the lagoons near the lake park, just inside the Point. We saw no damage to the water lilies, but suddenly, from nowhere, fish appeared in the shallows near shore, weak and gulping air. Here were fish we'd never seen before! Extraordinary fish from unknown trenches and secret depths. There were gars and pike and largemouth bass, bluegills broad as pie plates and catfish bigger than your leg. And they were helpless. Bobby threw off his shoes and waded in, reaching out, snatching a lazy, dazy northern pike behind its gills and lifting the monster triumphantly from the lake—holding it up, limp and unstruggling, with his bare hands.

Bonanza! In a trice, we were into the water after Bobby. Our shoes lay cluttered on the park grass. We rolled our dungarees up to our thighs, then got them wet, after all, splashing farther and farther into the lake after the gigantic, woozy whoppers.

Lake Tomah was not a clean lake. No lake close to a town, in Wisconsin, in the Fifties, was strictly pristine—although none were actually poisonous and none were unfishable. Lake Tomah, like most well-used reservoirs, had its oil slicks from outboard motors, farm chemicals from upstream on the Lemonweir, a tolerable level of piss-and-shit pollution from a few unsewered lake cottages, beer cans poking out among the water lilies. Most of all, Lake Tomah had broken glass. People picnicked by the lake, drank from Coke bottles, swirly Pepsi bottles, longnecked beer bottles and then—festively—chucked the empties into the lake. Most bottles just settled, intact, at the bottom, silting over, sinking, sinking, creating a smooth walking surface for the occasional daring lake-wader, swimless child or passing heron. On the other hand, the lake bottom was covered with rocks. Bottles hitting rocks break, a reality that occasioned mothers to tell their sons, "Don't go in there barefoot. There's glass!"

This was a warning we usually heeded, but we'd never before seen twenty-four-inch fish swimming, stoned out of their gourds, three feet from shore. We damned the glass, unshod, and plunged pell-mell into the blind, treacherous mud. I found my personal beer bottle about ten feet from shore while herding a world-record gar into my clutches. I felt barely a pinprick on my big toe, but I knew what had happened. Water close to the lake bottom was colder; it knifed my opened flesh with a shocking chill.

I limped to shore to examine the wound, trailed by Bobby, Danny and Bill. Blood, to boys, is every bit as interesting as big fish. We figured out quickly that my cut was fairly huge, because there was so much blood gushing from my toe that the contours of the laceration were indistinguishable. I wiped at the flow of blood, which instantly replenished itself. A puddle formed in the grass.

"Boy," said Bobby, "you better go back."

Reluctant to leave Lake Tomah's once-in-a-lifetime windfall of big fish, I considered the possibility of just throwing a sock onto my foot, to hold my toe together, then going back into the water.

"I don't know," I said.

"Jesus," said Danny. "You're really getting white."

"Yeah," said Bill, who saw the possibility of beating me out of something, for once in his life, "you better go back."

All little brothers are vipers. I thought I was hard up because I had Bill, following along, getting underfoot and then, when I finally needed him, betraying me. But Peg had it worse than me. She had two of us.

I stared at my toe. The blood was like a river.

I relented. I'd go back.

At this point, kid ethics kicked in. The Code made us all Darwinists. A more advanced species—say, baboons, or scorpions—would have delegated a member of the colony to accompany me home, in case I passed out from blood loss and shock. Kids, however—well, boys—recognize no known fraternal bonds. A kid who falls by the wayside stays by the wayside, unless he can pick his own ass up and get going again. That famous war scene where the wounded soldier says, "I can't make it. You guys go on without me," wouldn't work with kids. There wouldn't be anyone for the wounded kid to say this to; every other kid would be way ahead already, not looking back.

So, without further sentiment, Danny, Bobby and Bill (first putting their sneakers on, just in case) plunged back into the lake. I shoed my good foot, wrapped the cut toe clumsily in a sock, and mounted my bike. My grandma Annie's house was a mile off.

At about the halfway mark, I noticed my bike wobbling oddly and the path along the lake edge forking off in two different directions—something the path had never done before. I decided to pull over and rest up. I laid down my bike, gently—nothing was as precious as my bike—and sat on the curb in front of Tomah Hospital. My head swam ever so psychotropically. My toe throbbed. I watched my sock fill with blood until a steady drip began puddling on the pavement. This was pretty fascinating. It never occurred to me that I was twenty steps from an entire hospital full of nurses, doctors, candy stripers and other professional caregivers. In my universe, hospitals were not a place people went with problems like a toe that was shredded from stepping on a busted Meister Brau bottle in Lake Tomah. Mothers had babies in hospitals. Old people went to hospitals, mainly to die. Kids only got dragged, bawling, to hospitals—for hypodermic needles.

By and by, my wooze subsided. My blood puddle was an impressive six inches in diameter and beginning to form a stream in the gutter. I climbed back into the saddle and pedaled forth.

I was still dizzy when I got to Annie, who looked at my face—white as albumen—and said, "Oh my God."

Once in Annie's care, however, I was in clover. She bundled me indoors, tipped me over, studied my cut, cleaned it with water and peroxide, wrapped it in twenty yards of gauze and put the word out around the neighborhood that the boy needed emergency medicine—right this minute! Mrs. Konicek across the street picked up the bulletin and made a call. Most of Tomah's doctors worked down the street at the clinic, next to the hospital. On weekends, they stood around the sidewalk, leaning on a rake and talking with Papa. When an emergency landed on Annie's porch, they came to Annie's porch, rather than ordering up transportation to the ER. A half-hour after my legendary bike ride from Lake Tomah with a big toe "split open like an overheated cuke," Dr. Konicek was at Annie's, unwrapping my gauze and reviewing Annie's first aid.

Dr. Konicek didn't have to do much, but his touch was immensely reassuring to Annie. Me, too. After the crisis had passed, I got a week's worth of luxurious convalescence on Annie's porch, with all my meals served on a tray, with a pile of books to keep me amused and the Milwaukee Braves on the radio. Danny, Bobby and Bill all got reamed royally for not helping me get home, and they had to throw away a pile of the biggest fish they would ever catch in their whole lives because every grownup on Pearl Street agreed that the fish had been poisoned.

The incident with the broken bottle, of course, had no effect on my loyalties. I remained, mainly, a lake kid. The Keeton boys next door, because their father was a Serious Fisherman who drove Up North (a mist-shrouded Camelot), were not lake kids. Some of the kids who lived way out of town were, more or less, cranberry bog kids—which made me envious. The cranberry bogs, full of snags and snappers, teemed with ravenous catfish and capricious black bass. Once, angling in twilight at the cranberry bogs, I yanked my line and gaped in awe as my fish soared from the water with, clamped angrily onto its tail, an immense snapping turtle—twelve feet from wingtip to wingtip, two hundred pounds, shooting sparks and cursing gutturally in what sounded like German. In three breathtaking seconds, the half-eaten fish and trailing snapper straightened my hook and plummeted into the swamp with a prodigious splash.

As I grew more adventurous with my bicycle, I did a little exploring among the stony streams and ponds that flowed on every side of town, but they were either barren of fish, or the fish were too finicky to sniff my humble bait. My loyalty always brought me home to Lake Tomah. I never evolved into a creek kid.

Still, I learned a lot from creeks.

The Epic Lone-Wolf Trout of Council Creek

One summer, after fifth grade, I fell under the spell of an eighth grader, a loner like me, named Kevin. Kevin wasn't a lake kid. Because he lived near it, he had become obsessed with Council Creek (pronounced "Crick"), a fetid stream meandering along the north edge of town. Kevin's dubious conviction was that Council Creek was an unheralded "trout stream."

Kevin's trout stream delusion contained, although minuscule, a kernel of truth. Upstream somewhere, in a sloping pasture on the Ridge, Council Creek burst from the earth, spring-fed and ice-cold. It meandered and burbled among cowflops and maple groves, nurturing little pockets of stunted trout where swirling water formed hollows in soft bottom soil. This was miles and miles away from town. The minute Council Creek hit the Tomah city limits, it grew whiskers and needed a bath. Inside town, first off, Council Creek became the sluiceway for the Tomah Creamery. A few times a day, the Creamery would vomit several thousand gallons of warm whey into the passing stream. Whey (the stuff Miss Muffet poured on her curds—God knows why) is a rich dairy waste product that tends to encourage the riotous growth of algae.

I got to know the Creamery, and its relationship to Council Creek, after Mom had moved us out of our little bungalow on The

Alley, to T.J.'s house, way up on the north side of town off Highway 12. When my cousins Danny and Bobby found out Peg and
Bill and I were living upstairs in T.J.'s house—T.J. right downstairs
listening to our every footfall and waiting for us to make one false
move—Bobby said, "Jee-*zus*! Are you scared?"

"Shitless!"

Bobby and Danny were surprised I was still alive. For all of T.J.'s
grandchildren—there were dozens of us—T.J. himself was the
boogeyman. He was Vlad the Impaler. He was the Sheriff of Not-
tingham.

"Holy shit! Upstairs from T.J.!" said Bobby. "Ho-oly *shit*!"

The consolation in our banishment to T.J.'s house was Grandma,
the undisputed ruler of a kitchen where no fear or discord was
conceivable, at the risk of blaspheming the food. Grandma was
short and round, shaped like a cookie jar, with an endless mane
of gray-brown hair wound tight to her head and hidden, mysteri-
ously, somewhere in her clothes. Grandma, except when she shuffled humbly to St. Mary's in some shapeless bag of a dress, was
always in an apron, thus signifying her vocation. Unlike everyone
else on earth, Grandma never got any lip, never a critical word (unless he happened to be bitching about somebody else) from T.J. He
spared Grandma because he judged her as having done her job. In
less than twenty years, she had borne thirteen children, twelve of
whom had survived. She had kept immaculate a huge, rambling
bluff of a house, filling it thrice daily with cooking smells that would
have tempted a Carmelite to give up self-mortification for roast
chicken and buckwheat pancakes.

Now and then, Grandma would give me a dollar bill and a four-
quart stoneware bowl, and dispatch me to the Creamery. I hurried
across Highway 12 and down a side street. I'd enter the Creamery
through an unmarked door, and hand the bowl to a man in the office. He'd lead me inside, to a great silver vat, from which he
scooped butter into the bowl until it heaped three inches over the
top, like ice cream in a giant cone. I handed over my dollar and said
thank you. Then, wrapping my arms around the bowl, I carried

home five pounds of butter so fresh that it beaded up with oily dew before I handed it to Grandma. I knew that butter could also be bought—at grocery stores—in little quarter-pound blocks wrapped in wax paper, but I made sure never to tell Grandma.

Starting from T.J.'s house and going down behind the Creamery, I could follow Council Creek a half-mile or so to the Monowau Street dump. There, the foamy brown waters wended their way through rusting Maytags, slippery heaps of rotting cranberries and mountains of threadbare truck tires. On the shoals of garbage that had come to rest more or less permanently in the creek, whey stains recorded the high-tide mark.

Farther on, where pastures touched the shore, grazing Holsteins made regular pause, plopping fertile additions into the thickening soup that flowed ever westward toward the Mississippi. Children rarely ventured near these pastured stretches of Council Creek. They were frightened away by stories of immense snapping turtles who now and then wandered ashore and devoured entire calves by clamping crocodile jaws onto their legs and dragging them under-water. A similar fate, grownups warned, awaited wayward kids. And if the snappers didn't get us, the white-slaving gandy dancers would.

Most of us never did figure out what a gandy dancer did, other than murder children, and we often wondered why society so casu-ally tolerated their proximity to nice little towns like Tomah.

It was downstream from all this horror where dwelt—Kevin assured me—the ruggedest trouts in all the Midwest. These mean-street trout hung out in a murky pool, preying on any edible organ-ism that entered their domain, feasting on rotten tomatoes and PCBs and flinging loud, filthy underwater slurs at Mother Nature.

According to Kevin, this deep and dirty stretch of Council Creek was the relict of some long-dead farmer's efforts to create a reservoir for his livestock. On the upstream end of the "trout pool" was a makeshift concrete dam. Downstream, two felled trees held the water back—as well as a tangle of brush, twenty or thirty bleached beer cans, a few spent rubber condoms undulating like jellyfish, a jumble of oxidized farm equipment and a permanent slick of motor oil and yellowish foam. A dirt road, the halfhearted denouement of Saratoga Street, passed nearby, lending a certain Erskine Caldwell finality to the locale. The pool and the little-traveled strip of dusty Saratoga were the only clear spots in a swaying field of horse nettle and timothy, burdock, milkweed and wild asparagus that sprawled and buzzed for a hundred yards in three directions. There was a cluster of trees close to the pool, black willow and elm, fine for climbing but an impediment to any sportsman trying to cast with an eight-foot spinning rod and a push-button Zebco reel—the redoubtable Kevin's weapon of choice.

The singular and legendary feature of Kevin's "trout pool"—which kept it from real utility as a swimming hole—was its astounding abundance of a black, tubular species of leech, universally, respectfully, known as "bloodsuckers." There was a difference, you understand, between "bloodsuckers" and mere "leeches." A leech was flat and oval with ribbed skin, usually found living symbiotically in the armpits of turtles. Kids regarded your typical leech as sluggish and inept, bereft of the go-getter outlook that made its cousin, the true bloodsucker, the stuff of campfire stories, bad dreams and shivery-creepy scenes from *The African Queen*.

Knowing about this pool's bloodsucker glut, and incredulous that they would readily suffer coexistence with a fellow tenant as taste-tempting as a trout, I accompanied Kevin skeptically to his secret grove.

Kevin had his spinning ensemble. I still had bamboo and black line. Kevin was disdainful of my outfit, I apologetic. Assuming that this fishing trip was the same as all those that had gone before, I had brought my Campbell's can, full of nightcrawlers. Kevin rolled his eyes, called my worms a "last resort." With a measure of pomposity I failed to fully appreciate, Kevin explained that the compleat angler eventually outgrows the primal urge to merely harvest "fish" in the generic sense. As the sport fisherman matures, he fixes his expectations not on the lumpenfish that spill from one's wicker creel in gross and unseemly multitude, but on a peerage of specific fish whom he has come to know personally.

Kevin had a certain fish in mind. The quarry of Kevin's cerebral quest finned (he insisted) lazily beneath the surface of the polluted pool. I was dubious, but the prospect of matching wits with that "big trout" drew Kevin like a magnet and excited him, he said, like a beautiful woman unhooking her nylons.

The latter reference went by me like a speeding tractor, but I caught his drift. I silently guessed that this afternoon would not go down as the fishing highlight of my summer vacation. Of course, I'd heard rumors of Kevin's trout, but the rumors had attracted no fishermen, ever, other than Kevin. The consensus around town seemed to be that if there was indeed a fish in that toxic hole, there was only *one* fish.

When one plays *kemo sabe* to a prophet like Kevin, one learns not to hasten eagerly to any site of mutual recreation. It came to me early in our relationship that I was not authorized to ever commence anything. Much of the instruction I picked up from Kevin along the way consisted of encouragements like "Hold this!" and "Now, stay back and watch this!" and, most often, "No! What are you *doing*? Wait for me and I'll show you! Don't touch it again!"

Such admonitions applied, implicitly, to our pursuit of the epic lone-wolf trout of Council Creek.

In this case, however, it was tough standing back reverently waiting for Kevin to dispense knowledge and reveal technique. I knew how to fish, and my cane pole was the closest thing to instant fishing that the hand of man has ever conceived. Within sixty seconds, I had unwrapped the necessary ten feet of black nylon and two-hundred-pound-test fishline. I'd guessed the depth of the pool at about fifty inches and set my bobber appropriately. I strung a fresh worm on my hook. I was beginning to swing my line toward the center of the creek when Kevin halted me in mid-cast, reminding me harshly of his proprietary rights in this domain.

Stifling a sigh, I withdrew my cast.

Meanwhile, complications developed. The first was a Gordian tangle of monofilament line inside Kevin's Zebco. He responded with all the scatology known to your average devoutly Catholic eighth grader—which isn't much—and then sat back on the bank, in the shadow of a huge half-dead black willow, to untangle. As the process extended to forty-five minutes, then to an hour and beyond, one might picture Kevin's faithful sidekick fretting and fuming at his side, eager to press the piscatorial quest, hovering over the tangled line and offering advice.

Not so.

I had dared such meddling only once, during a U.S. commemorative–sorting session in our period as philatelic entrepreneurs. Kevin's resulting rage was sufficiently pathological that I resolved thereafter to schedule alternate activities for whenever Kevin might find himself immersed in some exquisitely delicate manual operation subsequent to some screwup for which Kevin customarily fingered me as the half-witted perp.

"Look what happened," he growled broodingly as he plucked at his hairball of fishing line. "I knew I shouldn't've let you carry this."

He hadn't, actually, let me carry anything belonging to him, but this wasn't a point to argue.

Instead, while Kevin hunkered, I dug into Papa's creel for a scrubbed-out Welch's grape jelly jar. There were holes punched in the lid, as with every jelly jar I ever carried out of the house. By the time I reached fifth grade, my accuracy with an icepick was almost foolproof, and I was able to go several weeks without a puncture wound in my left hand (usually in the membrane between thumb and index finger).

The jelly jar was for grasshoppers. I especially enjoyed stalking those horror-movie-size green locusts who were capable of up-chucking gallons of "tobacco juice" the second you clamped two fingers onto their wings. So, while Kevin struggled (he eventually managed to unravel thirty yards of line in a sort of DNA helix run amok along the dusty surface of the access road), I disported among the chest-high weeds, sneaking up on grasshoppers and popping them, wriggling and ralphing, into my jelly jar.

By and by, Kevin hacked and spliced his line into about twenty feet of serviceable knotlessness. He hied me back to the safari, conveying a strong measure of censure for my failure to appreciate the gravity incumbent upon our circumstances.

Relaunching his fishing tutorial, Kevin stressed the importance of proper equipment, digressing deeply into the theology of the Artificial Lure. Kevin's choice in this day's hunt for the elusive lunker was one of the featured lures that were available at Olson's at a price range from 19 cents to $1.29. Kevin held before my eyes a big fuzzy yellow device known commonly as a doll fly, although nothing in its appearance was discernibly doll-like. It was actually quite hideous. I'm convinced that hundreds of abstract sculptures and more than a few B sci-fi movies have been inspired by an author's subliminal remembrance of the ubiquitous doll fly, but from that day to this I have never known a fish of any species—even in the full flush of a mass feeding frenzy—to pay any notice whatsoever to a doll fly. Nevertheless, here was Kevin ranting its praises. Such was my faith in his Waltonian expertise that I stifled all doubt and prepared to watch an artificial lure come to life in the hands of a pro.

At last, Kevin took rod in hand, placed thumb on Zebco, planted his feet and directed me to alertly observe the proper stalking of a trophy trout.

Kevin's first cast sang forth from his reel and lodged in a patch of horse nettle directly behind him, six yards back. I welled with sympathy. These, after all, were hardly the ideal conditions for the genuine artist of the spinning rod. I said as much to Kevin, supportively. Kevin replied by ordering me to rescue the doll fly from the stinging weeds. I tackled the job with such laborious caution (nettle stings your skin like a sleeveful of needles) that Kevin eventually had to come, cursing my chicken heart, to do it himself. I watched in admiration as Kevin, disregarding his own comfort, plunged his bare arm into the fronds of nettle. He emerged with his lure and an itchy inflammation that would rankle for hours.

Kevin's second cast was a fateful moment in his sexual development. To prevent another nettle patch mishap, he shortened his swing, going for the base hit rather than the bleachers. To an extent, this adjustment worked like a charm. His backcast swung well shy of the vegetation. However, Kevin had overcompensated. The doll fly swung in a compact arc, back, down and dead center behind Kevin, into the seat of Kevin's OshKosh B'Goshes. The shrill buzz of the Zebco's drag outsang the cicadas in the trees.

While cussing, Kevin suggested that this accident was my fault. I had been standing too close, crowding his backswing. He dispatched me to the seat of his pants, to remove the hook.

For my unschooled fingers, the barb proved inextricable from Kevin's butt. Excremental mutterings from Kevin were poor encouragement, especially from my vantage point. After a few tentative efforts of his own, Kevin concluded that he could not simultaneously fumble with and wear the seat of his pants. The fact that I then suggested the obvious expedient—that he simply cut his line and go on to the next artificial lure in his tackle box—also had an unfortunate effect on later events. Advice from me tended to propel Kevin toward whatever choice lay in the opposite direction.

With this, Kevin boldly skinned down to his Fruit of the Looms and plumped onto the creekbank to extricate his doll fly from his jeans.

I intuited the peril of hanging too close to Kevin during this operation. I withdrew to alternate activity number two, which was to climb the black willow that towered over Council Creek and its trout-rich pool.

Kevin labored on. Getting a hook's barb free from a pair of jeans is a hard job in the best of circumstances. Kevin was pissed off to the point of blindness, which increased the degree of difficulty.

From the height of the willow, I noticed the approach of a third party. It didn't occur to me right away that the plot might be thickening. For a long time, I didn't mention her to Kevin. Reticence, after all, was fundamental to the Code. Paladin never spoke unless he had something to say, and when he did speak, it was usually a line from Shakespeare or Byron. I didn't know any lines from Shakespeare. The only Byron I'd ever heard of was a kid in my sister's grade who got a lot of ribbing because he had a dumb name. All the more reason to keep my mouth shut.

Watching her approach, I supposed that she might be in Kevin's grade in school, or thereabouts. There was something familiar about her. Prominent in her aspect, from a distance, were a wispy blondeness and a pronounced flounce.

It was too late for escape. "Someone's comin'," I announced to Kevin, in a stage whisper.

She was so close, in fact, that it was too late for Kevin to get his pants back on.

"It's a girl," I added.

Over the next few minutes, I learned the depth of agony possible in an eighth-grade boy caught with his pants off by an eighth-grade girl who has been, for a period of time as long as the history of human passion (about three months), the secret object of his most fevered longings. From up there in the willow, I remained undetected and saw it all, and derived more insight from this than I had from my entire previous accumulation of Kevinic pedagogy.

Kevin—turning to see the pubescent incarnation of Doris Day as she rounded the bend and bore down on him like a violin crescendo from the original soundtrack of *Pillow Talk*—took the only remaining course available to him. He flung himself, headlong, trailing pants, fishing gear and doll fly, into the middle of Council Creek.

Kevin's splash deepened his dilemma. It drew the thus far oblivious maiden. She strode directly to the shore.

My immediate thought was to picture Kevin's naked feet, sunk into the muck, rusty fence wire and glass shards on the creek bottom, as hordes of delirious bloodsuckers circled his ankles and hugged each other with the delight of this sudden, miraculous banquet. In Kevin's place, this thought would have gotten me out of the water like Daffy Duck with a hotfoot. Kevin, made of sterner stuff, held his ground . . . er, water. Although he could not escape the certainty of ravenous leeches inflicting an artfully random pattern of small bloody circles all over his freckled form, he was preoccupied with an even profounder terror—of being seen in his underpants (soaking wet and transparent) by the woman he someday wanted to bear his children.

"So," said the girl, whose name turned out to be Susan, "what are you doing in there?"

"Swimmin'." Kevin's mask of nonchalance trembled.

"With your shirt on?"

Kevin faced a fresh torture. Bloodsuckers were not known to eat their way through cotton. Some would be foiled by the shirt. Suddenly, however, the shirt was untenable.

"Oh," said Kevin, "the water just looked so good, I guess I forgot to take it off." Then, he took it off, tossing it to the shore dashingly, not entirely unlike Cornel Wilde casting aside a bothersome scabbard.

"Gee," said Susan coyly, "I didn't know you could swim in here."

"Well, uh, sure," said Kevin. "It's sort of my secret spot."

From above, I watched, one by one, black bloodsucker silhouettes, just below the surface, squirming ecstatically toward the endless bounty of Kevin. A series of twitches in Kevin's flesh, which then grew into a brief involuntary shudder coursing from head to toe, indicated when a new bloodsucker had docked. I gaped at Kevin's self-control, wondered whatever on earth could compel him to endure this supreme suffering.

"Gee," said Susan, "it's awful hot. Maybe I should come in for a little dip."

At this proposal, Kevin momentarily disappeared underwater. I saw a bloodsucker making swiftly for Kevin's eyes. Kevin resurfaced with a half-inch to spare. The bloodsucker settled for Kevin's throat.

"Uh, well," Kevin said, spluttering.

"I mean," continued the ruthless coquette, "there's nobody around. I could just slip off my shorts and top and jump right in. I bet it's real cool, huh?"

Kevin, too early in life, had one of those insoluble moral crises— the sort from which few grown men emerge unscarred. Should he succumb to his baser self and agree to Susan's indecent proposal, to splash with him in the toxic cauldron of Council Creek in naught but her training bra and lollipops? Or must he travel the high, hard road: admit that he had thrown himself in amongst the swirling bloodsuckers merely to protect his sullied dignity, a confession that would come at the probable cost of losing Susan forever in a torrent of girlish sniggering?

Even to my fifth-grade sensibilities, this was an entertaining scene. Something about women taking off their clothes stirs interest even in the numbest male skull. Almost breathless, I watched as Kevin reddened with indecision, his complexion altered stunningly from the pastiness that had swept him when he first dove into the leech swarm.

"Of course, if you *told* anybody that I came in the water with you . . ." said Susan. "You wouldn't tell, would you?"

"Oh no!"

" 'Cause if you did tell somebody, then I'd be in big trouble. God, I bet I'd be grounded for the rest of my life."

Kevin floated in a troubled silence. Suspense hung in the air. Bloodsuckers lunched quietly.

Susan prattled on. "But it looks so cool. And I feel so *hot* . . . Well, why not?"

At this, suddenly, Susan's blouse came off. From my angle, the almost empty bra seemed more bandage than underwear, a homely superfluity. For Kevin, the effect was thrombotic. He bit his lip, nearly severing it from his face.

"Uh," he managed, "this isn't really a good place for girls to swim. It's sort of dirty."

She waved her blouse brazenly and cocked a curveless hip, flaunting her partial nudity and giving me, after years of confusion, a definition of the word I had uncomprehendingly heard Frankie Laine wail maybe a hundred times from the bowels of T.J.'s forbidden hi-fi cabinet: *Jezebel*.

"Oh, heck," said the temptress, "it can't be any dirtier than the lake. I swim in the lake all the time."

Susan, I dimly suspected, was the sort of woman who liked to be talked out of doing things she never intended to do.

Kevin soldiered on, with the last of his strength. His blood was draining fast. "And, well, I've heard there might be bloodsuckers in here. Well, you know, guys don't mind a little bloodsucker, but girls—"

"Oh," said Susan, gasping theatrically. "Bloodsuckers? Ick!"

She allowed this evocative syllable to echo for a moment across the waving meadow. "Are there really bloodsuckers?"

"Well, a few," Kevin replied, recovering—as she wavered—some of his customary suavity. "I might even have one on me now."

Then he delivered the clincher, a flourish that made me proud to be Kevin's private lickspittle.

"You wanna take a look and see?" Kevin dared.

Susan's response was a second, definitive "ick." In a moment, she had bid Kevin a regretful adieu and was retracing her route, her blouse once more demurely in order. There was something in her departing demeanor that told me she had exerted some extraordinary force she had barely begun to fathom.

I had plenty of time to ponder Susan's aura because Kevin was whispering frantically that I should watch her like a hawk and let him know when she had cleared the horizon. I was scrupulous. I even gave her a little extra time after she had topped the crest of yonder hill.

When finally I signaled the all-clear, Kevin exploded from the bloodsucking pool like a tethered tarpon. He hit the shore running, his voice a tortured squeal that wrung the sultry air. Stumbling through the horse nettle and clawing at the leeches that speckled his skin like bloated black boils, he fled Council Creek, my tree and most of his clothes. The only desire left in his suddenly shrunken existence was—a four-minute mile away—the salt shaker in his mother's kitchen.

After the last strains of Kevin's screaming had died in the distance, I climbed down and spent a few minutes snagging his pants and fishing tackle off the bottom of Council Creek. Then I settled back with my cane pole and can of worms. It took me about a half-hour to catch Kevin's private mobydick, a yellowish thirteen-inch rainbow trout with a scar over one eye and a four o'clock shadow. After all, the prize fish came easily enough, grabbing the worm in one gulp and flying, unprotesting, from the water in a quick snap of my line.

Then, I did something strange. Instead of taking it home for supper, I unhooked Kevin's trophy trout and dropped it back into the water. The fish didn't seem real pleased to be there, but he eventually flipped a lazy tail and slid back down among the bloodsuckers.

Maybe I freed the trout because my experience with Kevin and Susan and the bloodsuckers was a moment in my coming of age, which needed somehow to be commemorated. Probably, though, I did it because I knew better than to eat anything that came out of Council Creek.

By the Shores of Lake Monona

I don't remember exactly. But the way I figure it, one day this other kid—Bob—and I were unacquainted cells in the swirling juvenile protoplasm of Waunona Way in Madison. The next day, I was Bob's family's unofficial summer vacation parasite, tracking dirt on the living room carpet, mooching meals and leaving, on almost every receptive surface, telltale fingerprints in fish slime.

In July the previous year, despairing of career opportunity in the Tomah tavern industry, my mother had forcibly removed sister Peg, brother Bill and me to a brick fourplex in a former cornfield in the state capital. It was a blessing for which all three of us would be eternally indebted to Mom—for liberating us from the stifling microculture of Tomah—but our first impression was that she had destroyed our lives and blighted our future. The move almost killed Peg. She was a recent eighth-grade grad of St. Mary's and eager to start her freshman year at Tomah High School. She had built, within her endlessly invaded room above the S&Q Hardware, a pink and fluffy fortress, guarded by stuffed animals and stacked with velvet jewel boxes, each one stuffed with tacky keepsakes. Her boon companions were Rosie Schappe, daughter of Tomah's wealthiest Realtor, and Jeannie Westphal, a wild girl and a dubious companion, but I thought her rather fetching. Jeannie was strangely stirring in her nightgown when Peg held sleepovers in our place. Peg's ability to hold sleepovers at all, to lure other girls into the stark decrepitude of our family penitentiary, was a tribute to her social tenacity. I suspect that other parents trembled when they heard of their daughters venturing downtown, among all the bars and GI's, to stay with that Benjamin girl. By aspiring at last to Tomah High, freed of the thrall of Sister Terence and the other nuns, Peg was joining a social whirl of spectacular breadth and variety for which she had groomed herself exhaustively. She had spread a net that stretched from the V.A. Hospital on one end of town to Oak Grove Cemetery on the other end. There wasn't an eighth-grade kid in Tomah who hadn't heard of Peg. She was in Girl Scouts. She was in 4-H. She was a member of the Tomah Saddle Club. She had already started playing the clarinet, in anticipation of joining the Tomah High School Band (which was a fallback option if she didn't make varsity cheerleader). Her friends included numerous Public School girls. She had known associations, although perfectly innocent, with Public boys. Her evenings were squandered over the phone with Rosie and Jeannie, endlessly reciting lists of boys, deficiencies in girls, rumors of liaisons, hair talk, makeup talk, horse talk and hours of other teenage girl crap—while Bill and I made rude noises, shouted, "Hiya, Rosie!" and yelled, "Get off the phone! Get off the phone! There's a fire! There's a fire!"

All this crashed into shambles and despair the day Mom said, with cold finality, "We're moving to Madison. I have a job. I found a place."

Peg fought like a cornered badger. She said she could live with our grandparents, Papa and Annie, down on Pearl Street. Papa and Annie said okay. Mom said, "Absolutely not! Let that woman poison my own daughter against me?" Peg tendered an offer from Rosie's parents to let her live with them, if Mom gave her consent. Mom, suddenly swollen with working-class pride, snorted contemptuously at the suggestion of these rich people taking possession of her daughter. Peg threatened to run away. Mom called her bluff. "Okay, go ahead," she said. Peg stayed. After we got to Madison, in the summer of '63, depression ruled our carton-stacked house for weeks. Peg pouted in her room and slowly rebuilt her pastel castle. It was soon the only neat room in the new apartment. To cheer us up, Mom's new boss, Clyde, brought his smarmy son and daughter over to play "Yellow Bird" on their accordions, over and over. After they left, all we could think of, for hours, was rushing outdoors, finding a goldfinch, ripping off its head and tearing it to shreds.

Peg summoned Papa to Madison repeatedly. Despite Mom's open hostility, Papa would drive Peg back to Tomah, leave her at Rosie's for a few days, then bring her back, bitchy, weepy and inconsolable.

Peg suffered worse when school started. Bill and I were bused to a public grammar school full of multicolored classmates and secular adventure, called Franklin School. But Peg, a high school kid new in town, irretrievably friendless and not prone to make friends with anyone who wasn't from Tomah, was sent all the way across Madison to the richest, snottiest public high school in the tri-state region—Madison West. West kids treated Peg like a shitkicker from the countryside. In retaliation, she renounced every aspect of West High, then came home and hid all night in her room. She spent every weekend in Tomah. Papa wore out Fords and risked death in blizzards to make sure Peg saw Rosie once a week. Peg suffered, visibly, melodramatically and accusingly, every minute of every day for more than a year, a period at least four hundred days longer than either Bill or I could sustain our worst possible tantrum. Peg was a paragon of bitterness.

Bill and I were Peg's brothers, close to her throughout her pain. We stayed true to our kid Code and sibling mission. We didn't give a rat's ass.

Bill and I had other jobs to do, exploring our neighborhood, finding fields where we could play, discovering Lake Monona, exploring Waunona Way.

Waunona Way proper—a street on which we did not live—was costly shoreline acreage on Lake Monona, habitat for doctors, lawyers and manufacturers. Long after I started hanging out at Bob's house, I ascertained that his father was a dentist. Well, maybe a podiatrist. Or astrologer. Since I never really spoke to him, just walked past him, stepped around him, wolfed wordless meals next to him, ignored him as blindly as he ignored me, I never exactly pinned down his occupation—nor did I care. What grownups did for a living had no bearing on kid life. Ants and aphids were infinitely more intimate.

Where we did live was a Simpson Street brick fourplex—a form that represented the architectural apotheosis of mid-century Madison, dull, square, cheap and practical, the grist of rapid growth. Simpson was one of a hundred short, bare residential streets between Waunona Way and the edge-of-civilization Beltline, across which one could still see crops and swamps that were doomed by the fourplex virus.

To get to Bob's house, I would each day get on my bike, pedal two blocks down Hoboken Road, past old man Ashman's forbidden orchard, and hang a left onto Waunona Way. As I turned, I always kept an eye peeled for the six-foot saber-toothed Great Dane who often prowled the stretch of road across from old man Ashman's haunted manor (where, honest to God, in darkest Wisconsin, Spanish moss hung gloomily from the gnarled talons of Ashman's Tolkienesque oaks). Bob's house was a mile away, where—after a while—if I didn't show for twenty-four hours, Bob's mother would ask if I had been sick.

Bob's mother was tall and healthy, the mother of four kids and overseer of a constantly rumpled household. She was one of those women who kept life under control by good humor rather than discipline. She had an instinct for chaos and somehow kept her family—and all their hangers-on—just shy of it. In all the time I hung out with Bob, his house was never neat, never a mess. There were never just four kids at home; there were usually twice as many, from all over Waunona Way. Bob's mother fed everyone, found a blanket and a pillow for any kid who stayed over, and never got spooked when she found a strange animal asleep on the couch. The interesting thing to me was that she knew kids' names. She flouted the silent gulf that separated kids from grownups. She talked to me like a person. I found myself talking back, even smiling. I started to talk to her like Papa talked, mimicking his genial line of small-town main-street over-the-counter badinage. While this was going on, Bob would stand by tapping his toe. Finally, he'd say, "You comin'?"

Yeah, I'm comin'.

The very first time I saw Bob, I guess, was on the raft.

The raft was a platform on empty fifty-five-gallon drums, anchored about sixty yards offshore from Waunona Way's so-called beach. This was a beach on which no self-respecting kid lingered long. It was reserved almost exclusively to young mothers, who brought their toddlers to grub in the gray and gravelly sand—which doubled as a toilet for most of the cats within a three-block radius. The beach's only redeeming feature was a girl in my class, named Donna, who did all her sunbathing there.

There were two things significant about the raft. One was that Donna never went there. As far as I recall, Donna never swam. Even then, just out of eighth grade, Donna had somehow intuited the incongruity of putting her body to any exertion as frantic and indecorous as the Australian crawl. Water did not become Donna, although it probably wanted to. No man—even one as small and incipient as I was then—could encounter Donna barefoot in her two-piece on Waunona Way, her skin aglow, her hair like cornsilk, her flow of line from breast to thigh a sculpture in French vanilla ice cream, and regard her as a fellow kid. Puberty had lifted Donna so far above the rest of us that we were but featureless specks, watching her soar, powerless and irretrievable, into the brooding clouds of adulthood.

When I got to high school, the luck of the draw made me Donna's partner in Mr. Sherman's biology class. Together, we fertilized frog eggs. Like many girls then, in the emerging Sixties, she wore short dresses of clingy fabric that hugged her like Saran Wrap, and sheer hose of material that laddered easily and had to be repaired—quickly before they were ruined—by applying clear nail polish to regions of her thigh 20,000 leagues above her hemline while I held the little bottle and kibitzed gapishly.

There was no way to behold Donna dabbing her pantyhose, save with a sense of awe so deep that the rest of the world fogged over, until the only things visible were Donna, her nail brush and me. If Mr. Sherman had called my name, I would have been deaf. This was true of every boy within sight of Donna, their mouths open, their eyes glazed. Even girls nearby were a little breathless. We didn't exactly grasp the phenomenon then—because, after all, Donna sat with the rest of us on the bus, carried her own books and got Bs in gym like everyone else—but for most of us, Donna was the first traffic-stopper we had ever seen outside the movies. As high school went by, she rarely dated and never went steady. The boyfriends she had were older guys, from other schools, or law firms—who knows? If the thought had ever occurred to me, I could have asked her out. Her dance card was always clear. Just by asking, I might have become her boyfriend—by default—kind of like walking hand-in-hand with Botticelli's Venus. But, like everyone, I was dumbstruck, reduced to small talk and belittled into sudden flight by the unspoken mockery of Donna's luminosity. Later in life, too late to offer Donna even the slightest succor, I realized how lonely she must have been in high school, denied her teens by an unsought, transcendent, petrifying beauty.

The other thing about the raft was that there was no way to reach it unless you swam there. And you didn't belong among the Waunona Way kids if you couldn't get to the raft. My problem wasn't just that I couldn't swim a lick; I was also terrified of the water. I had come by this terror reasonably, before my eighth birthday.

Getting back to Tomah.

As a little kid, I wasn't substantially brighter than most of my peers. But I knew a few things for sure.

Tomah—flat on the edge of the Great Plains, lying in the swath of an Ice Age glacier that had ground our hills into humps and drooled for a million years into a ragged rut that became the

Mississippi—was, in summertime, a dusty and humid ordeal. I knew this. I knew also that winter put us in the path of winds and snow that started at the North Pole and built up speed and moisture all the way down Canada, past International Falls, Minnesota, where Sears tested DieHard batteries, and right up the main drag of town, which was Superior Avenue, Highway 12 and also, unfortunately, my bedroom—where, if there really were monsters beneath my bed, they would've froze their asses off by Thanksgiving.

I knew for sure that Tomah was somewhere in the less glamorous outskirts of Nowhere. I knew this because we only got one TV channel. I'd heard that big cities like Chicago had three channels, maybe even more. But these were wild rumors. I didn't know for sure.

What I did know for sure was that death was my co-pilot. One of the things I heard from child psychologists later in life is that kids have no appreciation of human mortality. These, clearly, were not psychologists who had sat with me in my grandmother's kitchen every morning of the year, listening to Dale Lundquist on WTMB, as he concluded the farm report and commenced ticking off the daily body count in Monroe County (some of them old folks who'd run out of fuel "out in the country" in February and weren't discovered until they started to thaw and stink in May), piling corpses like cordwood at Oak Grove Cemetery. Annie knew every last dead person in town, where they had lived, what they had done for a living, who they'd married, whether the husband had outlived the wife or if they were now going to be reunited in the Great Beyond. Annie's daily postmortem sometimes took more than an hour. On any given day, I'd hear more disparagement of the dead than I heard gossip about the living.

Clued in by Dale Lundquist, I knew for sure there were people dropping like flies all around me. The obvious implication was that I could kick my private bucket anytime, even coming down the hill on my bike after school. Another kid could clip my handlebar and pitch me out of control, flying off my bike and sliding on the pavement, my flesh peeling away, until I stopped abruptly under the wheels of an oncoming car that had swerved to avoid my careening bike only to squash me instead.

But my bike was the least of the threats that conspired to snuff out my existence. Trains roared through town a dozen times a day, often sneaking up on the careless kid who wandered oblivious onto a grade crossing. The weather could kill you. Snow that caught you in the woods, disoriented you, covered you like a blanket and smothered you in your sleep. Cold that ate at your fingers, numbed your legs, dropped you in your tracks and left you beside the road stiff as a fish stick. Tornadoes that exploded from the heat of summer and strewed buildings, livestock and little kids, in ghastly twisted pieces, all over the landscape.

Ice could kill you, as you set foot on your stoop, or slid along a slick sidewalk, your feet suddenly zipping out from beneath and your head splitting open as it hit the frozen ground, like a grapefruit dropped from a balcony.

You could die from tractors that tipped over or combines that sucked you in and chewed you into mulch, or livestock gone berserk, leaping its fences to trample you, gore you and rip your stomach open. It could happen. Dale Lundquist told the tale a thousand times.

Your old man could come home drunk, pull you out of bed and whang you against the wall like Raggedy Andy. Or he could drive into a bridge abutment and send you through the windshield like a howitzer shell. Parents were death traps, and every kid knew it.

So were deer hunters, wandering shitfaced through woods and backyards every autumn, blasting at anything that moved. There were hoboes, there were strangers, there were gandy dancers, there was a mass murderer over in Plainfield who made lamp shades out of little kids and bedsheets out of naked women.

Plus, there was polio.

If you went out to play, Tomah was a minefield of towering monkey bars, merry-go-rounds that would drag you underneath and mangle you so badly that only your dentist could identify you, and teeter-totters that could drop like lightning and crush your skull like a duck egg. Every local body of water had secret, fatal "drop-offs," and at the Tomah Municipal Swimming Pool, a kid could easily stumble into the bottomless deep end, drown unnoticed in a mob of swimmers and not be discovered 'til the next morning, white and swollen, plastered up against the filter grate.

Kids knew about death. We practiced dying every day, when we played war, cowboys and Indians, cops and robbers. We knew how to hit the ground like a sack of trash and lie deathly still, mimicking death with eerie verisimilitude, breathing so shallow that our lips went blue—just in case, someday, a murderer with a shotgun headed down Superior Avenue, killing anything or anyone that moved.

The only exceptions to this healthy fear were high school kids. Not all high school kids, just the best ones, the unpimpled cream of the crop. The prom queens and team captains—cheerful, athletic overachievers who taught swimming at the Tomah pool every summer.

Swimming lessons started in May as soon as school got out. In Tomah, May was not spring. It was winter's long epilogue. The water in the pool was pumped from springs and wells in the earth that had been frozen rock-solid until only a few weeks before. It entered the pool as cold as the ground at Oak Grove Cemetery. There it waited, not for recreational swimmers, who would not touch it until the heat of mid-July. It waited for us, tiny children, to take swimming lessons, in the weak light of early morning, before the sun had cleared the trees.

They lined us up at the pool's edge, like revolutionaries in front of a firing squad. I was naked but for wrinkled swim trunks that ballooned at my hips. I clutched my arms around my body uselessly, sinking my fingers deep into the spaces between my ribs. I shook so violently that the pool, a turquoise sheet blanketed with icy fog, danced spastically before my eyes. There was a shout. From our instructor, some cheerleader named Bonnie, ordering us into the water. I could see her breath, exploding in white bursts from her head. I could see the goose pimples on her thighs. Her nipples stood out like termite hills on the Serengeti.

As I watched her smile and twitter and goad us toward the rimes of ice that edged the pool, I recognized dimly that death was something not dreamed of in Bonnie's philosophy. Nor could Donny, Bonnie's fellow instructor, summon the insight to picture himself sinking like a stone, inhaling water and feeling his lungs implode. Neither of them had ever done anything in life but float. I was all by myself and I knew it.

Someone prodded me toward the water. I turned to look. It was Donny, calling me "little guy" and grinning macabre encouragement. I dug in my heels but the edge of the pool was like glass. The water clutched my toes like giant waterbugs with claws of venomous ice.

Numbly, I sidled into the arctic pool, knee-deep. Bonnie was hollering out orders. Trembling with terror while shivering with cold, I deteriorated into a midget hoofer rendering St. Vitus' Dance, which continued until Donny, noting my failure to cooperate with the group's unison dunk, simply placed his enormous hand behind my head and plunged me face-first into the well of death. My every muscle in rictus, unable to move, I sucked up the Tomah Municipal Swimming Pool like a lush in a vat of muscatel. A watery gagging cough saved my life, blasting from my mouth so hard that it lifted my head clear of the water. I stood leaning over the surface, hacking, spitting and gushing with tears.

"Great, little guy," said Donny, his voice distant and gurgly in my flooded ears. "Now! Again!"

Again?

I did this ten or fifteen more times, never once figuring out how to not inhale convulsively as soon as my face hit the water, never getting accustomed to the paralytic chill of the pool, never for a second ceasing to quake like a spaz and keen like a beaten puppy. Summoning courage I could not fathom, I went back to Bonnie and

Donny's morning torture the next day. On the third day, I hid in bed, whimpering and clutching the covers until my mother gave up.

My sister somehow survived Bonnie and Donny and actually learned to swim. Summer after summer, she moved up the scale from Beginner to Intermediate to being allowed in the deep end, among the diving boards and pubescent bathing beauties and Donny's throngs of roughhousing showoff jock buddies. My brother, Bill, the baby of the family, benefited from my example. By the third kid, parents get gun-shy. Mom didn't even think about sending Bill off to the pool for immersion torture.

Since Bonnie and Donny, I had been in the water a thousand times, but never in a place where I couldn't touch bottom, or hang on to the edge. The raft at the beach on Waunona Way was different. The edge of the raft was sixty bottomless yards away. I scanned the vast channel that lay between my incipient Waunona Way friends and me. They splashed merrily around the raft while I stood on the beach, among the rugrats, casting the occasional sly glance in Donna's direction. It was either swim to the raft, or retire to a lonesome summer of reading in my room, or bouncing a baseball off a brick wall—if I could find a brick wall. Waunona Way was not a brick wall kind of neighborhood.

I waded in as far as I could wade. It was June. The weather was warm, but my onset of full-body shakes was familiar. Around armpit level, the bottom changed from sand to muck. At neck level, the bottom was still sloping downward and I had no choice. In a frenzy of kicking and flailing, I launched myself toward the raft, resigned to death. I clawed panic-stricken at the water, hyperventilating, swallowing Lake Monona in quart-size gulps, then violently spewing out anything I found in my mouth—water, algae, seaweed, my tongue. I gasped. I plunged. I spluttered. I leapt like a carp. After five minutes, I reached the point of no return—thirty yards both ways and nothing solid beneath my feet for twelve or thirteen frigid miles. Meanwhile, not one kid on the raft—true to the

Code—paid one second's attention to my distress, or even noticed that I was floundering out into the lake to join them. Every last callous one of them would have been shocked—shocked—days later when my body was found rhythmically rocking against the shore, my eyes nibbled out by sunfish.

"Benjamin?" they would have said. "Yeah, I remember him from the school bus."

As I was pondering this pathetic epitaph, my hand clanged, painfully, into the raft. Sinking, I reached for something to grip. I found only the smooth round surface of an oil drum. I went down, gently, toward my watery grave. I imbibed a liter of Lake Monona, roused myself from despair and kicked upward, lunging from the water, seizing the raft's edge and clambering back to life. I'd done it.

Activity on the raft, as I recall, consisted largely of games of which I didn't approve, because they involved jumping back into the water, treading water (which my body interpreted as sinking like an igneous rock) and chasing one another (which required actual swimming). My role in this frolic was to cling to the raft, shiver copiously and occasionally venture out bravely, four or five feet, into the sucking waves, before flailing back to safety where I would spit up water and cough for a minute or so, whereat someone would tag me and I would be "it" and the game would bog down for ten minutes.

I'm not sure why Bob invited me to his house, but I assume it had to do with fishing. Fishing and puberty were the main things Bob and I had in common. Bob was the sort of totally average kid with whom I had never hit it off in Tomah. Bob's averageness captivated me, and initiated me into a whole host of mainstream, run-of-the-mill fascinations from which I had been previously excluded— like catchphrases. Bob cultivated catchphrases, like "way out" and "hang ten." Bob spent that whole summer waiting for opportunities to say, "Hang ten!" Few of these cropped up, as "hang ten" was a surfing term, and Wisconsin is a predominantly nonsurfing state. But Bob would practice for the opportunity, sometimes just sitting in reverie, muttering "Hang ten!" again and again, working on his delivery, adding flourishes. "Hey! Hang ten!" . . . "Hang ten, man!" . . . "Hang *all* ten, baby!" Bob had more success with the sentence he eventually adopted as his unofficial summer motto: "You got me hangin'!" The first time, probably on TV or in a scrum around the raft, that Bob heard someone say, "You got me hangin'!" he just split a gut. This terse little rejoinder hit Bob as the adolescent *mot juste,* the I-don't-know-and-I-don't-care that fixed his mildly impertinent place in the universe. He savored every question that came his way all summer long. He got to a point where, even if he knew the answer, Bob would come up empty, just for the chance to snap off his topper.

"Excuse me, son. Which way to the Beltline?"

"You got me hangin'!"

"This is Waunona Way, isn't it?"

"You got me hangin'!"

"Are you as stupid as you look?"

"You got me hangin'!"

Another of Bob's contributions to my cultural education was his reverence for pop music. Until Bob, I hated rock 'n' roll. I hated it for the best reason in the world.

My sister loved Dick Biondi.

Every night from around her eleventh birthday on, Peg had made a nightly ritual of commandeering the bathroom, dressed in her flannel nightgown and giant mohair slippers, armed with hair rollers, face cream, Q-Tips, twelve pounds of Kleenex and an Arvin Bakelite radio, where she would undertake a three-hour *toilette.* Her routine brooked no deviation. Her only companion was Dick Biondi—known to Bill and me as Dick Head. WLS Radio in Chicago had the most powerful AM signal in the Midwest, so powerful that you could drive from Syracuse to Sacramento and never have to touch your radio dial, unless you couldn't stand one more second of Dick Head. Biondi was the most beloved disk jockey west of Murray the K, but I hated him—and I hated rock 'n' roll. They kept me out of the toilet. Peg would station herself at the mirror, performing endless ablutions, swaying gently to "Earth Angel" or "Love Me Tender," allowing no one to enter—not even Mom—until she was completely finished and ready for her bedtime four-hour phone call to Rosie. If I addressed Peg while Dick Biondi was speaking, Peg would turn on me, viciously, and hiss, "David! Ssshhh!"

Because of Dick Biondi, I peed off the porch every night for three years.

I still hated rock 'n' roll when Bob undertook my reeducation. Bob's absorption in the intellectual content of that summer's Top 40 proved to me that life's lessons might be found anywhere, even in the lyrics of Bobby Vee, Little Eva and the Ronettes. Bob believed that the greatest artistic achievement of the summer of '63 was "Surf City" by Jan and Dean.

Bob, who was deeper into his sexual emergence than I, went glassy-eyed every time "Surf City" came around on the radio, promising "two swinging honeys" for every guy capable of winking. He pictured a paradise of bouncing Funicellos in French bikinis, oiling his hairless chest on the beach, offering him beer and whispering their irresistible desire to go all the way, right here, right now, two-on-one. Among teenage boys, the debate that raged all summer was who exactly, in the last verse of "Surf City," Jan and Dean were "checkin' out the parties" for. Was it a "surfer girl," as many listeners averred? Or was it, in the interpretation Bob preferred, a "stripper girl"? Anyone could have settled the argument simply by dropping into a music store and looking up the lyrics. But this solution demanded more academic intensity than rock 'n' roll merited. Bob would have been unconvinced in any case. "Well, yeah!" he would have replied. "They had to censor it when they wrote it down. But that's not how they *sing* it!"

Momentous debates like these kept us rolling for hours. Our usual companion in discourse was Bob's dog, Buster, whom I found strangely disturbing.

Buster was an aloof dog, not hostile but only actually friendly toward people bearing food. He was a rawboned, speckled German short-hair with prominent genitalia. Male dogs of Buster's sort have always bothered me because of their penises, which are glaringly obvious even when sheathed and recumbent. When, every thirty seconds or so, on the mildest provocation, such dogs experience an erection, it becomes the social responsibility of every human being present to pretend the unpretendable—that this huge naked dog is not prancing and slavering around the living room with a raging red hard-on. Since my own personal pecker was a source of private perplexity throughout the entire span of my adolescence, I found dogs like Buster, in those days, doubly troubling. I wondered, frankly, why people even kept male dogs around the house, exposing themselves habitually, in front of girls. I wondered why girls weren't embarrassed. They didn't even seem to notice.

Eventually, Bob and I went fishing.

Bob had a spot. Every fisherman seeks a spot, dreams of a spot, roams the waterways of the earth pursuing his personal spot. Kevin's fetid pool in Council Creek, crawling with bloodsuckers, had been his spot. Bob's spot put Kevin's spot to shame. For one thing, it was a real spot. It lay straight across Lake Monona, about a mile's motoring in Bob's outboard skiff, behind the Fauerbach Brewery. Fauerbach's made a beer called Fauerbach CB, which was, by popular acclamation, the Midwest's worst. No one with any self-respect in Madison drank Fauerbach CB. This consensus was validated, within several years, by the bankruptcy of the Fauerbach Brewery and the closure of the plant. When Bob and I were tooling across the lake, however, Fauerbach was still brewing and, when they did so, the brewery would release a steady flow of body-temperature water into the lake. Chances are that the warm water coming from Fauerbach was an ecological sin of mortal proportions, but these were days before the word "ecology" was known either to teenage kids with fishing poles, or to white bass.

White bass, probably attracted by the bloom of edible plankton that flourished in warm water, flocked to Fauerbach's effluent. At some point in his explorations of Lake Monona, Bob had found the

Fauerbach warm spot. He had learned that catching Fauerbach white bass consisted simply of attaching a lure called a pinkie to the end of one's line, dropping said pinkie to the bottom of the lake and waiting, say, six seconds. Inevitably, a ravenous white bass would spot the bright gewgaw, regard it as food and glom it greedily, before a rival bass could horn in. From there, after a brief and amusing struggle, the white bass would be flopping on the floor of Bob's boat and the pinkie would be heading back toward the Fauerbach undercurrent.

Dangling a pinkie behind Fauerbach with Bob was certainly the easiest fishing I've ever done. The white bass supply was infinite and the fish were impatient to sacrifice themselves. In an hour of dropping our lures and hauling in white bass, Bob and I would harvest sixty or seventy fish. We stopped only when the prospect of cleaning so many fish overbalanced the delight in catching them. Then Bob would fire up the outboard and we'd skim back toward Waunona Way, the aluminum boat dancing on the light chop that constantly riffled the summer surface of Lake Monona. The fish all ended up in Bob's family freezer. White bass is a delicious pan fish, but I don't recall eating any of the several thousand fish Bob and I took from the Fauerbach bonanza. I suspect that Bob's family might still be slowly eating their way through the prodigious summer of '63.

Besides the brewery, Bob and I tried other spots, all around Monona and through the locks into Lake Mendota. Sometimes we didn't fish at all. Madison in summer is a watery sprawl that cries out for boys to go down to the shore in dinghies. Madison occupies an isthmus surrounded by lakes—Mendota and Monona in the city, Waubesa, Kegonsa, and Wingra nearby. Creeks, rivers, canals and locks link the lakes. Tired of catching white bass, Bob would simply set off for an opening in the edge of the lake, motoring up channels, under bridges, through locks, into swamps, wasting a day and a tank of gas in aimless navigation. At lunchtime, we would buy a fish sandwich and a Coke off a dock. At dusk, which didn't fall 'til nine at night, we'd motor slowly up twinkling corridors of light toward Lake Monona, listening to laughter from tavern terraces and party boats. A pair of ill-bred towheads, neither of us possessed the couth to exclaim on the beauty through which we idled. But it captured us, wordlessly content, all the same. Something about all of this was better than fishing.

Bob liked to go to the terrace at the University of Wisconsin Memorial Union, where summer coeds would lie tanning on the pier, doing all the things that Surf City stripper girls might do, except stripping—or showing the least interest in fifteen-year-old Bob. It was on such an excursion that we hit one of those summer squalls that suddenly sweep over small lakes in the Midwest after a hot spell.

Bob's boat wasn't big, perhaps twelve feet from stem to stern. It wasn't heavy. Stamped out of aluminum, it attained wind-whipping, face-stinging velocity despite being powered by a mere sixty-horse Evinrude. It wasn't exactly loaded. There were no oars, no life jackets, no life preservers, no flares. This made the squall an anxious experience, especially after the engine suddenly went "Snap!" and then fell silent, and Bob said, "Aw, shit."

At this point, the wind was howling. The once softly lapping Lake Monona waves were six feet above the boat. We wallowed helplessly in a watery tilt-a-whirl. Bearing in mind that I couldn't swim, I grew swiftly irrational.

"What happened?"

"Sheared a pin."

"What? Sheared a what?"

"Pin."

"What does that mean?"

"What does that *mean*?"

"Yeah, yeah! What's it mean?"

"You know a lot about outboard motors, dipshit?"

"Nothing."

"So shut up."

I looked around. The sky was black and spitting rain. The waves were monsters out of Jules Verne. Without the motor, we had no control over the boat. We could be swamped any second.

"Jesus, Bob! Whaddya gonna do?"

"I think I have another pin."

"Where?"

"Shut up."

Bob, inexplicably calm in the face of what I knew were our last few minutes on earth, reached down and opened his tackle box. Pitching back and forth with the turmoil of the lake, he started rummaging through a pile of rusty lures, mangled sinkers, tangled leaders and dried-up worms.

"There's no *pin* in there," I shouted, giving in to terror.

"Here it is," said Bob. He held up a short steel cylinder. "See?"

A wave splashed over the side, depositing ten gallons of Lake Monona around our ankles.

"Great," I said. "What're ya gonna do?"

"Put it on."

"Put it on what?"

"The engine."

I looked at the engine, clamped to the rear of the boat, pivoting and thudding in the maelstrom.

"How?" I wailed.

Bob treated this question as unworthy of response. He popped the pin into his mouth, slid to the back of the boat and started detaching the sixty-horsepower Evinrude engine from the back of the boat. An outboard motor is not a particularly heavy device. It weighed perhaps fifty pounds, and Bob was a burly fifteen-year-old, big-shouldered and outdoorsy. But an outboard is ungainly to maneuver from point A to point B, even on solid ground. In a skiff in a gale, with waves tossing the boat violently from one forty-five-degree angle to the opposite fifty-five-degree angle, and then pitching the bow so high it almost touched my chin several times, removing the outboard from the heel of the boat without dropping it to the bottom of the lake, well . . . to me, this was like trying to catch an oiled hippo in midair from a trapeze.

As Bob recklessly unscrewed the clamps that held the motor to our boat, I lost all hope. I scanned the horizon for another way, any way, out. Bob seemed to be whistling while he worked, an attitude that seemed to me either profoundly stupid, or remarkably brave. Or something. Bob, after all, was the most normal, unexceptional kid I had ever befriended. He had no enemies. Nobody even disliked Bob. He floated on the hormonal hell of modern adolescence like a gull in a gale. He had never experienced, as far as I could determine, an examined moment. He cruised. He was destined to a life of modest ambitions, moderate attainment and agreeable mediocrity. And yet, in this fragile boat, assaulted by the wind and water that were his heritage as a lakeshore suburbanite, Bob approached heroism. Trapped in a violent storm, his life apparently in danger, badgered by a panicky partner, Bob was imperturbable and supremely competent.

> *... His fast gun for hire*
> *Heeds the calling wind . . .*

Or maybe he just wasn't worried because it didn't matter if he dropped the engine and the boat sank. Bob could swim.

Clutching both sides of the bow, I looked beyond the mountainous waves. We were, I saw, somewhere in Squaw Bay, the same thumb-shaped inlet of Lake Monona where, a few years later, Otis Redding's plane would crash, silencing the greatest R&B voice of my time. As I looked for escape, it appeared, incredibly, that the immense swell might have done us a favor. It had driven the boat within perhaps 150 yards of the shore. I vaguely recognized a house on shore, nestled behind a vast verdant lawn. We were about to die, I surmised, somewhere offshore from the intersection of Hoboken Road and Waunona Way. If I could walk on water, I could walk home from here.

Or die trying.

"Bob," I ventured.

"Ssh."

Bob was working. Astounded, I saw that he had somehow yanked the engine from the stern without losing his balance in the wildly rocking boat. The Evinrude was on Bob's lap. Its innards were exposed as Bob poked it with a screwdriver. Rain splattered all over the naked motor. I could hear the pin in Bob's mouth, as he clicked it rhythmically against his teeth. I recognized the beat: "Surf City." The boat slipped sideways, parallel to the waves. An eight-foot whitecap all but capsized us. Bob almost dropped the engine. He caught it deftly before it crushed one of his feet, and he plopped it back onto his lap.

"Jesus God," I said.

The giant wave had moved us ten yards closer to shore. I measured the distance. This was the raft all over again, but this time, it was life-or-death, sink-or-swim, hell-or-high-water. Without even taking off my sneakers, without so much as a fond farewell to my former friend Bob, certified idiot, I dove off the boat and pointed myself toward the shore.

The water was like a huge hand, squeezing me.

"Hey!"

This was Bob's voice—a tone of mild surprise. I heard no more. I flailed, I splattered. I wallowed, I gullied, I kicked, I squirmed. I fought death with a savage and hopeless ferocity.

Then I stood up.

As it turned out, the offshore shelf in that part of Squaw Bay extended about ninety yards before tapering abruptly downward. I had churned for about six chaotic yards before reaching it. The water was up to my waist. The rocks were sharp but they did no harm. I had had the foresight to keep my shoes on while leaping to my death.

I turned to look for Bob, who was near enough that I could see him slip the pin from his mouth and delicately position it inside the Evinrude—just as another wave hit the boat and spun it 180 degrees. But I didn't care anymore what Bob did with the motor. I was safe. I started walking toward the edge of the lake. I was deciding whether to go home, or walk down Waunona Way, to Bob's house, to tell his parents he was probably dead, drowned while trying to mount a sixty-horse Evinrude onto a skiff-stern in a cyclone.

I was twenty feet from shore when I saw it.

The dog.

I knew this dog. It was the Great Dane, the one whose territorial imperative extended so far beyond his own yard that he would sometimes follow me two blocks down Waunona Way, breathing on my neck and snarling phlegmily, waiting for me to utter one sound, or make one sudden move so he could bite me in two like a Milk-Bone.

Here he was, standing on the edge of his yard, legs splayed, lips curled back, growling, slobbering, waiting.

"Aw, shit."

I altered my route to shore, angling toward a landing farther to the right. The dog turned and followed, breaking his growl with a wet baritone woof. He shadowed me along the shore. This was easy for the dog. All the lawns along Waunona Way were unfenced, a rolling greensward that one could stroll—if not for the Hound of the Baskervilles—for almost a mile at any given stretch. The dog bounced and growled. I caught sight of his genitals. His dick was hard.

"Oh, goody."

Lucky for me, about five lawns down from the Baskerville compound, there was a fence that reached to the very water's edge. Beyond it, I could climb ashore and the dog couldn't reach me. Shivering, slogging in thigh-deep water, I hastened toward the fence. The dog kept pace. Fifty yards short of my objective, my shelf ended. The lake went suddenly twenty feet deep; I went with it, ten feet under before I started kicking and clawing back up.

I popped to the surface, scraping myself on the rocky lip of the drop-off, gasping as I reached the air again. The bloodthirsty dog welcomed me with a frenzy of barking. He had jumped into the water, and now he was pacing the shallows, strings of drool hanging from each jowl.

The dog feinted toward me, charging twenty terrifying feet before halting and snarling. His collar was festooned with glistening steel spikes.

"Oh, Jesus."

It was hopeless. I looked back to Bob. Calmly, like one of Snow White's dwarfs finishing a job well done, Bob was just guiding the engine back onto the stern plate. He started to tighten its clamps.

I heard splashing. The dog, accustomed to the water now, was closing in. He was going to eat me offshore, like an oyster in Newport. His footsplashes grew louder, his growl closer. I thought of dodging the dog and sprinting toward shore. This was a fleeting notion. The dog's legs were roughly twice as long as mine—and he had four of them.

Galloping, then floundering, I headed back toward Bob. At the drop-off I went down, inhaling a greenish lungful of lake. I struggled to the surface, retching and flapping. The boat was only fifty feet, or five minutes, away. A wave hit my face and added two minutes to my trip. I struggled, sank, fought back to the air again, spit out more water and heard the Evinrude. It was running.

Bob pulled up beside me a moment later. "Hop in," he said.

I tried, but a swell struck the boat broadside as I was reaching for Bob's hand. The boat bucked and the hull bashed me in the head. I drank more lake and I headed half-conscious for the bottom, finished this time once and for all—except for Bob, who grabbed me by the elbow, like a tired bass. In a single smooth lift, Bob draped me over the side of the boat and said, "C'mon. Let's get home."

After I'd caught my breath and assessed the swelling lump on my head, I lay in the bilge and considered Bob. I was seeing him in a new light, as a sort of taciturn hero, like Bart Starr or Ben-Hur— except he was talking.

"Why the hell'd you jump out of the boat? That was stupid. Dja think I couldn't fix the damn motor? Jeez, Dave—"

Bob was the only friend I ever had who called me Dave. I interrupted.

"D'you see that dog?" I said.

"Yeah," said Bob. "His name's Caesar. He doesn't bite. He'll try to fuck you right up the ass, though. If you turn your back."

The storm died before we reached Bob's dock. I went home to change but got back in time to mooch supper from Bob's mom.

Two years later, in high school, I had nine weeks of swimming lessons in Coach Breitenbach's gym class, all of which I spent either two feet under the surface or clinging to the deck, coughing violently. Somehow, although I never mastered a stroke in class, Coach Breitenbach's prolonged failure to drown me changed my outlook. While I wasn't tending to it, my fear of the water dissipated. One day, a summer later, without struggle and without understanding why, I could swim.

Bob and I didn't last. At the end of August, starting up at a brand-new high school, we reported to different home rooms in different grades. Bob hooked up with friends he had met in ninth grade, other boisterous guys in the lower ranges of the college-prep track who thought the Angels' lyrics were witty and Surf City really existed, somewhere in California, full of girls so dumb and so willing that they'd put out even for uncombed doofuses from the Great White North. While Bob cruised, I bumbled through my freshman year, trying to figure out what to wear, writing war comic satires and helping Donna mend her nylons in biology class. After the first semester, Bob and I barely noticed each other. We sat apart on the bus. We stopped saying hi in the halls. I never saw his mother again, never said goodbye to her or thanked her for all the free meals. She might have thought I died.

PART III

"Awjeezma-a!"

"Awjeezma!" was the universal dissent, whined—repeatedly if necessary—at an unreasonable mother who wanted the vacuuming done now-not-next-year or a pile of encrusted dishes washed or the sputtering heater refueled.

"Awjeezma! Do I gotta?"

"If I have to tell you one more time—"

"Awjeezma! Awright! Jeez!"

When Mom told us to get out of the house, resistance was instinctive.

"Awjeezma! There's nothin' to do out there!"

Grownups didn't care. A kid could grow old outside and die with nothing to do in his whole life, and it was no skin off grownups' nose. Besides, they knew our weakness. No kid had the willpower to sit still more than ninety seconds, even with nothin' to do. Pretty soon, I'd be on the move, seeking sidekicks.

My first steady sidekick, Chucky Dutcher, was the heretic of nothin'-to-do. He thrived outside. He had a million things to do. At age eight, he was more worldly than Homer Price and more inventive than Henry Reed. He could crawl, fearlessly, through a blind opening barely wider than his fist. He had a hideout in every berry patch and a secret entrance to every empty building in town. You could tie up Chucky Dutcher, gag him, blindfold him and dump him down Timmy's mine shaft and Chucky would have a plan before he hit bottom.

Even more than he loved it outside, Chucky hated the inside, especially school. When he could, he waged anarchy. Otherwise, he hibernated at his desk, deep in a funk that lasted 'til Saturday when there were movies at the Erwin, or all the way 'til summer when there were three months of Saturday.

School had its moments of going outside, each too short and too mundane to interest Chucky. At recess, the nuns would order us outdoors regardless of the conditions—into rain, blizzards, arctic cold and imminent cyclones. Three times a day, we faced an asphalt tundra whose only diversion was the world's dullest collection of playground apparatus.

"Awjeez!"

But the clock was ticking. We only got fifteen minutes. Then we'd be snatched back inside—for fractions, subjects and predicates, goiter pills and catechism. We had to move, quick! If we just stood there, Sister Terence might suddenly swoop down, line us up, count us off and organize us. Make us play jacks, with girls. Or hopscotch! Fear drove us out, into the gale, onto the glacier.

. . . Where we forgot there was weather, and we lost track of time. We skidded along the ice, playing pom-pom, or king-of-the-hill on a precipice of packed snow or kicking a red ball into one another's faces—all of us clammy with sweat under twelve pounds of woolknit, nylon pile, cowhide and thermal long johns.

But then, just when we were having fun . . . the bell.

"Awjeez! Already?"

Chucky Dutcher, Ben-Hur
and Tommy Ducklow

Chucky Dutcher was my first romance.

We were thrown together prior to second grade, in St. Mary's special intensive July remedial religion program for spiritually disadvantaged boys, taught by the Brothers of St. Dominic instead of the Dominican nuns who stalked the corridors during the regular school year. Neither of us had gone to parochial school as first graders. Due to a family holy war, between my Lutheran-bred dad and my papist-indoctrinated mom—which was eventually resolved by Mom leaving Dad, on various theological and moral grounds (plus a lot of drinking and fighting), and moving in with her parents—I had attended kindergarten and first grade at the public school. Chucky Dutcher's excuse was simpler. He had moved to Tomah from some heathen village Up North that had no Catholic school. It was the mission of the Brothers of St. Dominic (a murky figure to us, this Dominic guy—some sort of medieval sadist obsessed with thumbscrews and immolation, whose writings Stephen King evidently lapped up in his impressionable youth) to instill in Chucky and me a proper fear of the eternal damnation we would suffer if we ever wavered one millimeter from the Church's rigidly drawn behavioral objectives. Without Chucky, my whole three weeks of catch-up catechism truly might have been a stroll through hell. In those days before Vatican II, the Church—especially its Dominican *sturm abteilungen*—was a merciless engine of fear. Chucky and I learned, our first day, from Brother Ferdinand, that we were both festering vessels of sin and corruption, and that our fate—almost inevitably—was to die young and be flushed unceremoniously into the boiling bowels of perdition, where giant dull pitchforks would be employed by goat-footed fiends to rip out our entrails over and over and over, for millions and millions of years, while rats and rabid dogs gnawed our nuts and nibbled our lips from our faces, and jolly red giants pounded our arms and legs to jelly with sledgehammers before tearing them from our arm sockets and leg moorings, after which they would crouch over us and shit in our lipless, toothless mouths—and wash it down with endless streams of rancid piss.

This was actually one of the cheerier images that Brother Ferdinand—whom Chucky immediately redubbed "Ferdinand the Bullshitter"—conjured, before handing out crayons and commanding us to draw a colored picture of it. I might have swallowed all of this reefer madness whole, if not for Chucky, who seemed incapable of visualizing anything more abstract than his next Milky Way. Death was, for Chucky, a possibility too distant to contemplate, and hell a notion too hypothetical to entertain. His first drawing of hell was a sort of cartoon, with Goofy as the devil, and the fiery skies abuzz with World War II dogfights in which a squadron of U.S. Army Air Corps Corsairs obliterated a larger complement of Mitsubishi Zeroes. We both piled up C-minuses, but Chucky made me oddly indifferent to my grades. Remarkably streetwise for a country kid, Chucky presumed—accurately—that summer grades didn't count. We weren't supposed to progress. We were simply expected to serve our time and be terrified.

The first time we played hooky from Ferd's Inferno, Chucky took me to the big field across the street from his house, where we dug holes looking for turtle eggs. Chucky, who heard the call of the wild more clearly than I, had somehow sensed that the painted turtles and snapping turtles from Lake Tomah were sneaking into the big meadow to lay their eggs. Crawling through the weeds and rooting in the stony soil all day, Chucky and I found two egg nests. We carefully unearthed the leathery eggs and moved them to a dirt-filled box behind Chucky's woodshed. They eventually hatched, and Chucky made a small windfall in the first days of school that year, selling baby painters and snappers at ten cents apiece.

The next summer, there were no turtle eggs in the field because Chucky's dad, a frustrated agronomist, decided to grow peanuts in Wisconsin. He actually harvested peanuts, not one of them bigger than a caper. Chucky's family spent that winter loyally snacking on tiny peanutoid pellets.

Except for Brother Ferdinand's class, Chucky and I were never really friends in school. While I worked hard and strove against the social order, Chucky was indifferent to the whole scholastic scene. He seemed to disappear into the back row, only renewing his bond with me when we were both outdoors again.

I never knew exactly where Chucky came from, but he gave off the sense that he had been raised in the hills, where he had suckled 'neath raccoons and disported with bobcats. He treated town like an untracked wilderness. Each street was an overgrown path through a neglected woods. He attacked every wild patch he encountered, as though it held secrets unnoticed by ordinary mortals. He knew, for instance, that there must be turtle eggs in that field. He knew that, above the dam in Lake Tomah, if you went out at midnight and sank a doughball forty feet to the bottom, and waited, you could haul up a catfish bigger than a yearling hog.

Chucky was way ahead of me in street smarts, woodlore and deep background because he had instinctively grasped—and gleefully embraced—the concept of benign neglect. By not staying where he wasn't wanted, he mostly got to do whatever he wanted.

I was slower coming 'round to this brainstorm. In fact, as adult interest in me steadily declined, after about age two, I was miffed. I started noticing—with mounting dismay—that, except to yell at me or feed me or send me off to pester my grandparents, Mom and Dad had almost no use for me at all. If I was indoors, I was "underfoot."

I should either "go outside and play" or "light somewhere." Often, stung by these brush-offs, I would repair righteously to the front stoop, where I plumped down on the cold concrete, put my chin in my hands and pouted. In a good snit, I could even squeeze a tear. My strategy was to stay there, rooted to the stoop, airing out my bottom lip, until a passing grownup sensed my misery and bent down to kiss away my tear.

It was a lonely damn vigil. In years of resolute pouting, I never got one kiss, or even a passing snigger. With so little appreciation, my average pout usually petered out in less than five minutes.

But it seemed longer.

The alternative to being banished outdoors to amuse myself was the occasional opportunity to "tag along." Tagging along consisted of staying close to a fast-moving grownup, but not so close that you might get in the way. Above all, you kept quiet. No stupid questions. No smart remarks. No lip at all. No wandering off. Keep pace. Sit there. Shut up.

I'd tag along with Dad when he took a lot of old paint cans to the dump, or when he went up to the Carlton to stock the bar, and I'd sit on a stool in a vast, empty tavern in mid-morning, sucking ginger ale through a clear straw. I'd tag along with Annie down the backyard path to the trellis by the garage, and I'd watch her mole around under the morning glories until Tillie, next door, came to the garden fence and drew Annie into conversation about the drunks and sluts and thieves and wife-beaters who infested our seemingly placid neighborhood. I'd tag along, best of all, with Papa to Burnstad's or Shutter's for lunch meat and Sealtest ice cream, or over to the A&P for fresh-ground coffee, or up to Uncle Bob's shoe shop, and wherever Papa went, he talked, with easy charm and bottomless bonhomie, and I knew there were, after all, no drunks, no sluts, no thieves and not one wife-beater in all of Tomah.

After I found Chucky Dutcher, though, tagging along lost a lot of its luster. Why trail mutely after a grownup when you could simply hit the streets, disappear into the woods or jump in the lake? And you could say whatever you wanted! I learned from Chucky

Dutcher that if a kid just wandered off by himself, nobody came looking for him. The kid was out from underfoot, and the grownup world was relieved. You were out of sight, out of mind, and everybody figured you'd show up eventually, if you ever got hungry. Meanwhile, I embarked—sometimes with Chucky Dutcher, sometimes all by my poutless lonesome—on a career of unfettered and unmonitored discovery.

Chucky lived, literally, on the wrong side of the tracks. His family occupied a rickety rental house just across the Milwaukee Road, a block from the Lake Tomah floodplain—filled with water holes, sand flats, willow groves, mosquito larvae and wood ticks. One year, they dredged the lake, pumping tons of silt, muck and clay in amongst the willows and sandbars in Chucky's neighborhood. When the dredge pipes began spewing clay into giant mounds, kids emerged from all over town and filled their bike baskets with lakebottom. It was perfect, uncontaminated, slate-gray modeling clay, readily moldable into any shape a kid's mind could conjure. Mostly, we conjured ashtrays. For a brief period, Tomah became the world's foremost manufacturer of garishly painted, handcrafted unfired clay ashtrays. These all, inevitably, disappeared before school started, because they proved even more fun to smash than they had been to sculpt.

Chucky Dutcher and I played war in the willows and speared bullheads in the shallow channels that trickled toward the Lemonweir River—until we got a little older and discovered independent movies. Kids in Tomah had two standard moviegoing methods. One was your basic family outing, when the whole brood would head for the Erwin on a Friday or Saturday night, or the old Tomah Theater (before they shut it down and renovated it into the Tee Pee Supper Club), and all line up in a row of seats to watch Robert Taylor or June Allyson with popcorn and Jujyfruits. The alternative was the Saturday morning riot. Twice every school year, for two dollars per kid, the Erwin would issue a sheet of ten movie tickets. The schools distributed these. Saturday morning movies were a blend of second-runs and golden oldies, all wholesome and approved by the omnipotent Legion of Decency, and well suited for kid audiences, who were assembled in an unruly mass at 11:00 A.M. every Saturday for ten straight giddy weeks. Everybody in town appreciated the Saturday movie riots—kids were dazzled by Hollywood and grown-ups went back to bed—except for the teenage ushers at the Erwin, who emerged at day's end, frazzled, existential and sticky with orangeade.

For Chucky Dutcher and me, these two approaches did not yield nearly enough moviegoing. We were among the first kids in our grade to venture into the Erwin unsupervised, uncurfewed, independent. This was possible because Chucky and I both had mothers who worked and fathers who passed through our daily lives in a series of chance meetings that might be spaced weeks apart. Chucky and I saw more flicks in a month than most other kids saw in a whole school year of Saturday morning riots. Chucky and I were barely ten years old when first we went to the Erwin on a nonriot Saturday and paid full price—25 cents—to watch the movies without parents, brothers, sisters or the entire grade school population of town. It was just the two of us, me and Chucky, immersed in the darkness of the Erwin, nothing to sustain us but jawbreakers, root beer barrels, Milk Duds, M&M's, Raisinettes and green pop, from the first showing at 1:00 P.M. until the Erwin finally emptied out at 11:00 P.M. We saw every movie five times. We memorized *Journey to the Center of the Earth,* both fell in love with Arlene Dahl (whose understated cleavage foreshadowed for us a whole new level of aesthetic awareness), argued violently when I switched my allegiance to Doris Day in *Calamity Jane* and never—even after two whole Saturdays and ten viewings—failed to cringe and shiver at the first appearance of the Morlocks in *The Time Machine,* starring Rod Taylor and the torn-bodice, breast-delectable Yvette Mimieux.

Our biggest movie outing, not long before Chucky's family blew town never to be heard from again, was *Ben-Hur.* Here was the biggest movie ever made, the biggest in my whole life that I will ever see. Here, for Chucky and me, was the pinnacle of our cinematic careers. When the arrival of *Ben-Hur* to the Erwin was rumored, I thanked God for a whole host of special blessings that accrued to me as a pupil of the town's Catholic grade school. Unlike public school (or even Lutheran school) kids, I possessed an almost encyclopedic command of the abstrusities of the New Testament, derived from daily memorization and regurgitation of whole sections of *Father McGuire's New Baltimore Catechism and Mass No. 2.*

1. *Who made us?*
   God made us . . .

3. *Why did God make us?*
   God made us to show forth His goodness and to share
   with us His everlasting happiness in heaven.

Me and Jesus, thanks to the *Baltimore Catechism,* Father Mulligan, Ferdinand the Bullshitter and all the nuns, were pretty much on speaking terms. I knew his trials and tribulations, his miracles and triumphs, his tendency to go off on endless parable jags, his temptations, his moods, his hassles with the twelve stooges and the Stations of his Cross. He sat up in heaven on his eternal throne, watching my every move, reading my every thought and—assuming a good confession and a sincere Act of Contrition—absolving my every fib, cussword, impure thought, juvenile erection and act of disobedience. Me and Jesus were pals.

84. *Was the Son of God always man?*
    The Son of God was not always man, but became man at
    the time of the Incarnation.

85. *What is meant by the Incarnation?*
    By the Incarnation is meant that the Son of God,
    retaining His Divine nature, took to Himself a human
    nature, that is, a body and soul like ours.

Jesus knew all the people in my life, better than I. He certainly paid more attention to my annoying sister than I did. He knew about Chucky Dutcher, and he wasn't real happy about our ditching remedial religion class to dig up turtle eggs, but I'd been to Confession and Jesus had forgiven me for that sin a long time ago. I knew about Jesus' mom and dad and family, and all the weird stuff that went down on Annunciation Day.

> 87. *When was the Son of God conceived and made man?*
>   The Son of God was conceived and made man on
>   Annunciation Day, the day on which the Angel Gabriel
>   announced to the Blessed Virgin Mary that she was to be
>   the Mother of God.

> 88. *Is Saint Joseph the father of Jesus Christ?*
>   Jesus Christ had no human father, but Saint Joseph was
>   the spouse of the Blessed Virgin Mary and the guardian,
>   or foster father, of Christ.

I was so well prepared by Father McGuire that, in *Ben-Hur,* when Jesus first showed up, ladling out water to Charlton Heston, the subtlety of director William Wyler—who only shot Christ from the rear—didn't throw me for a second. I knew my Savior, front-forward, ass-backwards and six ways from Sunday.

I turned to Chucky and said, "That's Jesus, y'know."

"Shut up."

The thing that almost got me kicked out of the Erwin was Intermission. I had never heard of Intermission. Nonetheless, *Ben-Hur* had Intermission.

"What's Intermission?" I said to Chucky.

"I'n'no."

"Oh."

The movie screen read "Intermission," the lights in the Erwin were on, patrons were streaming back and forth to the refreshment counter and the toilets. The omnipotent ushers were prowling the aisles.

Movie ushers used to be one of the most powerful institutions on earth. Enlisted by movie theater managers to enforce absolute silence in the auditorium, to keep everyone's feet off the seat backs in front of them, and to brook no lip from patrons—especially minors—ushers operated under no Constitutional restraints. Democracy stopped at the door of the Erwin. Movie ushers, all of them recruited from the ranks of the officious and insulted at Tomah High School, were the last gasp of the Gestapo. Ready to defend to the death against any defilement of the basilica of the Silver Screen, they skulked the Erwin's inky aisles with hair-trigger spotlights, stalking the mildest transgressor. Overheard in mid-whisper, caught with your feet up, spotted with your gumwad slipping beneath an arm rest, you had no options. There was no court of appeal. You were rousted bodily from your seat by the triumphant usher, hauled to the lobby—crimson with shame—and rudely cast out.

I know, because it happened to me, at the Intermission of *Ben-Hur.* Bored by this inexplicable interlude of ponderous religious music, Chucky and I had begun goofing around, tickling each other and occasionally kicking the seat in front of us in our rambunctiousness. We might have gotten away with this impiety, because the movie wasn't exactly running and the lights were on. But then, we stepped over the line.

Raisinettes were my favorite movie candy. Alternating with jaw-breakers, I had nursed my Raisinette supply through the first two hours of *Ben-Hur.* Chucky spotted my candy stash and lunged for the box.

"Just one," I said.

"Okay, okay, okay," said Chucky. And then he tossed the Raisinette high in the air. Confidently, he settled under the airborne chocolate-covered raisin, opened his mouth and caught it. Nothing but tongue. Chucky chewed smugly.

"Ooh," I said.

I took out a new, fat Raisinette and flipped it upward, hastily. It landed three rows forward, on two snuggling teenagers who paid it no mind.

"Whoops."

I tried again, overcompensating. I almost sprained my neck stretching backwards to catch the Raisinette, which landed in the lap of a man seated behind me. "Thanks," he said, and ate my raisin.

One more time, I decided. After a couple of Cornbread Maxwell phantom tosses, I launched Raisinette No. 3. This one was perfect. It went up straight over my upturned face. It seemed to hang in midair, turning gently, the striated contours of milk chocolate brightening momentarily in the glow of projector light. I opened my mouth to receive the Raisinette. Suddenly, a hand swept past my nose, snatching the prize. The same hand grabbed my collar and lifted me, weightless, from my seat.

"Awright, kid. You're in deep shit now."

The usher, seventeen and pustulous with acne, yanked me away from Chucky, who didn't move but watched my departure with appropriate sympathy. The usher had me in the lobby, head spinning, before my feet had once touched the floor. Suddenly, I was staring into a wall of blue serge.

Mr. Erwin himself.

I looked up. Mr. Erwin, bigger than God, scowled down.

"Kid was throwin' candy, Mr. Erwin."

"Well then," said Mr. Erwin.

Oh, God, I thought. To be kicked out of any movie was a disgrace of epic dimensions. But to be torn from *Ben-Hur,* for which I had paid three times the normal admission price, which was the greatest movie ever filmed, the only movie truly loved by God the Father God the Son and God the Holy Ghost, winner of 250 Academy Awards, and the movie that I knew and appreciated more sincerely and devoutly than anyone else in all of Tomah and probably Monroe County because, after all, I was personal friends with Jesus Christ His only Son, Our Lord, who was conceived by the Holy Ghost, born of the Virgin Mary, suffered under Pontius Pilate, was crucified, died and was buried; He descended into hell; the third day He arose again from the dead; He ascended into heaven, sitteth at the right hand of God—

I was being dragged toward the door.

"No! No! Wait! Mr. Erwin!" I shouted. "It's a mistake!"

"Shut up, kid!" said the usher. "No candy throwin'. You know the rules."

"I wasn't throwin' candy!" I shouted. "I was just eatin'!"

The usher, my collar balled in his fist, my coat over his arm, reached for the exit door.

"Jesus!" I screamed desperately. "I love Jesus!"

I felt the cool air of the evening sweep into the lobby.

"Jesus!" I sobbed. "Forgive him, Jesus! For he knows not what he does!"

"Shut up, kid," said the usher.

"Wait."

Incredible. The voice of Mr. Erwin.

The usher paused in my bum's rush. I looked up. The ruthless usher's pimples flushed indigo.

"I'll talk to him, son," said Mr. Erwin to the usher.

The usher, obediently—he was, after all, a military man—unhanded me. Only under his breath, unheard by Mr. Erwin, as he retreated, did the vengeful underling mutter, "Your days are numbered, you little fuck."

I trembled at the exit doors, tears shining on my cheeks. Mr. Erwin crouched, like a glacier sliding into the sea. He faced me.

"Will you make me a promise, son?"

"Oh, yes. Oh sure! I will, Mr. Erwin. I promise I promise I will I will! I'm sorry. I didn't—I wasn't—I didn't mean—"

"Calm down. Calm down."

"Yessiryessiryessiryessiryessiryessir—"

"If you promise not to ever—"

"Oh, I do I do I do. I'm sorry. I'm sorry. It was just an acc—I mean, I didn't mean—"

"If you promise," Mr. Erwin began once more, patiently, "to be-have, like a gentleman, whenever you come to my theater—"

"Oh, I do! I do! I do!"

"Well then, all right," he said. He smiled tightly and rose back to his full height of 37,500 feet. "You may go back to the movie."

"Oh, thank you! Thank you, Mr. Erwin. Thank you! I promise—"

"Quietly," Mr. Erwin added.

I tiptoed back to *Ben-Hur,* backwards, my only sound a litany of thank-yous directed toward Mr. Erwin, whose smile had turned slightly crooked.

The movie had begun by the time, my sleeves damp with tears, I reclaimed my seat. Chucky, who had already dumped his coat into my empty seat, moved it back to his lap. He stared at me in amaze-ment. He hadn't expected to see me 'til Monday in school. As soon as the usher snatched me, Chucky had written me off as a goner and scavenged my Raisinettes.

"Holy shit!" said Chucky, momentarily losing all interest in *Ben-Hur.* "What happened?"

I caught my breath and stared up raptly at Charlton Heston. The voice that answered Chucky Dutcher wasn't mine. It was Paladin's.

"Oh," it said, "nothin'."

Moviegoing, outside of family bounds and the Saturday morning riots, was a major economic commitment for a kid. A movie, if you paid by yourself—which kids didn't usually do—cost a quarter, which was a lot. It was enough to buy a haircut! A quarter was a normal week's allowance. It was two and a half comic books. It was what T.J., my "other" grandfather, would pay for mowing his enor-mous lawn—if he paid anything at all. T.J. didn't readily liberate 25 cents. A quarter was serious money. But a movie was worth it. A movie was Doris Day singing "Once I Had a Secret Love." It was Roy Rogers whipping the reins across Trigger's withers and run-ning down some bushwhacking bastard in a black hat. It was *Looney Tunes,* Johnny Mack Brown and Francis the Talking Mule.

There were only two other known human pleasures worth as

much as a quarter. One was the annual triple-length, perfect-bound special edition of Superman Comics.

The other was basketball at Tomah High. And that was where I actually got tossed into the street by Management. There was no appeal, no Mr. Erwin to save me, no divine intervention.

But no shame, either. I accepted the bum's rush with my chinless chin held high, a crusader for justice in an unjust world.

Basketball at Tomah High also cost a quarter, but somehow it seemed cheap, probably by virtue of its scarcity. Movies came along all year round, but basketball had a brief season—a bitter depressing season, the dead of winter, when fun came with frostbite and homework nagged at your conscience. Tomah High basketball was a secret to most little kids. Grownups went to games. High school kids knew about the games. But little kids weren't in the loop. Unlike the Erwin, there was no marquee mounted on the facade of Tomah High School, no announcement in class that there was a game that night, no Saturday morning riot.

I knew, vaguely, that there was basketball at Tomah High. I knew it must be magnificent. But I had no idea when it happened, and how I could get in. I asked Chucky Dutcher. He didn't know, didn't care. Winter was Chucky's dormant period. School slowed his metabolism. "Basketball?" he said. "So what?

"Besides," he added, "I bet it costs a lot."

Hence, I was deeply dubious when Dougie, the stupendously dirty-mouthed little kid who lived next door to my grandparents, told me it was only a quarter to go to a game.

"Nah," I scoffed.

"Shit, yeah," said Dougie, spraying me slightly.

"Is that all? A quarter?"

"What'd I tell ya, dipshit?"

"Jeez. Only a quarter. Honest?"

"Goddamn right, peckerface."

Even though Dougie had crossed his heart and hoped his mother to die, I figured he was lying—because Dougie lied almost as much as he cussed, and besides, paradise had to be a lot harder to get into than just forking over a quarter. Cautiously, I posed the issue to Papa—who expressed dismay that a mere basketball game could be so expensive, and commenced reminiscing about a time when admission was only a nickel. He remembered especially the cordial race war waged annually between the white kids of Tomah High School and the Chippewas, Winnebagos, Menominees and Sauks who had been sentenced to separate but equal education, by the Bureau of Indian Affairs, at the Tomah Indian School. In years when the annual Indians-vs.-Indians game transpired at Tomah High's home gym, said Papa, decorum reigned. The festering resentment that had marked a half-century of second-class Native American citizenship dissipated in the vast spaces of the town's ultramodern gymnasium. But when the white Indians of Tomah High had to enter the lair of the red Indians on their own reservation, vengeance was the agenda. The Indian School gym was a veritable box, with barely enough space beyond the sidelines for two rows of folding chairs. Most spectators were squeezed into the ends of the gym, where they stood cheek-by-jowl, damp and musty in their winter coats, straining to see over one another's shoulders. The seats not occupied by players were reserved for the young ladies of the Indian School, clad from head to toe in black wool dresses and starched white collars, each wearing a simple straw hat with a black band and a bow, secured by a nine-inch hatpin honed to hypodermic acuity.

Every spectator at the game understood the placement of the young ladies of the Indian School and the significance of the hatpins. Every Tomah High player had been warned; each boy knew not to dribble too close to the sideline. To chase a loose ball into the crowd was an act of courage comparable to going over the top of a trench into No-Man's-Land. The poker-faced young ladies of the Indian School, Papa recalled admiringly, could slip the pins from their hats and plunge them bone-deep into a human ass or a milk-white male thigh with a speed and deftness that defied detection. The careless Tomah High School player would stagger away from his encounter with the young ladies of the Indian School bleeding in red droplets from a dozen neat punctures. These would often seal up within seconds, concealing the seed of a pus-swollen infection or a case of blood poisoning that wouldn't erupt until days—or weeks—after the game.

The Indian School players were never as skilled or as well coached as the kids from the high school. But they never lost a game on their own court.

I listened with awe and envy to Papa's tales of those Indian wars, to which admission was but a nickel. However—for all his historical knowledge—Papa couldn't confirm that the latter-day games were only a quarter. He hadn't been to a game in decades. I was afraid to broach the issue with anyone else, for fear of bursting the bubble. I resolved to investigate for myself.

When the basketball season finally arrived, and Tomah had its first home game, against Reedsburg or Richland Center or some other enemy hamlet, I took my wretched little brother, Bill, along. He made no protest. Going out in the dark on a Friday night, walking all the way from home to the high school gym, was an oddity of spectacular appeal.

Bill would follow anywhere that was even vaguely interesting, but Bill was hard to dislodge if he sensed that people wanted him to hit the road. When that happened . . . well, it wasn't like those heartwarming movies we watched on Saturday mornings at the Erwin Theater, starring Roddy McDowall or Jackie Cooper. Grownups rarely ever said to me, "Now, you take care of your little brother. He depends on you."

The usual exchange was something like "Take *him* along."

"Aw, Mom!"

"Take him."

"No!"

"Yes!"

Here, Bill would chime in. "I don'wanna go!"

"Get him out of here, before I kill him."

"Aw, Mom!"

"Now!"

"Crap."

"What did you say?"

To Mom: "Nuthin'." To Bill: "C'mon, stupid."

"I don'wanna go!"

"Mom, I'm gonna kill 'im."

"Fine. But do it outside."

The night of that first Tomah High basketball game, however, Bill tagged along willingly. And he always came willingly after that. He liked the games. He liked to watch me go bananas.

That night, I carried two of Papa's quarters to get us into the game. I knew, with the deep-seated pessimism of kids who get turned down, turned away, left behind and pushed aside as a condition of their existence, that the quarters wouldn't work. Some scowling thug at the door would curl his lip at the sight of my two damp overheated coins and say, "What's this, kid?"

"I wanna go to the game."

"Uh huh. Where's the rest?"

"The rest?"

"The rest of your money, kid?"

"You mean—?"

"Shit! You stupid brat! Get the hell out of here! You think you can get into a Tomah High School basketball game for a lousy quarter? Twenty-five stinkin' cents? Are you kidding? Who do you think you are? What do you think this is? Amateur night? Get the hell out of here! Beat it, kid, you miserable snot, before I beat the hell out of you!"

This is what I expected. This was life. I knew about life.

The ticket seller was a high school boy in a yellow-and-black varsity cardigan. He bore a vague resemblance to Bobby Rydell, but with black-rimmed glasses.

I laid down my two quarters and said, "Two . . . uh, children."

The boy looked up pleasantly, tore off two tickets, handed them to me, swept away my two quarters and said, "Have a good time."

The next thing I noticed, after what seemed like an hour—in

which I could hear choirs singing and angels sobbing with joy, during which I waited for several football players to seize us and toss us into the frigid night laughing at our gullibility and the richness of their joke—was Bill tugging at my sleeve.

"Come on, stupid! Whaddya doin' just standin' there?" he nagged. "We gotta get seats!"

Unimpeded, I entered the gym, which seemed roughly the size of St. Peter's. This was the biggest arena I had ever seen. I didn't know until years later, after it had been razed, that the gym floor was actually about ten feet short of the regulation ninety-four feet. One basket was mounted directly to the wall, with a mat hung from the wall five feet behind the backboard to prevent death-by-driving-layup.

Like most gyms of its time. Tomah's gym doubled as an auditorium and theater. On one sideline was a stage, where school plays, student assemblies and graduation ceremonies were held, where prom queens were crowned and Christmas pageants were staged. Bleachers were mounted on the stage for basketball games, and this is where the student body sat—raucous, sociable, empyrean.

Opposite the stage was a bank of permanent grandstands, elevated above the gym level. Here is where grownups, families, townspeople and visiting spectators gathered in dignity. Underneath the grandstands and extending out to the sideline were movable bleachers. These were the peanut gallery. Bill and I recognized our place immediately and headed for the bleachers. From that night on, we always sat in the same spot—exactly.

An evening of hoops in the brilliant shell of the Tomah High School gym unfolded before me like the Mass. The breathtaking music of the pep band, blasting out John Philip Sousa and "How Much Is That Doggie in the Window?" was pipe organs in the rafters and celestial choirs. The cheerleaders—Debbie Reynolds, Jane Russell, Rita Hayworth and the June Taylor Dancers—swirled around the gym like bare-legged acolytes, chanting the liturgy and warbling ritual responses.

"Come on, Tommy,
Put it in!
Take that ball, and
SIIIINK IT!"

"Are Ee Bee Oh You En Dee!
Rebound, rebound!
Yessirree!"

The junior varsity game, its slightly undersized players, a coach who was a little too close to his players' age and too frantic in his Sears & Roebuck blazer and half-tucked shirt, and the fans still filing into the bleachers, chatting and flirting and shlepping refreshments, was the Offertory.

The Eucharist came slowly, suspensefully, as the varsity players arrived. There was a fresh explosion of sound; the cheerleaders spun upside-down, all saddle shoes, palomino ponytails and golden panties. The players were not people, they were skyscrapers, totem poles, Apollo in his underwear. They broke into extraordinary coordination, lining up with drill team precision and performing layups that, incredibly, never missed. On a December Saturday under the plywood backboard of the St. Mary's playground, in my winter coat, reindeer sweater, farmer cap and rubber galoshes, I could spend a half-hour shooting a hundred layups and missing ninety-eight. Here were magicians who could simply amble up to the hoop, flip a wrist and spin every attempt, unerringly, through the net. And this was only a drill. They could perform this same unthinkable miracle at full speed, in heavy traffic, with the clock ticking, whistles blowing, fans screaming and starlets cartwheeling. They could probably do it in straitjackets, under mortar attack from the Red Chinese Army. I sat transfixed and ecstatic in the cheap seats, my ass in the footwell, my arms spread, my feet up—as the warriors of the *Iliad,* the knights of the Temple, the paratroopers of the 101st Airborne saving France for democracy streaked past me gigantically in short pants of gold and ivory, sweating out gallons of milk and honey. I reeled, I glowed, I guffawed.

Holy Communion began with the tipoff. Two titans, one a Tomah Indian, the other some Antichrist from Baraboo or Sparta—wearing hideous colors, with great black dirty hair all over his legs—would leap together, scraping holes in the ionosphere with their fingernails. Most games I don't remember. They were too magnificent for specific recall. High school hoops, especially in those days, when gyms were always full and pep bands were preposterously peppy, were Carnival. The players were the toast of the town, the standard-bearers of community pride—and they were the long winter's only entertainment. Each game was a festival of bright, clean, shimmering colors—from the gold and blonde of the cheerleaders to the violent contrast of Tomah's white-clad heroes to the blue or black or scarlet of the enemy to the vibrant orange of the ball. Scores I forget, but not the great players of Tomah High.

There was Chuck Ludeking, a buzzcut behemoth who played center, scored thousands of baskets and fought hand-to-hand against the colossal farm boys and elbow-swinging thugs of Black River Falls and Portage High. I remember the nimble and cerebral Ducklow brothers, who played one magical season side by side at guard and who astounded me doubly because their mother was Mrs. Ducklow, my fourth-grade teacher. After seeing Jimmy and Tommy, her sons, in action, I changed my view of Mrs. Ducklow. She was not a middle-aged lady in a chalk-dusted print dress and a permanent wave. She was a Norse goddess who spawned Vikings. Above all, the most heroic of all the Caucasoid Indians was a silky forward with sandy hair, who destroyed girls with a wink of his eye. His name was Toy Grovesteen, but he was Elvis.

Basketball games at the Tomah High gym were the closest I ever came to pure abandon. I slipped my moorings, lost all sense of time, place, restraint and proportion. I rolled in the bleachers, pulled out my hair, flushed purple and spoke in tongues. If Toy swished a clutch J, or Chuck put back a key rebound and got fouled in the act, I would leap from my seat and jump on the bleachers, waving my parka and clipping total strangers across the chops with my zipper tab.

The game that got me tossed from the Tomah gym was the best I had ever seen. The visitors were the Blugolds from La Crosse Aquinas, a big school in the big city. Moreover, Aquinas was a Catholic school, with Jesus in its locker room. The fact that I was also Catholic, also attended a parochial school, also conversed regularly with Jesus and got my sins directly forgiven every week by God the Father God the Son God the Holy Ghost and Father Mulligan— none of this even nicked my loyalties. I knew that in sports, you stood by your hometown team, above all other gods. Besides, I knew Jesus had bigger fish to fry than to get privately involved in podunk basketball.

I was twitchy and hoarse by the end of the first quarter. Incredibly, the Indians and the Blugolds were tied, and tied again at halftime. I fibrillated with excitement. My eyes bulged; my hands shook; my popcorn spilled. The impossible was transpiring. We were beating the toughest team that had ever entered the Tomah gym. The game stayed razor-close to the waning seconds, when Toy broke another tie. He sliced between two Blugolds on the baseline and coaxed a floater into the hoop. I erupted from my seat, flapping my arms and jumping up and down in the bleachers, screaming praise at Toy and spewing spite at the beaten Blugolds. An usher, a dignified adult in a brown sport coat and tie, noted that the people surrounding me, mostly kids, were looking my way fearfully and leaning away from me. The usher encroached a few steps and motioned me to calm down. I did so marginally, while my ecstasy simmered. There were ten seconds left in the game. Aquinas took a time-out. I built up steam for my climactic detonation. Aquinas took the court. The dangerous Blugold point guard collected the inbounds pass and streaked upcourt, only to be foiled, brilliantly, by Tommy Ducklow. As the two players rushed past the bleachers, a few feet away from me, Tommy flicked a hand at the ball and bounced it off the Blugold's knee. The ball skittered away. The Blugold lunged and touched the ball, but couldn't control it. It rolled, excruciatingly slow, out of bounds. It bounced off the bleachers, so close I could almost touch it. Joy engulfed me.

Our ball!

From some deep recess of my senses, I heard a whistle blow. I looked up, expecting to see the referee pointing to my right and shouting over the roar of the delighted throng, "White ball!"

But I saw something else, something unfathomable and diabolical. The referee's upraised hand was closed in a fist and his other hand pointed directly, accusingly, at Tommy Ducklow's dewy and innocent face.

"That's a hack," I heard him say.

That's a what?

"Two shots," said the ref. "Blue."

"Blue? *Blue!*"

Here was madness. Here was a ref who was not only taking the ball away from Tomah after Tommy Ducklow had stolen the ball fair and square, but taking Tommy Ducklow away, too. This was Tommy's fifth foul! He was gone. I looked desperately for the other ref, fairer and purer, to rush over and correct this horror, to overrule his rogue comrade and restore balance to the scales of justice.

But he stood there. Just stood there, passive in the presence of evil. How could he?

"No!" I cried. "NO NO NO NO NO NO NO!"

"Boo!" said Bill beside me, helpfully.

"You're blind! You're blind!" I wailed, bounding on the bleachers.

"Yeah! Blind!" shouted Bill.

"Booo!" I keened. "Booo! Booo!"

A few others joined my booing. My usher, visible but irrelevant in the corner of my bloodshot eye, stirred.

The offending referee, short, plump and striped—a penguin in sneakers—took the ball and directed the Blugold guard to the free throw line. Then he motioned Tommy Ducklow off the floor. This was the last straw. My heart broke audibly in my chest. Something snapped in my brain. I knew about injustice. I was a battle-scarred veteran of injustice. I knew injustice from being the odd kid in choose-ups at recess and I'd be left off both teams, and Gunderson or Overacker would say, "You wait here, Benjamin. You can be the sub, and you'll get in as soon as somebody gets hurt, or gets tired." And I knew I was screwed because nobody ever got hurt or got tired.

I knew injustice from all the way back in second grade, when stupidhead Kippy Kamperschroer couldn't remember the Apostles' Creed and our teacher, Mrs. Poss, made all of us sit silent at our desks—even though the bell had rung—and do twenty rosaries, and we missed most of lunch hour. We all knew the Apostles' Creed by heart, every one of us except for stupidhead Kippy, who never remembered anything. And Mrs. Poss knew it!

I knew injustice from the movies, from when Messala sent Charlton Heston off to die as a galley slave, because Messala was rich and powerful and mean.

And I knew injustice from the Bible, terrible unspeakable injustice. Pontius Pilate could have saved Jesus from the bloodthirsty mob, but he pardoned Barabbas instead and then washed his hands and walked away.

Injustice gnawed at my soul and festered in my bosom. I knew injustice was out there. I was vigilant for any sign of it. But in the Tomah High School gym, I believed I was safe. Injustice here was inconceivable, because here was unblemished sport, played by Adonises, officiated by priests of fair play who were fallible and human, but deeply sincere.

But here, suddenly, in the midst of the Benediction, was a fallen priest exposed. Here was a Pharisee, possessed by Beelzebub, pointing his cleft hoof at the face of pure and sinless Tommy Ducklow, and casting him into the darkness.

This travesty could not stand. As silence fell in anticipation of the tying free throws, with two seconds on the clock, I drew myself up to my full forty-nine inches. The vast vocabulary of Dougie scrolled willy-nilly through my fevered brain as I directed the cracked relic of my prepubescent alto toward the corrupt, myopic referee.

"You're blind," I squealed. "You fat prick!"

No one heard me. I was drowned out by the klaxon that blew to announce a substitution and summon Tommy Ducklow to the Tomah bench. Tommy obeyed, his shoulders hunched.

I'd missed my shot. I couldn't do it again. I couldn't cuss in front all those people twice. Desperate, I looked around. I saw my coat behind me. Yes! I seized it by one arm, swung it once over my head and flung it toward the evil ref.

It floated weightless, rising gently, falling on the sideline barely noticed—except by one increasingly restive usher.

I needed more ammo. I grabbed Bill's coat.

"Hey! That's my—"

Bill's coat went farther, mainly because he had stuffed his mittens into his pockets and it was heavier. But I still lacked distance. The evil ref's back was turned, thirty feet away, oblivious to my rage.

I spotted my hat, a knit navy blue stocking cap. I winged it with all my puny might—and missed by ten feet.

"Shit!"

All I had left were my gloves. In the corner of my eye, I saw the usher closing in, fast. I had inspiration. One glove wasn't enough. I stuffed my right glove inside the left. I reared back. I wound up, and with all the wrath that God's faithful reserved for a thousand martyrs unjustly flayed, grilled and killed by heathen tyrants, I pitched a whistling strike right at the number on that son of a bitch's back.

Thump.

"Jeez-*us*!" said Bill, struggling to conceal his glee.

The referee made a little leap. He turned to look at me. My clothes and my brother's coat littered the pristine floor of the Tomah High School gym. Everyone—except the Aquinas kid about to shoot the free throws—turned and stared. What they saw was the long arm of my avenging usher swipe me, like a wet leaf on a windshield, from the bleachers. The usher, growling and inarticulate, transported me bodily toward the lobby. Once there, he dumped me onto the tiled floor. A student dropped a heap of winter clothes at my feet, and hurried away.

"That," said the usher, "is not the way Tomah fans behave." His ears glowed red and his eyes trembled with outrage.

"Oh yeah?" I replied lamely.

"Get out!"

I fought to keep tears back. My chin trembled. But this, I knew, was no time to break down. I collected my parka and straightened. I looked him in the top button of his shirt.

"Now!" he said.

I didn't mention injustice, nor Ben-Hur, nor even Jesus and Pontius Pilate. Kids didn't argue ethics with strange grownups. Kids, if they knew what was good for them, didn't argue anything with any grownups. We lived, after all, by the Code.

"I won't do it again," I said. "Promise."

"Out."

"What about the next game?" I asked, dawdling over a coat sleeve.

His fury was entirely official, thus ephemeral. I looked at his face. He was a little older than my dad, sandy-haired, clean-shaven, lean and slightly rumpled—the way high school teachers looked in movies. His sport coat was corduroy, a button missing.

He looked down at me and took in the fact that, outside the gym, I was small and scrawny and cuter than the average psychopath.

He shook his head and sighed.

"We'll see," he relented.

He pointed to the door.

I didn't try to beg my way back in. This wasn't Raisinettes, after all. This was important. This was justice. I sensed that to return to the gym now, on any terms, would diminish me, my sad-eyed usher, and my team.

I separated my brother's coat and mittens from the pile and gave them to the usher.

"These are my brother's. He's still . . ."

The usher took them, nodded.

"Bye," I said, and went into the January night, where a light snow was beginning to dust the walkways on the campus.

I waited there until the game was over. I could hear the waves and bursts of crowd noise, like organ music overhead through cathedral doors. Torn suddenly from my transports of emotion, I felt both emptied and chastened. I knew I had sinned mightily. I had stood against my fellow churchmen, the Blugolds of St. Thomas Aquinas, I had denounced authority, and I had talked dirty, at the top of my lungs—or at least tried to—before a thousand witnesses.

But the old trusty guilt wasn't there, soiling my soul and demanding contrition. Instead of ashamed, I was exultant. I could almost hear the ethical contradictions slugging it out between my ears, and they felt good. For cussing and throwing clothes, in the name of truth, in the temple of basketball, I was banished. But this turned out to be the same penance you got for throwing candy, for no good reason, at the Erwin. Was this fair?

A few minutes later, the building gave out its last muffled roar. I snagged the first kid who came out of the gym and asked the final score. Despite my recent notoriety, he didn't seem to recognize me.

"Sixty-three to sixty-two," he said. "We lost."

I murmured knowingly, collected Bill and walked home, looking about me with eyes of wonder. The night was black, the snow was white. But the rest was shades of gray.

The Hotpads

One year, we came back to school and the playground had been paved. The red dust was gone, and the sandburs had lost their purchase. But most devastating, the tree was missing. It had been neither a healthy nor a comely tree—merely a scabrous claw of scrub oak clinging to a riddled mound of naked orange sand and dropping dead branches like a leper losing fingers. Nonetheless, every spring, it had been a sort of Maypole for boys. The eroded hump on which it stood was the playing field for our annual marbles frenzy. Answering some unspoken male urge—I suspect the female equivalent had something to do with jacks—one Monday in May, when at last the cold through the parka's fold no longer stabbed like a driven nail, we all brought to school a fat pouch full of marbles. These were the conventional variety: cat's eyes, clearies, aggies and steelies, especially steelies. In Tomah, steelies—elsewhere precious—were a glut on the marble market, because of the frog shops down at the Milwaukee Road railyard, where ball bearings were as common as timothy between the ties.

We didn't play the chalk-circle-on-the-sidewalk marbles game that monopolizes American folklore. Ours was pitch-and-putt keepsies, where you dug a shallow pot in the dirt, ante'd a marble or two into the pot and pitched your shooters from a fair distance away.

After that first toss, your putter was your index finger, with closest-to-the-hole shooting first, and the last man into the pot lost his marbles. Every recess in the spring, 'til barehands softball captured our fickle fancy, we swarmed the mound 'round the arthritic tree, pitching and crouching, shuffling back into class at the bell with muddied knees and filthy knuckles. Marbles under the tree were a small rite of passage in which kids learned the truth: if you staked too much on the roll of a hard little orb on a rutted field that was mined with crazy rocks and treacherous depressions, you could lose your best shooter, your prettiest pebbles and your self-respect in one fifteen-minute recess. Your best friend could take you to the cleaners, and you didn't have the option to snivel about it afterwards. In marbles, you were either a man or a spectator.

> *. . . A Knight without armor*
> *In a savage land . . .*

The paving of the playground was another passage, I guess. It was our own little Industrial Revolution—nature succumbing to the march of asphalt and the erection of deadly machines, including a merry-go-round which, if you didn't watch your feet, would catch you between its whirling edge and the unforgiving pavement and rip your leg off at the knee. Once they had paved the playground and eighty-sixed the scraggy oak, we never moved our marbles season to a new venue. It just died—which makes me suspect the marbles urge might have been something in the tree, a spell it cast or a mystic drug in its meager annual gasp of acorn pollen. The kids over at the public school might have still had a marble season. They still had acres of dirt and a veritable forest of moribund oaks. But, after the paving, us Catholics just cold-turkeyed into softball season.

However, softball was a spring thing, and here it was only September, all of us staring at asphalt where dust annually turned to snow, then mud, then dust again just before school got out. Naked asphalt. There it was, sloping down from the upper (girls') playground, which had always been paved (the better for hopscotch), stopping forty yards yonder at a gleaming new chain link fence, and new chain link backstops at each far corner of the playground. They even put up a nifty plywood backboard and equipped each grade with a neoprene Voit basketball. An unexplored vista lay before our gaze: chain link, plywood, leg-eating merry-go-round. Shazam.

Our first impression was that it stunk. This was a big change. Kids are reactionary. We wanted the old playground back—or at least someone to explain what the hell was *wrong* with the old playground. But then, this was the Fifties, when kids didn't talk to adults. Heck, we barely talked to each other. We stood atop the slope, staring at this new recess environment, speechless, scowling.

Gradually, we began to cope, each of us, privately.

For a while, we suffered a kind of group kid identity crisis, groping to change from a rural gang of sodbusters to a sleek, orderly team of urban hustlers. Grudgingly, we broke in the asphalt—with mob basketball. Thirty midgets milling frantically under the hoop, winter clothes flopping, clawing at one another and occasionally whanging the Voit off a corner of the backboard. We moved on to touch football—a stupid game. When the first winter winds started screaming up the hill and swirling around the church steeple, we retrenched. For a bitter week or so, we reduced our recess activity to huddling.

Huddling is an instinctive response to winter in Wisconsin. One Indian summer day, you're cavorting on the playground in shirtsleeves. Next day, it's 10 degrees below zero, with winds from the north at twenty miles an hour, running up your pantlegs. The shock of that first really arctic day, usually mid-November, is like spinal trauma. We stopped playing, left all our balls indoors. It was all we could do to filter meekly onto the shelterless, treeless, merciless, wind-whipped asphalt. One or two kids hunkered pathetically by the monkey bars, seeking relief behind its leafless pipes. A few others found some respite beneath the slide, whose tin surface sang weirdly in the frozen blast. Everyone else just huddled, shivering bleakly and counting the hours 'til recess was over and arithmetic indoors was a welcome alternative. Huddling became a subtle dance, in which each member of a four- or five-kid cluster shifted surreptitiously, seeking an angle where the wind hit another sufferer directly and dealt him only a glancing blow.

While we were huddling, the playground entered a new season, taking on a new aspect. Its pool table uniformity had already proved to be an autumn illusion. In the fall rains, it had betrayed shallow channels which wound downhill toward the fence, and dips where puddles built. In November, the puddles froze into an invisible patchwork of hazards. When snow coughed from the sky, some of it would bond, cold with cold, and outline the ice patches. The early snow, driven by rapier winds, huddled like we did, clinging to edges of the fence, the lee side of the slide, the struts of the leg-ripping merry-go-round. With the first accumulation of the winter, it lay like a thermal coverlet on the asphalt, roughly textured by tiny pebbles trapped in tar, suggesting undulations beneath. The wind moved the thin snow efficiently into cracks and hollows, denuded its swells and exposed its subtle eskers. Snow lent life to the dead asphalt. One day, the snow was thick and tempting, begging to be trampled, demanding an end to our cowardly huddling, needful of a game.

Somehow, that winter, we chose soccer.

This was the Fifties, when soccer wasn't supposed to exist in the United States, much less in its northern climes, much less played in the dead of winter by unsupervised boys. We only knew there was soccer because we played it. We had no idea anybody had heard of it in Europe, or that people in South America were killing each other over World Cup bids. We didn't know there was a World Cup. What we knew was that one team kicked the ball that way, and the other team kicked the ball this way. And if you kicked the ball across the edge of the playground (we had no goalmouths, although each team had two goalies, patrolling the vast expanse of available goal), you scored. Later, we found out our game was called "two-line soccer," the modifier suggesting that there might be another variety of the game. No one discovered, until years later, what that hypothetical variant might be.

Meanwhile, we kicked and ran and scored goals in heaps, usually wearing buckle-up rubber galoshes, on a field of rock-packed snow that couldn't be dented with a pickax.

On Monday, every week, all winter, all the boys in our grade would gather on the lower playground and we'd choose up sides. Team captains were the usual handful of alpha males, Kiegel, Fin, Gunderson, Overacker. Out of tradition, they chose me late. The same team then stuck together through the week.

No one kept score. We just played, a horde of faceless bundles ebbing and flowing across the ice in pursuit of a textured red ball designed for no sport in particular. Just a red ball you could kick and it would ping hollowly if you connected square—your galosh finding the ball's sweet spot—and it would take off like a bat out of hell. After five minutes on the ice pack, the ball, though still bouncy, would freeze, its skin gone leathery and skid-prone, the air inside gone icy, slightly deflated.

I remember intimately the texture of the frozen ball because my specialty was blocking in-bounds kicks, which involved angling deviously toward the in-bounder on his blind side, waiting for him to cock his kicking leg and then flinging my body toward the ball just as it went "ping" and took flight. Sometimes, when I succeeded, I'd deflect the ball with a hand or arm. Otherwise, I'd get it in the face. Nose-first impact with a frozen kickball is a singular effect. Suddenly, beneath the impassive surface of my numbed kisser, bodily fluids erupt, rather like poking a torch at a sprinkler system. The ball careens away, my body hits the ice, tears blind my eyes, saliva squirts through my chapped lips and snot gushes from ice-caked nostrils. On a good hit, my nose bleeds.

Why do this?

Most kids didn't, of course. Most kids, understanding the effect of bitter cold on a neoprene ball, had no desire to fling themselves teeth-first into its path. But, as a known associate of Koscal and the perpetual odd-kid-out, I saw it as my duty to shoulder the most onerous role in the daily soccer game. I was proving my mettle to the elite males; I struggled for worthiness. The fact that no other

kids ever acknowledged my sacrifice, as I staggered to my feet drooling and draining, the fact that no teammate ever patted me on the
back or said, "Good block, shrimp!" or ever showed a glimmer of
appreciation—all this inattention deterred me not a whit. This was
Catholic school; I knew about martyrdom. There were saints, bar-
becued over hot coals, flattened like pizza dough or twisted like wet
towels, who never got a word of thanks 'til three or four centuries after they were dead. Someday, someone would be paying five
figures to get a sliver of my femur embedded in a crucifix. I could
wait.

Actually, there were more immediate gratifications. On a typical
in-bounds kick, everyone on two teams, thirty kids, would be leaning in one direction; my block would send the ball skittering the
other way. Usually, being the perpetrator of the anomaly, I was
closest to the ball. If I could get back to my feet, waggle my head
and clear my vision of mucus and tears before the liquid buildup
froze my eyes shut, I had a scant moment alone, just me and the
bouncing ball. Ideally, I was a few steps from the goal, where—
inevitably—a goalie was hopelessly out of position (goalie was the
position reserved for the irretrievably uncoordinated; these guys
went on to high school careers in the Projectionist Club). I scored
most of my goals while peering through a scrim of bodily fluids.

No one noticed my goals. Soccer for me was a solitary endeavor,
despite the galloping, tumbling, clambering mob around the ball.
By myself, I created my niche in the game, exploiting my social in-
visibility, prowling the sidelines, waiting for a kick-in, battering my
unloved face and wobbling after the ball like a derelict following a
wind-blown stogie.

Secretly, I kept score of each day's game. My team was always
called the Hotpads. This is not a dignified name for a team, especially
one that never played a game in temperatures above 0 degrees C.
I know that now. I didn't know it then. I thought "Hotpads"
sounded cool. In the field of asinine team nomenclature, I was a
prophet.

My opposing teams had no names. I only corrected this oversight later in life.

I kept a notebook in my desk where I recorded scores, recess-by-recess. Each day constituted one game, three periods (morning recess, lunchtime, afternoon recess). Final scores were pleasingly higher than your average triple-overtime 0–0 World Cup nailbiter. In one Hotpad victory, which probably ended 31–24 or thereabouts, I scored nine quiet goals. In my career, I guess, I had hundreds of goals. My notebook, which I revealed to no one, was the only proof of this. It was the only record of any of the exploits of the Hotpads in the St. Mary's Winter Two-Team Two-Line Soccer League. Once, Gerald Seitz, who sat next to me in class, noticed me filling in columns of statistics in my Hotpads notebook.

"What's that?"

I slammed it shut.

"Nothin'."

"Come on. Show me."

"Nope."

"Whatcha writin'?"

I thought fast. "It's a story."

"Oh. You gonna read it to the class sometime?"

I did that regularly—read my stories to the class. They were preposterous stories, but they served to postpone geography tests.

"Yeah. When it's done."

The kid was quelled. "Oh. Okay."

As winter deepened, so did the ice pack. We'd come back to school on a Monday and the giant pile of snow that had been plowed against the chain link fence eventually grew taller in places than the fence. It was a fortress of ice, eight feet high, six feet wide, fifty yards from end to end. When an alpha, Kiegel or Fin, gave the ball a mighty kick, sometimes it would clear the ice fortress on the fly, evade the snaggleteeth of the chain link barrier, land outside the playground and skid down the icy hill to Hollister Avenue. Once, though, it bounced atop the ice fortress, hit chain link and stopped, trapped sickeningly on the teeth of the dragon. The ball hung, impaled on a fence prong, leaking cold air.

Someone retrieved it, looked at it dubiously and threw it back into the game. It didn't bounce.

Hopefully, a kick.

The ball went several feet and settled crookedly on the side that had been caved in by the kicker.

"Jesus. Look what you did!"

"I didn't do that. There's a hole in the ball."

"Who kicked it onto the fence?"

We all knew. No one took credit.

"What are we gonna do?"

Two-line soccer was always a silent—introspective—game, each kid pursuing the ball in his own style, with his own deeply private passion, barely speaking, his lips tight to prevent his teeth freezing, grunting evocatively with each kick. At this moment, though, individualism was impossible. The Code had to be temporarily waived. Suddenly, all of us, alphas and journeymen, toadies and weenies, were knit together by the crisis of a punctured ball. Without it, we had no soccer. There was only winter, harsh and life-sucking, stretching out in an imponderable eternity of wine-dark sky, arctic wind and huddling.

"We could tell Sister."

Our nun that year was Sister Claveria, which did not bode well for the repair or replacement of the ball. Sister Claveria thought the proper use of the red ball was a girls' game called four-square, which could be played, without endangering the ball, 'til hell froze over. Of course, only four people at a time could play four-square, assuming that the four players were either girls or sissies.

The fact that we had punctured the vital red ball in a game other than four-square precluded any sympathy from Sister Claveria.

One boy, a rank-and-file myopic named Four-Eyes Fuchs, volunteered to attempt a repair. He took it home at lunch, patched the hole with three or four pounds of black electrical tape, and re-inflated the ball, gingerly, with a bicycle pump. Miraculously, it worked. With ten minutes to go in lunch recess, we kicked the ball cautiously around the ice pack. The tape held; the ball bounced. Four-Eyes Fuchs was a hero.

In three minutes, the tape froze, the adhesion relaxed, the tape curled away from the hole and when Gunderson swung his leg for a prodigious kick into the enemy goal, the ball stuck on his foot.

"Shit."

Gunderson wasn't just cussing over a punctured ball. There was a bigger issue here. "No grownups allowed," after all, was the principle that defined every kid's kidhood. You took orders from grownups. You ate the food they gave you. You went to bed when they said. You got stuff from them—clothes, allowance, Christmas presents. But they had their problems; we had ours. You didn't bring grownups into a kid problem.

Our dilemma was whether the ball was a kid problem or a grownup problem. Clearly, we kids had busted the ball. But, technically, it wasn't our ball. It was the school's ball.

Someone realized that our fundamental anti-grownup theology was, in this situation, in conflict with another basic kid rule: "Everybody has their own stuff." You didn't mess with somebody else's stuff. Strictly speaking, we had messed with the school's ball, and we had broken it—which made us responsible for the punctured ball. Simple. However, the school let us use the ball. The school had balls because the school had kids. Without us, there would be no balls. The nuns weren't going to use the ball—not even for four-square. So, it wasn't our ball, but it *was* our ball. So, what happens when you bust the ball? We'd never busted a ball before. Was this a grownup problem because, technically, the ball was the school's ball? Or was this a kid problem, which we would have to solve by ourselves regardless of the ball's true owner, because it was *our* game?

We never answered these questions. Instead, we considered Sister Claveria.

Fin, the brightest alpha male, said, "She won't buy us another ball."

"Why not?" said Kiegel.

"She ain't got'ny money."

This was true. Nuns are notoriously penniless. They collected money, from kids, in piles. But they never had any to spend.

"Yeah, well," said Overacker, lamely, "the school could—"

"Yeah?" interrupted Fin. "How?"

We pictured the process. Sister Claveria might relent so far as to submit a request for a new ball to the principal, Sister Terence—who was cheerful and affectionate but, like all nuns, impoverished and thoroughly devoid of fiscal authority. For a major nonreligious expenditure, especially something as secular and frivolous as a red neoprene ball for a bunch of ne'er-do-well fifth-grade boys to play soccer on a glacier, there was only one avenue of appeal.

A priest.

If we could get to Father Mulligan, we were in like Flynn. Father Mulligan, the pastor, was Santa Claus in a cassock. To see a band of boys without a ball would fill him with Irish sentiment. Father Mulligan would have us back in business in a heartbeat—which is exactly why the diocese had installed Father Rourke as the gatekeeper to Father Mulligan. Father Rourke was dour, middle-aged, judgmental and abstemious. He would not see our punctured ball as an accident or a tragedy. He would not recognize the snaggletoothed chain link fence as a dragon lurking on the fringe of the asphalt plain. He would see our busted ball as the sin of juvenile carelessness, an inability of the young boys of our day to take proper care of the playthings bestowed so generously upon us—without thought of reward—by the Holy See of Rome, gifts which we were shamelessly prone to squander and destroy while better Catholics around the world, in destitute outposts like Korea and France, went not only without balls to play with but without bread to eat or beds to sleep in or prayers to comfort them in their throes of infant death. To have recess with no ball and no soccer—this would be a fitting penance, in Father Rourke's pitiless philosophy, for our negligence.

"Even if Father Rourke let us have another ball," said Fin, stretching everyone's credulity, "it would take forever."

This was true. We knew that the school had no money, and the church had less. There would have to be some sort of special appropriation—details beyond our comprehension. To us, building a new rectory or buying a red kickball were financial challenges of equal magnitude. By the time the school could free up the funds for our ball, the ice would be gone and the soccer season history.

"What if," said Koscal.

Koscal was such a dipshit! Always shooting off his mouth. He put on the lordly airs of an alpha male, bristled with self-confidence and battled the best jocks to a standstill in every sport, but he had never cracked the alpha brotherhood—and nobody liked him. Not even me. And I was his best friend. The worst part was that he sometimes had a good idea. He pissed everyone off.

"What if what?" said Overacker, pointing his chin threateningly at Koscal.

Koscal, who could beat Overacker at everything but football, didn't back down. "What if we buy a new ball ourselves?"

This was an unprecedented presumption.

The ball belonged to the school. It wasn't our ball. Koscal was saying we should buy a new ball, but whose ball would it be? Our ball? Or the school's ball? Why would we want to buy a ball if it wasn't ours, even though we were the only ones who used it?

Think about it. Everybody has their own stuff, but this wouldn't be anybody's.

Koscal was talking Communism.

We recoiled.

But then, Fin nimbly leapt the ontological abyss. He said, "Where would we get the money?"

Practicality, once more, transcended politics. It even stifled our aversion to Koscal.

The money, it turned out, was in our pockets and piggybanks. I had 13 cents on me at that moment, 5 of which I had mentally reserved for a Milky Way after school. But that left 8 cents for the common cause. How much would a new ball cost?

Koscal, at lunch, found out. Risking accusations of hooky,

he stole away downtown (after, of course, eating his usual forty pounds of food in less than a minute). Before the lunch recess was over, Koscal had returned to the playground with a report that the identical mate to the very ball we had killed was available, at Burris's Dime Store, for a mere $2.99.

For a moment, a certain sense of awe affected us. We had ventured outside the paternal bounds of the school world, an entirely grownup realm wherein we operated without power or recourse and did so willingly. We had broached the possibility of sidestepping the byzantine grownup system of appropriations, requisitions, distribution and supply, and we had found this deviant route not only possible but ridiculously easy. The stuff they gave us at school was the same stuff they sold at the dime store. And it was cheap. For any one of us, $2.99 was a king's ransom, a year's savings, a whole day of midway and Tilt-A-Whirl and ecstasy at the Monroe County Fair in July. But split up among us to solve the red ball crisis, $2.99 was barely 20 cents a head. We could do this.

We didn't instantly dig into our pockets and count our change. We paused to contemplate the magnitude of our discovery. By taking a mere bagatelle of responsibility for ourselves, we could beat the grownup system, bypass the nuns and duck the brimstone breath of Father Rourke. We could have our ball and kick it, too.

Four-Eyes Fuchs was chosen—instead of Koscal, who volunteered enthusiastically—as our purchasing agent. The substitution was not a matter of mistrust. Koscal was probably more honest than Four-Eyes Fuchs. Trouble was, Koscal would have carried out the mission to Burris's Dime Store with so much officious self-importance and scrupulous integrity that he would have ended up irritating us beyond endurance.

The next day, with the new ball, the game was restored—with an air of unprecedented recklessness. The dragon, though he still crouched behind the ice fortress, spreading his thousand-toothed jaws across one entire border of our playing field, was foiled forever. If he ate the ball again, we knew where we could get a new ball—or even a better ball—with no help from anyone but ourselves.

Inexplicably, Sister Claveria noted the arrival of the new ball with approval, praising us for our initiative. She was apparently unaware that she had lost a grip on our minds that could never be restored. We had licked the nun, and she purred in defeat. Here was further evidence that grownups were incomprehensible.

Toward the end of the soccer season, when the ice pack every day grudgingly sweated out a thin slime of gray slush, I bumbled into the rare opportunity to deflate the mighty Gunderson.

Gunderson was not exactly my nemesis. This title was properly shared by Kiegel—a mean and stumpy sluggo who pleasured himself, now and then, by accompanying me all the way home from school, thumping the side of my head fifty or sixty times with his knuckles until my ear would bleed; and Feeney—the smallest kid in class, a conniver who sucked up to the alpha males and plotted humiliation for every outcast and half-pint who unwittingly reminded him of his own puniness.

Gunderson was too dumb to be mean. He was a humorless slob, coursing with gallons of premature testosterone, who—like most mesomorphic hulks—judged other human beings entirely on the basis of whether he could knock them on their ass. The ones he couldn't, or could do so only with difficulty, he horsed around with, rather daintily (you've seen those *National Geographic* clips . . . of male elephant seals, sparring playfully on the beach?), and occasionally exchanged manly *bon mots*. Everybody else, he knocked on their ass, dutifully—no hard feelings.

Gunderson, in the daily grind of recess, had knocked me on my ass—both physically and spiritually—countless times. The physical assaults, flattening me in a touch football game, elbowing me to the asphalt in a game of mob basketball, were a matter of routine. Stand up, dust off, plunge back in. The pain came during choose-up time, when, after almost everyone else had been selected, he would consider me, standing with the other dregs. Gunderson, dismissively, would wave all of us onto the other team, a mess of spare parts which—even assembled by a master craftsman—couldn't conceivably amount to one whole operational kid.

In a way, Gunderson shooing us all onto the opposition, fearless of being outnumbered, was a princely gesture. To us rejects, however, the experience lacked grandeur. To me, especially, knowing that Gunderson had never in his life deigned to block a kick-in and hence—on many days—scored fewer goals than I, it rankled. I harbored a chronic, subconscious resentment toward Gunderson and his kind, although I had no power and no plan for ever gaining vengeance.

Hence, my opportunity for payback was a happenstance. It was a March day, the temperature almost up to freezing. We played hatless, bootless, our shoes turning to sponge as we slopped across the melting ice pack, our coats open, our dungarees wet to the knees. The afternoon recess wound down. The weak winter sun already cast long shadows. The incomparable Fin, my Hotpad teammate this week, burst from a scrum and whacked the ball toward the goal. It hooked sharply, bouncing off the backstop and trickling into the deep corner of the field. It rolled almost to a stop at the foot of the ice fortress. Gunderson, a non-Hotpad this week, rumbled to the ball to clear it from the danger zone. I was faster than Gunderson; I stuck to his heels. He reared back for a mighty kick. I divined Gunderson's likeliest trajectory and launched myself.

The red ball caught me square in the chest. I opened my eyes in mid-flight, just in time to see Gunderson's shoe, following through. With a damp cowhide splat, Gunderson's kick caught my chin. My teeth snapped together like a car door. The impact spun me 180 degrees, so that I landed facing away from Gunderson. I spied the ball, through filmy eyes, skittering toward the edge of the backstop. I saw it nick the fence, slide to the right, teeter and then fall off the end of the playground—a goal!—just out of Nordling the goaltender's impotent reach.

This I saw. I heard a bell ring. Then, for perhaps fifteen seconds, no more, everything was black. Fuzzily, I heard feet on the playground, the whole class galloping back to school. Someone paused long enough to put a hand on my back and say my name. Obviously, he wanted me to get up and go into school, but I wasn't going anyplace 'til I found my head and screwed it back on. I just lay there, curled fetally, throbbing.

Through a dispersing fog, a moment later, a voice. Couldn't be, but it was. Gunderson! He shook me gingerly.

"Benjamin, c'mon. Hey! Get up. C'mon. Jeez, ya gotta get back into school. C'mon, the bell rang."

He kept talking, while it dawned on me. If I wasn't in class inside of two minutes, somebody would notice. Sister Claveria would ask, "Where is David?"

Silence would descend. Sister Claveria would dispatch someone to locate me, probably Stephen Lagerbloom, one of those uncannily blessed boys who were liked equally by kids and teachers. He would hurry away, then return in a moment to say, ominously, "He's out there, Sister."

"Out there? Out where?"

"On the playground, Sister."

"On the playground? Doing what?"

"He's just layin' there, Sister. Not movin'."

Then they would come—not kids. The kids would be left inside to study quietly, ponder their sins and wonder if, ever before in history, a kid had actually been kicked to death on a playground. Nuns would come, maybe even a priest. They would hurry across the playground, down the slope, rushing across the ice pack, splashing slush on their habits and cassocks, reaching me at last, prone, motionless and racked with pain. They would put a hand on me, say my name, make sure I wasn't paralyzed, then gently lift me, first to a sitting position, so that they could examine the contusion on my chin, check my jaw for broken bones and missing teeth.

Finally, someone—a voice already heavy with the weight of a dire punishment that must be meted out for mayhem this heinous—would ask, "David, who did this to you? Please, name your attacker."

Gunderson, finally, at my mercy.

"Goddammit, Benjamin, get up. They'll see ya. You're late. Come on."

Gunderson was begging, but I couldn't hear, couldn't move. As far as Gunderson knew, he had killed me, booted my brains all the way to next week.

"Awjeez!"

He fled, hurrying to get into class before his absence was noted.

I was alone on the playground, sprawled lifeless on the ice, slush and cold seeping through my clothes and into my bloodstream.

Actually, I felt fine. Kids have hard-rubber heads. I had recovered while Gunderson was still hovering, imploring me to get up and save his ass. But I stayed, inert. I waited.

Minutes passed. Five, maybe more. By now, they had discovered my empty seat where a living scholar, a bona fide A student—paying rapt and exemplary attention, raising his hand regularly, secretly doing intricate drawings of World War II dogfights—had once sat.

More minutes. They were massing at the school door by now, summoning perhaps an ambulance. Sister Caritas, who liked me the most of all the nuns, maybe even had a tear in her eye. I wished they would hurry. I was soaked to the skin and getting cold.

I began to despair. I had just decided to feign a sort of gradual, woozy awakening process, like the Lone Ranger emerging from a knockout blow, when I heard footsteps in the slush, measured and heavy. They stopped next to me. I opened an eye, imperceptibly. Huge black shoes. A voice. My name.

Father Mulligan!

Bonanza!

He crouched beside me, put a hand on my shoulder. I did my Lone Ranger impression, fluttering my eyes, shaking my head, slowly, foggily meeting Father Mulligan's gaze with a "Where am I?" look in my eyes.

"Are you all right, son?"

"I . . . I guess so, Father," I said brokenly. "I got . . . hit . . . in the head."

He nodded, helped me to my feet. I stayed shaky for a few steps as he led me toward school, long enough to prolong the illusion.

"Hit in the head?" said Father Mulligan.

Here it came!

"Who hit you?"

I stood at the crossroads of my recess career. Gunderson, a plague upon my days, was in my sights. A great deal of mayhem occurred daily on the St. Mary's playground, shoving, elbowing, tripping, trampling, pigpiling and hat snatching. All of this was routine contact. But hitting, an outright premeditated blow, particularly to the head—this was beyond the pale. Hitting was taboo. The unanswerable offense. If a kid accused you of raring back and socking him, on purpose, in the face, you were in as much trouble as you could get into. If you said anything, to deny your guilt or defend yourself, you just dug your grave deeper.

Technically, of course, Gunderson hadn't hit me. He had kicked me. And it was an accident. It wasn't really hitting. But who knew for sure? Gunderson's kick was a blow struck in the heat of battle on a gloomy day. No one could verify whether it was a follow-through or a sucker punch. No one would risk defending Gunderson, for fear of becoming an accessory after the fact.

Gunderson hung by a thread.

On the other hand, of course, there was the anathema of snitching. There have been, over the years, reams of bullshit written on the purity of the anti–stool pigeon ethic among small boys. In fact, like all other rules of kidhood, snitching etiquette followed a pecking order. Any kid could freely tattle on any other kid who was beneath him on the social scale. No kid in his right mind would think less of Fin or Overacker for informing on Bissell or Nordling, or on me, for that matter. Informing upward was betrayal, but informing downward was the equivalent of stepping on a bug. Being one of the bugs, I'd been snitched on regularly, by just about everyone, never resulting in any apparent stigma for the stoolie.

I'd never brooded over this sort of unequal treatment. I'd figured out long before fifth grade that life wasn't fair. If I had any beef with Gunderson, it wasn't that he'd been unfair to me. It wasn't that he had disdained me in front of my peers, or even that he had kicked me in the head and knocked me silly. I can't say that I even thirsted for revenge against Gunderson, who was to me less a human being than he was a force of nature—like hailstones or methane buildups.

If I resented Gunderson at all, it was mainly because he was an asshole.

Finally, I said, "I don't know, Father. Somebody kicked me accidentally, during the game."

"You're all right now?"

"Yes, Father."

"Well, good. Let's get you back to Sister Claveria."

"Yes, Father."

A chance to squeal on Gunderson, and I'd punted. How come? Squealing wouldn't have cost me any status in class; I didn't have any status. But as I walked along, Father Mulligan holding my hand, for a moment, I realized that life had rarely been better than getting kicked in the head by one of life's true assholes.

For a moment, Gunderson had treated me as a peer, even begged me to get up off the ground, so he could lend me a hand. I had disdained Gunderson and, in doing so, had filled his heart with trepidation.

I had gotten sympathy, personally, from Father Mulligan. When he walked me back into school, I was late for class. But there was no fear, no scolding, no punishment. Sister Claveria, hand on my arm, helped me to my seat and asked after my health.

"I'm okay, Sister. Thank you."

Others were envious.

Gunderson never thanked me for sparing him from the crushing disappointment of Father Mulligan and the wrath of Sister Claveria. But I never expected any thanks. And it never occurred to him.

P A R T   I V
"Swing, you stinkin' pussy!"

Once, in one of my adult jobs as a newspaper editor, I attended a Little League meeting. No kids were there—just parents, talking about kids, comparing their won-lost ratio, their athletic prowess and deficient skills. The parents were all preparing for something they called "the draft." They all had lists of kids, and each kid had a "bio," with notations like "bats right, throws right," "weak in the IF," "good arm from RF," "can't hit the curve," "turns 13 May 20." Birthdays were very important to these people, not because of gifts and parties, but because birthdays were a manpower issue. Certain birthdays meant a kid would move to a higher league. One too many birthdays and the grownups wouldn't let you play anymore. You were done.

That meeting pretty much explained to me why kids don't go outside anymore, among themselves, and play ball all day long. They've stopped because they're being watched.

When I was a kid, nobody watched. Kids were only done when it got too dark to see. Nobody—except a wacky old bag we called Mrs. Moose—knew that a bunch of us played ball, day in and day out (incompetently), on a potholed hillside not far from Council Creek.

Nobody knew about me and my cousins Danny and Bobby and my bumbling brother, Bill, claiming the Miller School field every evening after supper all one summer. The teams were always the same, Bobby and Bill vs. Danny and me, and we played with Civil War ferocity. We swung so hard our backs were bruised. We ran so hard our ankles popped. We dove for groundballs and swallowed sand. We stumbled through rocks for flyballs. We slapped mosquitoes and dodged deerflies. We tore dungarees, banged ribs, bled from the elbows and stood nose-to-nose, arguing at the top of our lungs in a steady mist of saliva. The air turned blue with novice profanity. Every day, we lovingly stretched a new layer of electrical tape around our only ball. Every night, we carried our stuff home in the dark, Danny and I smirking if we'd won, spoiling—hatefully—for vengeance if we'd lost.

Nobody knew, either, about Fin and Stitch, the two best players in our grade, putting together games between the Catholic school and public school. We were the only ones who knew which kids could hit, which kids couldn't and which ones ended up covering center field among the boulders and roots and oak trees. We shared gloves, because there were never enough to go around. We cherished our bats and taped them against breakage. We made bases out of the available materials, a stomped beer can, a flat rock, a slat from a peach box. We called our own pitches and settled our own close plays. We had our own sportsmanship. You could abuse any kid 'til you were hoarse—which is why a kid called Asswipe spent several years, every time he saw me, calling me "pussy"—but you had to play fair.

You had to play fair, because nobody was watching.

Field of Screams

Kids growing up in Wisconsin in the Fifties were blessed beyond the wildest fantasies of any children anywhere on earth—because right in our midst, just over in Waushara County, a few hours' drive from our very backyards and dark bedrooms, our rural and unsophisticated local culture had spawned the scariest son of a bitch in the entire inhabited world, a real-life monster more lunatic than Frankenstein, more bloodthirsty than Dracula, more savage than the Werewolf and more relentless than the Wendigo. He was every kid's ten worst nightmares all rolled together and tied up with human tendons still wet and shiny from the twitching corpse. He was Hitchcock's inspiration. He had caned his kitchen chairs with human skin. He had dressed out his headless victims and hung them in his rafters like gutted deer. He had kept a shoeboxful of keepsakes composed of women's private parts. He ate his corn flakes out of human skulls. He made a vest out of a woman's torso and danced in the moonlight clad only in Mary Hogan's skin. He had turned human faces into a private collection of Halloween masks. His deeds were so deliciously grisly that they defied belief and grossed out girls.

His name was a profanity on the tongue that sent chills through every kid's scrawny form. It was demons lurking just over your shoulder. It was waking up at 3:00 A.M. with no blankets and a cold hand squeezing your nuts. To scare yourself witless and set your friends to shuddering and hunkering, you had only to utter two blood-drenched words.

Ed Gein.

When I was barely ten, I had only a vague notion of what Ed Gein had actually done to all those victims in Plainfield. In fact, no one had actually told me Ed was from Plainfield. By the time Ed had become the most pervasive legend of any Wisconsin kid's existence, Ed was no longer from any *place*. Ed Gein was everywhere. Ed Gein was a fabric of hideous, palpable, gut-twisting rumors that expanded in the night and drifted through the deep dark countryside night like a toxic fog. Ed Gein was campfire terror and the Monkey's Paw. If you were abroad in the dark, Ed Gein was there, nearby, silent and stalking, ravenous, honing his fangs and fingering his bare bodkin. You couldn't see or smell him. The only sign was his breathing, which matched your own breath diabolically. He even held his breath when you held yours. And if you ventured an inch too far from your yard, made one false move, stepped on the wrong twig or got too close to the darkest shadow of the biggest tree, he had you. He would swoop and, before you knew it, you were in his laboratory, trussed up beside the big pot where you could smell human entrails cooking and see the leg bones poking up and the skulls floating on the scummy surface. He had been a local handyman—we knew that—with a toolbox from hell. Hot pokers to score your flesh. Melon-ballers to gouge your eyes. Meat-skewers to shove into your eardrums. Long glass needles to stick into your dick and smash with a ballpeen hammer. Razors to flay your living skin. Splintered fence posts to ream your asshole. Electric drills to bore your bones. Tin snips to clip off your fingers and toes, one by one. Screwdrivers to shove up your nostrils. Cherry bombs to cram into your mouth and blow your brains out your earholes. And bathtubs full of human shit to push you down and drown you.

Ed Gein was Lucifer and Ed Gein walked the Wisconsin night.

The worst horror of Ed Gein was that he was only the vanguard of a veritable army of similar psychos, kidnappers and cannibals. After Ed Gein's capture, every kid realized that there were more fiends just like him, in every neighborhood in every town, festering, biding their time, honing their rat-tail files. Partly, these local Geins were the natural offspring of Eddy's fast-growing legend. But the demons in our midst owed their power equally to the shadowy distance that kids and grownups kept between their worlds. Kids knew little of adulthood and grownups volunteered nothing. What kids knew about adulthood we saw through dirty glass, darkly. The grownups we encountered every day in the neighborhood and around town were kids' richest wellspring of mystery, wonder, envy and terror. Hitchcock and Boris Karloff were scary guys, but not nearly as horrible as the fiends and giants who walked— impenetrable and unpredictable—among us. Ed Gein's gory career merely confirmed the horror that lurked behind each door in Tomah.

For most kids, the scariest guy in Tomah was Old John Boone. Old John Boone lived a bizarre existence. Although he owned a huge lot on May Street, complete with a two-story house, an apple orchard, a raspberry patch and a yard big enough for football, he preferred living in a handmade lean-to, composed of plywood slabs and corrugated tin, in a corner of his property. He'd been shell-shocked, they said, in World War I and he'd never been quite "all there" afterward. He prowled the town in ragged clothes, barely speaking, buying his few staples at Shutter's Store, then sidling back into his wigwam.

Most kids avoided May Street because of Old John Boone, whose legend grew enormously after the discoveries in Ed Gein's house of horrors. But I never got the chance to demonize Old John Boone, because I had spent a hundred nights in the big house on his property, which Freda, my mother's favorite baby-sitter, rented from Old John Boone. From hanging out in Freda's house, I knew Old John as a kind and quiet and feeble hermit—irreparably hurt by his moment in the big war—and stuck in a time warp. Once, with my brother and our foul-mouthed sidekick Dougie, I had seen the inside of Old John's lean-to. It was a bleak and cozy cave. His only apparent furniture, a tube-steel and sheet-metal dinette, was strewn with packaged bread and jars of jam. As keepsakes of the war, Old John Boone had collected the huge brass casings of howitzer shells. They lined his walls. He let us handle one, and offered us peanut butter and jelly. As a demon, Old John Boone—his eyes hollow and his hands constantly, gently trembling—was a bust.

Mrs. Moose, on the other hand, was the real article.

Her real name was Meuser. Her husband had been dead so long that the only fair assumption was that she had murdered him—with her 12-gauge shotgun. She carried it everywhere, even when she went to Burris's Dime Store to buy thread and hairpins. It rode on her hip, tucked under her left arm, and my uncle Harold, the cop, made a habit of stopping her on Superior Avenue to make sure she didn't have any shells in the chambers. He couldn't arrest her or anything, because it wasn't illegal to carry the gun. This was hunting country, and she packed her heat right out in the open, unconcealed and big as a cannon.

Mrs. Moose, when she was out, walked bent over and hump-shouldered, her eyes flicking paranoiacally left and right, upward and down, sucking saliva audibly from the corners of her mouth. Rain, shine or snow, she always wore a threadbare cotton print "old-lady" dress with a thick food-stained cardigan and unbuckled galoshes on her feet that clinked as she moved. She was bareheaded and she never wore gloves, even in the dead of winter, her finger on the trigger of her 12-gauge. When Mrs. Moose was loose, kids always watched her gun. We knew it was loaded, all the time. She had some sort of trick, we figured, to take out the shells just before Harold tapped her on the shoulder and checked her load. She was quick and she was merciless.

We knew this from a public school kid named Zinsmeister, who had a numb hand. Mrs. Moose had roared from her house one day, caught Zinsmeister cutting through her garden and blasted at him, point-blank, with two barrels of rock salt. They said that after this, Zinsmeister's mangled hand was barely dangling off his wrist and it took doctors up in La Crosse twelve hours to save Zinsmeister from walking around the rest of his life with a hook. The hand looked disappointingly normal the first time I saw it. There were no scars or missing fingers, but Zinsmeister insisted Mrs. Moose had destroyed the nerves and he had to be careful in cold weather, because his hand could freeze and he wouldn't feel it.

Mrs. Moose lived out on the north edge of town, not far from T.J., my evil grandpa. Her house, a green-shingled three-room bungalow, was set into a hillside at the end of a dirt street. She had a multipane bay window that overlooked a vast expanse of meadow that stretched toward Council Creek. Most important, Mrs. Moose's garden was just outside her window. She grew flowers close to the window and vegetables down the hill. She guarded it with a fanaticism only possible in the homicidal mind. It was said that once, seeing a kid trespass among her tomatoes, Mrs. Moose didn't even bother to step outdoors and scream at the interloper, her usual pattern. She just rose up from the rocking chair in her parlor—where she sat brooding every day from dawn to midnight—and fired both shells right through the bay window, blowing broken glass thirty yards downhill and scaring the kid into crapping his pants.

Besides her husband, we didn't know how many people she had killed. But we knew where they were buried—the parts she hadn't eaten, that is. In her garden, under the cucumbers and beneath the zinnias.

Mrs. Moose, being nuts, was prone to weird and contradictory moods. When she was cheery, she made the best oatmeal-raisin cookies in town. We knew this because every year at the St. Paul's Lutheran Church bake sale, she'd bring a big batch and they'd sell out before anybody bought anything else. There were kids—we'd heard about them—who had been passing by Mrs. Moose's house, staying clear of the garden. And she had stepped outside, no shotgun, with a big plate of those famous cookies. And she had smiled. And she had beckoned.

Most kids, seeing Mrs. Moose with that crooked Richard Widmark grin and a plate of oatmeal cookies, just spooked, squawked and tore ass out of the neighborhood as fast as their spindly legs could carry them. But a few—little kids, morons and naïfs—who had heard of neither Ed Gein nor Mrs. Moose, accepted her invitation. They had eaten her cookies and she had patted them on the head with her bent, arthritic hand. Some had lived to tell the tale— amazed, in retrospect, at their incredible luck. Because there were other kids—there had to be—who'd been lured into the cookie-web of Mrs. Moose, who then quietly chopped them into bite-sized chunks, made a nice Mulligan stew, fed herself royally for several days and then used the bones and guts to fertilize the hydrangea bushes.

Kids disappeared all the time. We knew where they were.

Which makes you wonder why we made a baseball diamond in the field next to Mrs. Moose's house.

Actually, there was no mystery. In those days, a half-decent base-ball field was worth its weight in corn-on-the-cob. Grownups were not in the habit of building fields for kids to play baseball. Baseball was an accepted pastime for kids, and a good way to keep the mozniks from underfoot, but no parent with any sense went out of his way to encourage such outright idleness. Kids had chores. A kid who was finished with his chores, or didn't have any chores on his agenda, or was trying to duck his chores, stayed wisely out of sight of adults—lest they think up chores for him to do. Adults didn't re-gard baseball as a chore; therefore baseball—at least among kids— held no value for grownups. The idea of encouraging kids to go out and spend their days whacking a ball, instead of doing chores, was too peculiar to ponder. A father who made a conscious effort to coach his son in the finer points of pitching, hitting and turning the pivot at second base was universally regarded as a guy with way too much time on his hands.

Besides, kids learned everything they needed to know about base-ball from two sources. One was other kids. The other was Earl Gillespie.

I grew up in the brief Midwestern delirium when the arrival of

Warren Spahn, Henry Aaron, Joe Adcock, Eddie Mathews and Lew Burdette from Boston made the Milwaukee Braves a statewide religious experience. When the Braves, who won the World Series in '57 and lost to the Yankees in '58, then descended into mediocrity and fled Milwaukee for Atlanta in '65, I was angry and bewildered. The Braves' betrayal was one of professional sports' early insults to fans, the beginning of the end of the American romance. After a few teamless years, I did the only sensible thing a jilted baseball fan can do. I attached my loyalties to the one team in the major leagues that would never move, never triumph and never grow up. I became a Red Sox fan.

But during those heydays of the Tribe, I worshipped at the cords of the prophet, Earl Gillespie, voice of the Braves. The games came to me on a Philco radio that sat beside my bed and crackled into the night like cold bacon on a red skillet. I remember the birth of the Houston Colt .45's. I remember Joey Jay breaking in with the Cincinnati Redlegs (couldn't call them Reds in the afterglow—and home state—of Joe McCarthy) and mowing down Braves like tenpins. The Redlegs played at Crosley Field then, and I remember Gillespie gleefully describing the comedy of a rookie outfielder hitting the slope at Crosley and falling on his ass. I remember Frank Robinson. I remember the Mets in the Polo Grounds and the suspense of Marv Throneberry circling—in an exquisite prose-poem by Gillespie—under a pop fly. I remember Casey Stengel. I remember the games from the coast and the daunting mastery of the gods of California—Koufax and Drysdale and Podres in L.A., Mays and McCovey and Cepeda in San Francisco. I remember Juan Marichal. I remember Harvey Haddix, pitching thirteen no-hit innings against the Braves in Pittsburgh, then losing on an over-the-fence "double" by Adcock. I remember Roberto Clemente. I remember a game in Houston, when one of the Braves' bad Sixties pitchers, Tony Cloninger or Bob Buhl or Wade Blasingame, gave up four runs in the first inning, after which both sides played shutout ball way past midnight as I hoped and dozed, and the game ended up 4–0—a

wasted night with Earl. I remember Billy Bruton. I remember a trip
to Chicago, when I found out that it's possible for a television set to
broadcast a baseball game that did not involve Saturday afternoon,
Dizzy Dean and Pee Wee Reese at the mike and the sacred CBS
New York Yankees, always, on the field, always always winning the
game. In Chicago, there was non-Yankee TV! Chi had the Cubs, all
the time, in daytime, on WGN—162 days of Ernie Banks, Billy
Williams and Ron Santo and the worst pitching staff on the face of
the earth—and the Cubs became my second favorite team. I remember Gus Bell. I remember a sunny day in August, on Annie's
porch, and I was laid up with a cut on my foot, and a journeyman
outfielder named Lee May (or Maye—I forget) came to bat in
County Stadium in the bottom of the ninth, with two on and two
out, and he stroked the full-count three-run homer that won the
game in storybook fashion, 4–3. I remember Bobby Bragan, Birdie
Tebbetts and Danny Murtaugh. I remember reading a literary classic entitled *Bat Boy for the Braves*. And I remember the Mobilgas
station, down near the Tomah train depot, where every day the previous day's Braves result was posted, meticulously, on a handmade
scoreboard, complete with the up-to-the-minute National League
standings. And I remember when the state's love affair with the
Tribe somehow, secretly, started to deteriorate into a troubled marriage, because the scores at the Mobilgas station started to appear a
day late and the standings—with the Braves ten or twelve games out
of first—stayed unaltered and neglected for weeks at a stretch.

From the Braves, I learned all the positions on the field, from the
batter's box to the short porch. I learned about ground rules and
foul poles and Texas leaguers. I learned about the double play
(McMillan-to-Bolling-to-Adcock) and the infield fly rule. I learned
to read the distance of a flyball from the crack of the bat on the
radio and the tone of Earl Gillespie's voice (he never, ever hyped a
warning-track quail as a home run). I came to know what a manager was expected to do with a one-run deficit on the road with a
runner on first, no outs and the pitcher coming to bat (pinch-hit if
the pitcher is Carlton Willey, bunt if the pitcher is Spahn). I came to

understand the patient, poetic situationalism of baseball, of waiting through a seemingly endless series of momentary failures (strikeout, single, walk, pop fly, double-play ball to the shortstop) for the moment to be ripe, for the base runners to be in place and for Hammerin' Henry to be up against a tiring pitcher, nursing a one-run cushion in the eighth.

All my other baseball I learned from kids, none of whom gave a damn if I learned anything at all. Lesson No. 1 was if you didn't get out of the house early on a summer morning and get dibs on a playing field, you were out of luck. There were only three really good baseball fields in town. Two were down around Butts Avenue, where a few high school kids ran the town's embryonic Little League program. The whole town had only five or six Little League teams, mostly involving kids who were pathologically serious about sports. Most kids, in those days, recognized two jock tracks. The athletic minority consisted of a small elite who assumed—either because they were bigger than most other kids, or their dads were pushy ex–varsity stars—that they would grow up to become BMOCs at Tomah High. The overwhelming remnant were kids who knew they were never going to play high school sports (except maybe wrestling), so why get all bent out of shape about baseball if you're only eleven? Regardless of whether you were a serious jock or just a kid with a mitt and a taped-up bat, you needed a place to play. One of the town's great injustices was the Little League fields. Two nice flat dusty diamonds with mowed grass outfields, where most of the time kids weren't allowed to play because some stupid Little League practice was going on. Or even worse, some minimum-wage high school summer functionary was shooing kids away because the field had to be "saved" for Little League games.

Like the dirt was gonna wear out?

The other "official" field was down across the Milwaukee Road tracks on Glendale. This was a true ballpark, with tall chain link backstops and snow fences ringing the outfield, and here was where the town's semipro team played before cheering throngs of fifty or sixty fans on summer nights from June to September, and Toy

Grovesteen continued his brilliant high school career as a slugging outfielder and dangerously wild pitcher. But the Glendale Avenue field was even more inaccessible than the Little League fields, because its summer was monopolized by "big kids," known as Pony League. Besides, Glendale was way, way out of my neighborhood.

The best fields available to the disorganized masses were a pair of rocky sandlots at the Miller School. This was across Monroe Street from St. Mary's, where I went to school, but St. Mary's playgrounds were no good since the Catholic Church had paved them in asphalt. We knew they played baseball on concrete in the big cities, but Tomah was no big city and no kid I knew could afford to see his only baseball brutally frayed by the unforgiving pavement until the stitches tore and the whole cover ripped away in the fourth inning.

Baseballs were like jewels to us. My brother, Bill, and I had one, but its leather cover was a long-distant memory. It had bounced one time too many on the street beyond the Miller School field. We had replaced the cover in the standard way, wrapping the ball's naked strings with black electrical tape. Eventually, we had to patch the ball—where the electrical tape had sundered—with a constantly curling two-inch square of red duct tape. This ball performed selflessly through a thousand grueling innings before, finally, one dusk not long before Labor Day in my last summer in Tomah. That evening, my strapping cousin Bobby let loose with a Casey-like swing that sent the ball across two entire diamonds onto the middle of Monroe Street and up against the St. Mary's playground wall on one bounce, while the empty wad of black and red tape zizzed loopingly into my glove—on the pitcher's mound (well, not a mound, actually . . . more of a pit).

A lot of games ended like that one—with the destruction of the only baseball available among a half-dozen kids. Or losing it in the weeds, or hitting it into a yard surrounded by a fence and occupied by some horrible golden-ager (usually referred to as "the old bag") who devoured playthings and hated children. Broken bats never halted a game. There was always tape. Darkness could often be overcome by the proximity of a streetlight or a full moon. We would sometimes play into the night until some kid's parent finally drove up, got out of the car and screamed, "Jeffrey, what in God's name are you doing out here at this time of night?"

"Awje-e-e-ez, Ma! I'm jis' playin' ba-a-a-all!"

Numbers were never a factor. We could play a thirty- or thirty-five-inning game with as few as two kids to a side—although the gaps in the outfield tended to be vast, with singles far less common than home runs. With seven kids, or even six, you could start a good game of workup.

One of the things that always amused us when we dropped by the Little League fields on a July afternoon was the frequent postponement of games because the ump wasn't permitted to yell "Play ball!" unless there were eighteen kids present—nine to a team. This is one reason, I later realized, why parents in later years became so heavily involved in Little League. If you leave eleven-year-old kids to their own devices—as Little League did in Tomah in the Fifties—the kids'll think of a million things to do other than commit themselves devoutly to a randomly chosen baseball team with a lame nickname (Cubs, Twins, Cardinals) bound to a schedule of meaningless games that had to be played in wool-flannel uniforms and five-pound polystyrene batting helmets. As I recall, about half the official games ended up postponed or eventually canceled because neither team could field a full team of kids who hadn't forgotten there was a game that day, weren't playing Little League hooky or hadn't decided to quit the team without submitting a formal letter of resignation. The irony of all the delayed, aborted and put-off games was that, on any given day in July, there might be thirty kids hanging out around the Little League fields, leaning over the fence, jeering the idiots in uniform, razzing the sixteen-year-old umps and gassing up on pop and candy from Woodruff's Store. Loudly, half the spectators volunteered to take the missing kids' places, but we hadn't signed up officially. Our parents hadn't filled out permission forms and paid the insurance, so we couldn't fill in for the no-shows. And the officious high school jerks who managed Little League wouldn't let us use the field during absentee delays—or before, after or between games either. All we could do was hang on the rail and heap abuse—which we did well. Of course, we wouldn't have wasted our time there if Woodruff's wasn't a block away.

Tomah got its first "supermarket," a place called Cram's, when I was about ten. I'm still not sure what the difference was between a market and a supermarket, except possibly hubris. Cram's "supermarket" was noticeably larger than Burnstad's, Shutter's, the A&P and the Red Owl, but that wasn't much of a distinction. The difference between a store and a market, however, was unmistakable. A market had employees; a store just had a family. The family at Woodruff's was Mose and Betty, who not only did everything at the store from stocking canned goods to butchering chickens (my favorite memory of Mose is a tableau of him in the backyard, hatchet in hand, leaning over the chopping block, blood up to his elbows and a half-dozen headless fryers flapping and staggering at his feet), but they sold everything a kid could dream of desiring.

They sold Dubble Bubble bubblegum with Joe Palooka comic strips inside, and Topps baseball cards in which you could hope dreamily to find a team picture of the Braves, or Eddie Mathews in Technicolor, captured in mid-clout. Best of all, Mose and Betty sold all the provisions a kid needed to keep him nourished through a grueling July afternoon of hooting and howling at captive Little Leaguers. They had Popsicles, Fudg'icles, and Creamsicles, and wax tubes full of syrupy fruit drink where you bit off the cap, chugged the fluid and then chewed the tube like Red Man tobacco for an hour 'til your jaw ached. They had all the major soft drinks—7Up, Nesbitt's Orange and Tomah brand grape pop—in seven-ounce deposit bottles made of glass so thick you couldn't break it by just dropping it on cement. You had to climb a tree if you wanted to bust a bottle. But that would have been an unconscionable folly, because each bottle was worth two cents, making empty pop bottles one of the top four sources of kid revenue—right behind allowances, paper routes and birthday money—in Tomah. Pop bottle hunting was a major summer avocation, and every kid could remember the thrill of the first time he was walking down the alley behind the Red Owl or the A&P and he noticed that some rookie stockboy had placed a half-dozen cases of empties out behind the store, where they could easily be snatched, carried around to the front door and redeemed all over again for a whopping 48 cents a case. The elite drinks at Woodruff's—Coca-Cola, Pepsi, RC and Sun-Drop Golden Cola—came in ten-ounce mega-bottles just as thick as the seven-ouncers, with the added bonus that the Coke people had molded the name of an American city onto the bottom of every bottle. We would bet precious nickels on these cities.

"Okay, farthest west."

"Okay. Whatcha got?"

"Cincinnati, Ohio. What's yours."

"Ha ha, I win."

"Oh yeah? Whatcha got?"

"Knoxville, Tennessee!"

"Bullshit. I win."

"Bullshit. Tennessee is *way* west of Ohio."

"Bullshit it is!"

"Bullshit it ain't!"

"Oh yeah? And what grade did you get in geography, dipshit?"

"Who you callin' dipshit, dipshit?"

"You! Dipshit!"

"Hey, anybody got a map?"

"Yeah, I carry one in my shoe all the time." (This from a kid going barefoot.)

These sorts of arguments could last for hours, because no kid in the world (except possibly the ones in Cincinnati and Knoxville) had the remotest concept of the topographic relationship between Ohio and Tennessee, and no boy on earth ever thought to settle an academic debate by referring to published sources. Usually, after twelve or thirteen kids had horned into the battle, every kid had been called "dipshit" at least twice, and two kids (never the original bettors) had scuffled violently enough to scrape one knee raw and bloody one nostril, the bet was canceled for lack of conclusive information. Meanwhile, two more kids had arrived with fresh Cokes.

"Farthest east. Whatcha got?"

"Providence, Rhode Island. You?"

"Savannah, Georgia."

"Yay! I win!"

"Bull*shit*!"

Woodruff's stocked every sickening candy known to kiddom, including those sugary dots attached to long strips of paper that you bought by the foot, and licorice whips in red and black, Jujubes, Junior Mints, Rolos, all the Mars and Hershey's bars, Baby Ruth and Almond Joy and Zagnut and all-day suckers. In the summer, the heaviest traffic passed through the freezer, where you could get those nut-covered ice cream cones, or push-ups, Sealtest or Ranney's ice cream in cups, ice cream bars with chocolate or orange coating, and a half-dozen brands of Eskimo Pie and Eskimo Pie wannabes. Woodruff's pastries ranged from Betty's homemade doughnuts to the most cherished of all summertime kid edibles—Hostess cupcakes with chemical-cream filling and metallic orange frosting.

My grandmother was a devoted Woodruff's patron, although she probably went three years between visits there. Two or three mornings a week, she would call Betty, lingeringly, on the neighborhood party line, and put in an "order." Later that morning, Mose would pull up behind Annie's house and appear at the back door with a box of canned goods, vegetables, butter and bread. He'd rattle the door once, barge in, climb the steps to the back porch and bring the box into the kitchen, where he and Annie—the handsome grocer and the flirtatious old lady—would review each other's family news, assess the weather, reprise the obituaries and chew miscellaneous fat. If Mose didn't have too many orders, he'd stay long enough for coffee. Mose never collected a dime from Annie. Papa would drop into Woodruff's the next Saturday morning, pay Betty for that week's orders, gather some breakfast food and other staples and then, while stocking up on cold cuts, pass the time with Mose at the meat case. Woodruff's was a beautiful grotto, cool and dark with rolling hardwood floors, narrow aisles and provisions stacked so high that Wilt the Stilt would need a footstool to snag a roll of Charmin. Everything leaned precariously inward and blocked the electric lights. Papa and Mose, in the half-light of Woodruff's back room, leaning over the T-bones and boiled ham in the meat case, might have been two bootleggers in a cellar, deciding a new password for the speakeasy.

It's no overstatement to assert that Woodruff's kept Little League alive through its embryonic days in Tomah. Without Woodruff's cornucopia of sucrose and toothrot, no kid would've ventured near, nor lingered long, in that sunbaked basin of dusty lowlands. The same was true of the Tomah parks director, who drafted all the Little League "coaches" and umpires off the high school baseball team, with the connivance of the high school baseball coach. If a Tomah High baseball jock declined the honor of spending his lazy, hazy, crazy days of summer managing a transient population of unfamiliar and often unwilling little boys, he faced the prospect of warming the bench the following spring. Throughout Little League season, these adolescent coaches did very little coaching. A grim air of indentured servitude hung over each game.

A Little Leaguer who brought no knowledge of the game with him departed with only as much fresh expertise as he could gain from chance remarks and osmosis. But this was kid tradition anyway. Trial and error was how every kid, from Abner Doubleday forward, had always learned the game. Like most boys, my first taste of Earl Gillespie on the radio lured me onto sunny diamonds to try my hand at the miracles wrought by Aaron, Mathews and Spahn. The next educational phase was a stream of abuse and rejection from kids who were older, better, crueler. Either you gave up the game as too harsh and too intricate to suit your delicate sensibilities or you found kids who were roughly as clumsy and unenlightened as you. Among your bungling peers, you overcame your fear of the hardball, learned fundamentals and developed your arguing technique.

Among all the skills necessary to kid baseball, the most important has always been arguing. The feature of Little League that proved to us fence-hangers and Popsicle-guzzling skeptics that the games were lifeless, joyless and unimportant was their eerie dearth of heated discussion. Little League came with fixed rules, white lines, official balls, recognizable bases and "officials"—who arbitrated balls and strikes, outs and safes, fouls and fairs. There was nothing to fight about.

Without fighting, baseball is perhaps half the fun—maybe less. When you played on a baseball diamond shaped more like a squashed trapezoid, with boulders in short left, standing water that stretched from second base to deep center, flattened beer cans for bases, invisible foul lines intersected by visible patches of blackberry brambles and the odd erosion trench, you had something to argue almost every time somebody hit the ball. We usually played without a catcher, which precluded base-stealing or even leadoffs by base runners—but runners would lead off anyway, inevitably leading to cries of foul from spying outfielders, followed by a five-minute exchange of hostilities. We almost never had the luxury of a first baseman, which meant that "pitcher's hands" was an out. The furious debates that arose from this convention alone had the power to extend a nine-inning game (if we actually bothered to count innings) into a six-hour marathon—sometimes extending into the next day.

Street baseball, played on a two-lane avenue lined with parked cars—usually played with a tennis ball, a sponge-rubber sphere or a bona fide Spaldeen—was the most argumentative baseball of all. I recall games in which the average inning contained no fewer than nine five-minute disputes: one for each out, two for fair/foul calls and one for roster adjustments (usually involving dibs on a kid, arriving late, that both teams wanted, thus forcing the least-wanted kid on either team to head home, sniffling and embittered).

After Mom moved us into T.J.'s house, I spent one summer arguing baseball with my little brother, Bill, his pal Whelihan and a motley collection of runts and asthmatics who lived in the neighborhood. I fell into this crowd mostly because Whelihan dwelt nearby and he had found a promising pasture out on the north frontier of town. The field had a few hazards, including a cluster of rusted-out farm implements in right-field foul territory and, on the hill that dominated center field, a spreading scrub plum tree. Of course, the field wasn't flat—it had the natural undulation that occurs in ground that has been plowed for planting fifty springs in the last sixty years, but flatness was a virtue kids never expected out of a baseball diamond. A flat field was something you grew into eventually, like necking, auto mechanics and beer.

It wasn't until we'd stomped, torn and uprooted a half-acre of weeds and wildflowers that we noticed our neighbor was the dread Mrs. Moose. Her house and garden occupied a verdant hillside in deep left field. The third base foul line, if you extended it into infinity, passed right through Mrs. Moose's bay window, the window behind which she sat every day, looking out over the fields, clutching her 12-gauge and fondling its trigger. None of us had recognized Mrs. Moose's house—off in distant left—until suddenly, late that first morning, she showed up.

Staring at us.

Her gun nestled in her bosom.

Between our field and Mrs. Moose's distant garden was a ridge of raised ground planted with scraggly bridal wreath bushes. Mrs. Moose stood on that border, in bedroom slippers and her print dress, her hair a riot of steel wool and—on her face—a crooked, terrifying smile.

We'd all heard about Ed Gein's mother—that she was even worse than Ed himself, that she'd taught him everything he knew about skinning little kids alive and making them watch while she sautéed their livers in butter sauce and blood. They said Ed Gein's mother was dead, and her death was what made Ed go nuts. But what if they were wrong? What if she was alive all along, and she had snuck out of Plainfield the night the cops finally nabbed Ed? Ed would never tell where she'd disappeared to, because he loved her more than life itself, right? She could be anywhere, Ed Gein's cannibal mom. She could be in Tomah. She could be Mrs. Moose.

Mrs. Moose was the right age.

Mrs. Moose stood on the hillside, watching us. Smiling. We froze. We stared at her gun. We judged the range. How far does a shotgun shoot? Was it loaded—with buckshot or rock salt? Should we run? Should we hit the dirt? I looked over at my idiot brother. He seemed to be smiling back at Mrs. Moose. He seemed ready to do something fatal, like wave at her and shout "Hi." I tensed to pounce on my brother and strangle him at the first false move.

Our moment with Mrs. Moose dragged like High Mass. Bill kept his peace. Sweat and meadow chaff combined under our T-shirts and jeans to create an itch more powerful than chicken pox. We ached to scratch, too scared to move.

And she turned, deliberately, moving with that mixture of confusion and hunched menace unique to the criminally insane. She ambled back toward her house—never looking back again.

"Shit," someone finally said. "We can't play here."

We had just worked three hours to hack our field out of the wilderness. There were groans of dismay.

"Well, do *you* wanna be this close to Mrs. Moose?"

"But it's our field! Not hers!"

"Yeah, stupid! But she's RIGHT THERE!"

"Yeah, but it's daytime. She wouldn't do anything to anybody in the daytime."

"Oh yeah? She almost killed that kid in the daytime! What was his name?"

"Zinsmeister."

"Yeah. Zinsmeister. She shot Zinsmeister in broad goddamn daylight!"

"Yeah, but Zinsmeister was a dumb shit. He was in her garden! She doesn't let *anybody* in her garden. Everybody knows that. He was *askin'* for it."

"So all we have to do is stay out of her garden."

"Yeah. Right."

"Yeah. I ain't goin' over there."

"Me neither!"

"Yeah, but what if she suddenly has one of her fits? And she comes out of her house, shootin' at us?"

"Yeah!"

"Well, then we run, stupid! You think I'm gonna stand here while Mrs. Moose is comin' at me with a goddamn 12-gauge?"

"Is that a 12-gauge?"

"Yeah."

"I thought it was a 16."

"No, it's a 12."

"How do you know, anus-breath?"

"Because I seen it, dipshit!"

"Who you callin' dipshit?"

"Who you callin' anus-breath?"

After an hour or so, we decided to risk playing baseball next-field-over from Ed Gein's mom. But only after we had thoroughly aired the cookie rumor.

None of us had ever heard the word "schizophrenic," but everyone knew—thanks to the examples provided by Ed Gein and Mr. Hyde—that every homicidal maniac had two distinct and opposite personalities. Even though they regularly raved and snarled and butchered children, necrophiliac mass murderers often reverted to an aspect of disarming mildness and gracious charm. Mrs. Moose had the same sinister duality. Her evil side was the shotgun; her even deadlier "good side" was oatmeal-raisin cookies.

I loved oatmeal-raisin cookies. All kids love oatmeal-raisin cookies. Especially the extra chewy kind, loaded with fat raisins and crushed walnuts. Mrs. Moose used walnuts. As the days passed, Mrs. Moose lurking invisibly behind that blinding bay window, we thought less about the gun—its range was short—and more about cookies. Cookies could make a sensible kid helpless. Cookies could send tendrils of maddening fragrance across a summer mile, pierce a kid's nose, and turn his brain into a limpid pitcher of spit. Cookies were the food of Satan, strewn along the road to hell. Kids were small. Kids were weak. Kids were always hungry. Kids had no power against cookies.

For weeks, not counting her well-documented gun-totin' forays down Superior Avenue, Mrs. Moose almost dropped from sight. We played baseball in the meadow nearly every day, wasting our summer and only occasionally stealing a wary glance toward deep left field to make sure we didn't have an armed audience. Except for my brother and Whelihan, I've forgotten all those kids. All younger and smaller than me, they had names like Toony and Terry; there were a couple of brothers named Storck. And a few nameless others. They occur in my memory not as faces, but as shadows against a green background, big mitts hanging from their skinny arms, shoelaces trailing from their P.F Flyers. Perhaps one or two of them remember me, because—to my surprise—I turned out to be the slugger. I was proof of the proposition that even the last kid picked, if he moves downward in class far enough, can be for one brief aberrant moment a star. Served up the softly thrown pitches that were standard in kid baseball, I discovered my hitting stroke. I flailed uselessly at the ball on roughly two of every three pitches. But on the third, my focus sharpened by frustrated determination, I would often, inexplicably, connect. It was a lovely shock, that solid feel of the nicked and splintered bat striking the black-taped baseball flush on its chops. What an astounding discovery, realizing that in my bony torso and noodly arms, there was a hidden wellspring of power—strength enough to drive a baseball into the blue, toward the sun, beyond the backpedaling kid in center field and into the imaginary bleachers atop our ballhill, beyond the plum tree, while the imaginary men on base turned and watched the flight of the ball admiringly!

We played happy ball on that miserable diamond and would have gladly fallen into a ten-week routine of batting, fielding and debate from morning 'til twilight. Our only interruption was the periodic all-out, eight-kid search for the ball when someone fouled it into untracked regions of waist-high timothy. We only had the one ball, the one Bill and I nursed and mended every night and brought to the game every morning. We thought about saving up for a new ball, but other contingencies tended to interfere—the urge for an ice-cold swirly Pepsi, a flat tire on a bike, a new issue of *Sgt. Rock* comics. There was always something. So we bridged over into July, using the same ball and beating the weeds, on hands and knees, whenever it went astray.

The one time we almost lost the ball for good was when it was right in plain sight—when I hit the ball at Mrs. Moose's bay window.

First of all, hitting a baseball that far was impossible. When we laid our base paths, we started far enough downhill to preclude any incidental contact with Mrs. Moose, her garden or even her bridal wreath. We weren't taking any chances because, ever since Ed Gein emerged from the dead heart of Wisconsin with blood on his shirt and human heads hanging in neat rows in his broom closet, the barricades of kid credulity had crumbled. It had always been a chilly pleasure—from the age when a kid's imagination was able to first form fancies and images—to picture creatures beneath our beds, waiting to whip out a tentacle and drag us to our deaths. There had always been an element of pursuit, terror and escape in the summer night, when it was possible to spy the shadow of a wolfman in the trees beside the road, or to pretend there were vampires flitting on bat wings through half-open windows, hunting the tender throats and warm blood of sleeping boys. We enjoyed these horrors because, behind them, despite our loud and oft-professed faith in their existence, we knew we would reach adulthood without even a sidelong glimpse at a body snatcher, boogeyman or blood-drinking golem. We could believe, safely, deliciously, in the unbelievable awful. But then Ed Gein saw our awful, raised it to unspeakable, and went out into the night, prowling our neighborhoods and drooling over Aunt Martha's grave. Ed Gein, more sanguine and hideous than Frankenstein, the Thing and even Norman Bates, was real, was among us and was only prevented from adding us to his pile of putrefying victims by a single barred window in the loony bin over at Waupun. Worse than the prospect that Ed would escape and come questing for fresh, young blood was the knowledge that the deadly creatures of the dark were not just Transylvanian legends and literary nightmares. They could be regular people, born and raised in our midst, warped by a secret sickness within their own families and nudged into madness by the dispiriting cold, the routine hardship and the isolation of life in the Great White North. The once harmless eccentrics, like Old John Boone, who fringed the normalcy of quotidian Tomah could well be the clones, comrades and acolytes of Ed Gein. Which is why we made damn sure Mrs. Moose's garden was out of baseball range from our field.

We thought we had, anyhow.

Until I hit the ball perfect.

I mean *perfect.*

It was an even swing, with a little uppercut. I didn't shift my weight forward, into the pitch, until the split second of contact. The crack of the bat, slightly muffled by the layers of electrical tape on the ball, was musically sharp. I knew I had hit a Ruthian shot even before I saw it soaring, on a high and rapid arc, over third base and down, down, down the left field line.

Okay, ball. Wait!

"Awjeez," said Whelihan.

"Shit," said Bill.

It kept going. Too far, too far.

Too *fucking* far!

"Oh God," I said, racked with ambivalence. On one hand, this was the sort of hit that gives birth to kid legends. On the other hand . . .

"Oh shit oh shit oh shit. Slow down. Stop. Drop. Awjeez!"

It was going to hit her window.

Mrs. Moose's window.

"Oh, Jesus Christ," said the kid standing on second base, probably a Storck. "It's gonna hit her window."

"Oh, fucking . . ." said Toony before losing his voice.

The ball was above the garden—high, too high above the garden—and sinking. Still dead on course, for the window.

It had to hit the window. There was no alternative. Mrs. Moose's ramshackle western exposure was a flat-roofed annex sunk into the hillside, designed to catch the sun. From the earth to the roof, from side to side, it was all window, one hundred percent glass, in little panes puttied together on fragile strips of wooden lattice. One sharp blow and Mrs. Moose's entire crystal wall would collapse in an implosion of splintering glass.

Breaking a window with a ball was a catastrophe with few parallels. It meant parental fury, physical violence and weeks of house arrest. It brought on total economic failure—every allowance, every tip, every dime, every penny found in the gutter garnisheed to pay for the broken window. No pop, no candy, no comics, no piggybank stash for the Monroe County Fair. Nothing. The Great Depression. Famine, pestilence and exile.

Except, as we watched my epic home run home in on Mrs. Moose's window, the usual broken window considerations never entered our minds. We didn't think about lost allowances and belt-wielding dads. We thought about death and dismemberment, in broad daylight in a weltering pool of blood, on a weedlot baseball field. We didn't wonder whether she was carrying buckshot or rock salt in her 12-gauge. We knew that, ever since we opened our field for play, she had switched to buckshot and was waiting, invisible behind her glinting window, for one false move, one mistake, one pop-up into her cucumbers. And she would burst from her door and onto us like a police dog after a stray piglet. How many of us would she kill before her ammo ran out? What would she do with the bodies? Would any neighbors see her, dressing out our corpses like Bambi's mother and dragging us into her kitchen? Would our stretched faces be recognizable as lampshades?

We strained to watch the flight of the fatal fly. We tensed, ready to run pell-mell, due north, into the high grass and toward Council Creek.

And what if Mrs. Moose only winged us? Would she come up and taunt us while we tried to crawl away on bloody hands and broken knees? Would she torture us before slitting our throats and hanging us upside down to bleed out into a galvanized bucket?

"Oh my God," said Toony.

And then there was Ed Gein. What if he'd gotten out? What if

Mrs. Moose really was his mom? What if they worked together on our bodies, peeling skin, skewering eyeballs for shish kebab, cutting our juicy flanks into roasts and steaks and London broil?

The ball dropped. It was too late. We were dead.

Thud!

In the naked dust, two inches from the bottom of Mrs. Moose's bay window, the best-hit ball of my life struck, spun toward the glass and came to rest. It hadn't made a sound. A puff of dust quickly caught the breeze and blew away.

"Oh," said Toony. "Oh. Oh! Oh, God!" He sank to his knees.

For a moment, for all of us, life was sweeter than we had ever known. By the distance of two inches, we had ducked the combined calamity of a busted window and cannibal murder. The sudden contrast of profound terror followed by overwhelming relief filled my bladder almost to bursting. I gritted my teeth and clamped my legs to prevent pissing down my leg.

Bill, my idiot brother, interrupted my ecstasy and discomfort with an ill-timed practical point.

"That's our only ball," he said. "You gotta get it back."

Fresh fear prickled my skin.

"Oh no," said a Storck. "I don't think we—"

"It's not your ball," said Bill. "I want it back."

"So, go get it," I ventured.

Bill, who knew the Code, wasn't put off.

"You hit it there," he said. "You gotta get it. Or we can't play anymore."

"We can get another ball."

"Yeah? How? You got money?"

I shrugged.

"Anybody got money?"

Silence.

I sighed. I checked out Mrs. Moose's house. Nothing stirred. I waited a moment, my eyes glued to the black-taped ball, screwed into the dust below Mrs. Moose's bay window. Maybe she hadn't seen it fall, hadn't noticed the little puff of dust and the new foreign object in her garden. Maybe she was dozing, or astigmatic, or in her kitchen, baking—no!

"Whaddya waitin' for, f'Chrissake!" This was my brother.

"Shut up!"

"You goin' or not?" This from another kid, more reasonably, slightly plaintive—aware of the catastrophic economic impact of buying an entire new baseball when a perfectly good paid-for ball was sitting out in plain sight, not lost in the high weeds, or down a storm sewer, or through the window of a ball-hoarding grouch. Right out there, visible. All I had to do was go get it.

From Mrs. Moose's garden.

"Okay," I murmured. I had to go alone. Nobody to cover my back.

> . . . *Paladin, Paladin,*
> *Where do you roam? . . .*

I girded my loins. My loins cramped up.

"Ow."

How to approach the objective? This was the question.

I instinctively assumed a physical attitude that might be called haunted-house rigor. This was a posture of unnatural rigidity and stiff-legged gait. One threw one's shoulders back, literally leaning backwards as one inched toward the infernal doorway. In haunted-house rigor, your eyes bugged out of your head, you licked your lips compulsively, you clutched a useless wooden stake or a flickering torch. You shook all over. The full moon slid behind a cloud. Your knees knocked.

I once tried to make my knees knock. I managed it once, painfully, but concluded that causing one's knees to clatter repeatedly, like maracas, was anatomically preposterous. It was a fictional effect—like Wile E. Coyote spinning his legs in midair—invented by some hack writer or comic strip author to depict terror in the dumbest possible terms. To actually do it, you needed to be Lou Costello with a sound effects team.

Besides the knee-knocking issue, I sensed that haunted-house rigor would look silly in broad daylight on a sunny day in July. I switched quickly to war movie stealth, and lit out across the baseball field for the concealment of Mrs. Moose's bridal wreath. I crouched as I ran in quick, lightfooted crab steps, looking pointlessly to my left and right. I threw myself onto the earth just shy of the bushes. I looked back at my fellow ballplayers. They stood there like a game of statue tag, gaping, taut, saucer-eyed and ready to scatter.

I crept through the bridal wreath on my belly, wishing I had a bayonet clamped in my teeth. Aldo Ray always had a bayonet to bite. I gathered my feet beneath me and crouched hurriedly across the gap between the bridal wreath and the corner of Mrs. Moose's bay window. I flattened myself against Mrs. Moose's siding. My heart pounded annoyingly in my temples, like gongs at the beginning of a J. Arthur Rank movie. Wham, wham, wham! Through the bridal wreath, I saw my idiot brother waving me around the corner and toward the ball. I waved back, trying to express the idea that if he wanted to do this, I'd be glad to go back to the baseball field this second and then *he* could try sneaking up on Mrs. Moose without ending up in some slime-drooling stewpot with a meat thermometer sticking out of his eye socket. This sentiment was inadequately conveyed. Bill just kept waving. I gave him the finger, shakily.

I turned, slowly. Painstakingly, I stuck my head around the corner of the house, expecting Mrs. Moose, her shotgun staring up my nose. But the coast was clear. Twelve feet away, nestled in the berm below the window, there was our ball—the best damn hit of my life. I hadn't even thought to run the bases. My homer wasn't even official; it never would be. I tried, from an impossible angle, to peer into the window, to see if perhaps, somehow, Mrs. Moose was not at her customary battle station. But my angle was too severe. Besides, the glare off the window panes rendered the interior of the house invisible—unless I stuck my face up against the glass. Unthinkable.

Also unthinkable: the twelve feet of open ground between me and our only ball. But I had no choice. I'd hit it. I had to get it. The team was counting on me. I had to brave Mrs. Moose's shotgun and her ravenous blood hunger and her poison-laced—no!

I took one deep, spastic breath, crossed myself, ducked low and scurried, ratlike, across No-Kid's-Land to the ball. I grabbed it, felt its hot black roundness in my hand and felt a wave of ineffable relief. Another second, and I was safe. I could throw myself on the ground to avoid the gun's blast. I could roll back where I had come from. I could just run, zigzagging down through the tomatoes and beet greens to safety.

Instead—what was I? Nuts?

I turned, my head driven involuntarily by some death wish tumor growing in my brain, to see—to check on Mrs. Moose. Was she there?

I was blind. Shrunken to pinpoints by fear and sunlight, my pupils registered nothing inside the window but black. Okay, now I could run.

No. The suicidal maniac controlling my brain insisted on lingering, allowing my eyes to adjust. I crouched in Mrs. Moose's window, a few feet from where she usually sat cradling her blunderbuss on her lap.

Slowly, exposed, naked, I began to see. I could also hear Bill, then Whelihan and the Storcks and the others, shouting my name, egging me to cheezit while the cheezing was good. I couldn't move. The image was starting to form. There was movement inside the black room. The first thing I could see was her hair, a gray halo lit by diffused sunshine. Her face floated up like a disembodied head from the bottom of a well bucket. Smiling.

Oh, Jesus! Fangs?

Now I could see almost all of her, the lumpish body, the print dress, one flabby arm hanging at her side. No gun. A ray of sun caught the glint of the gun's barrel behind Mrs. Moose, lying across her chair. She was unarmed. A huge relief almost tipped me over, into the window—but too early—because then I cleared the murk from my vision and saw.

Her other hand was stretched toward me as she glided, ghostly, toward me, toward the door that would bring her into the garden. And in her hand she was carrying, proffering—brandishing!—a heaping, fragrant, steaming, fresh-baked plate full of oatmeal-raisin cookies!

The scream that cracked from my lungs, at the sight of Mrs. Moose's cookies, rent the summer air, set dogs barking for three blocks around and made pregnant women picture succubi gnawing their wombs. It also spotted my underwear. I fell backwards, scrabbling in the dirt, unable to distinguish my feet from any other body part. I was helpless on the ground like a tipped turtle. I could hear Mrs. Moose's slippered footsteps now, shuffling and soughing like cockroaches behind the sheetrock. I had to get up. I screamed again and started whimpering. I heard the calls of my brother and the other cowards change from encouragement to panic. I rolled on the ground until I was on my hands and knees. Behind me, a voice that went through my heart like Aldo Ray's red-hot bayonet.

"Hello, little boy. Don't be afraid."

This was enough. I leapt like a frog, landed on my stomach, somehow clambered to my feet, exploded through the bridal wreath and flew down the hill, barely touching the ground, falling once so violently that I did a midair somersault, rose shrieking and crossed the diamond—galloping toward Council Creek with oatmeal-raisin banshees nipping at my ass.

Neither Bill nor any of the other kids were anywhere in sight. Two of them I never saw again. Bill came home later that day, scratched, hollow-eyed and speckled with stick-tights. Bill drifted away from Whelihan after that, and we never played ball again within a mile of Mrs. Moose's house. The weeds got their field back.

But we still had our ball.

Catholics vs. Publics on the Sands of Iwo Jima

The kid playing shortstop kept calling me a "pussy."

I was accustomed to sticks-and-stones, but this one was new to me. I deduced that he was not comparing me to some sort of fairy-tale kitty-cat, but this—so far in my vocabulary development—was the only connotation I knew. Additionally distracting was the crowd reaction. Whenever he squalled this word, it drew a roar of prurient hilarity from every kid on his team and half the kids on mine.

"Benjamiiiiiin! Yer a pussy! Ya can't hit!"

The kid playing shortstop was a smug little towheaded prick with an angel face and a button nose. His name was Aston, known to intimate acquaintances as Asswipe.

"Swing pussy swing pussy swing."

I swung. I missed.

"Haaah! You PUSSY! You can't hit! Sit yer pussy ass down, Benjamin!"

Aston was playing shortstop because he had quick feet and good hands and he was what the radio baseball announcers called a "sparkplug"—meaning that he loved the sound of his own voice. Shrill and prepubescent, it registered on the naked ear somewhere between a worn-out brake pad and a raging gopher.

"Swing, pussy!"

I swung again, missed again.

"Pussssssseeeee!"

Under my breath, I said, "Shit," and stepped away from home plate (actually the tin lid from a ten-gallon can of roofing tar). Aston grinned at me and spat Dubble Bubble juice into the sand. I glared hatred at Aston. He cackled.

Normally, I didn't hate the kids from the Miller School, as a group. Hatred was against my religion. Jesus said love thy enemy. Besides, the Miller School kids outnumbered and surrounded us. Hating all of them was strategically impractical. Plus, in my neighborhood, most of the kids I played with went to the public school. They were generally likable. We only split into Catholic and Public camps during school hours—and baseball games.

Baseball changed everything—from peaceful coexistence to global thermonuclear war. The Publics were our sole rivals. We had no one else to play. Hating the Publics, for the duration of the game, was obligatory. Afterwards, tolerance returned and we all headed home to supper. Except, game or no game, I still hated Aston. He was loud and mean, and grownups thought he was cute as a bug's ear. He was Eddie Haskell in real life, disguised as Andy Hardy, with a garbage-mouth and an instinct for the jugular. I hated Aston with a low-key, health-giving consistency. Despising kids like Aston and Feeney, secretly nursing a hundred past indignities, was like niacin and riboflavin and all the other minimum daily nutritional requirements on the side of the Wheat Chex box.

If it weren't for hatred, most kids wouldn't make it through childhood. Too much nurturing love will soften a kid, expose his crybaby underbelly and leave him vulnerable to crippling disillusionment and lifelong cynicism. Hate is the balance. Kids are designed for hatred. Kids—smaller, weaker, prone to infections and never taken seriously—have lots to hate. Food. Parents. Horseflies. Rules. Clocks. Teachers. Religious services. Exposed nails and tetanus boosters. Other kids, especially other kids. Kids have an emotional agility that would kill a grownup. They can hate someone, or something, with blinding ferocity, for short bursts, after which their animosity plummets into quiescence—or reverts completely, into love. I used to hate my favorite cousin, Bobby, and my idiot brother, Bill—homicidally—whenever we played baseball.

My last summer in Tomah, Bobby, Danny, Bill and I played four-kid baseball at the Miller School sandlots. Playing a whole baseball game with only four players was almost impossible, which made each game fierce, angry and thick with hate. On defense, Danny and I on one team, Bobby and Bill on the other team, had to range over an acre of rubble, sand, humps, stubborn weeds and potholes. Even if you could reach a flyball before it hit the ground, you were often foiled by the terrain, by the deepening shadows of dusk, by outright darkness, by a cloud of ravenous mosquitoes, or by the sudden terror of getting hit in the chops with the ball and left to spend the rest of your life in an iron lung. There were few horrors as imminent and gruesome to kids in the Fifties as life in an iron lung. Every day, the March of Dimes reminded me that somewhere out there was an iron lung with my name on it.

Several rules made four-kid ball both possible and difficult. We played "pitcher's hands." There was no stealing. The critical rule was that "imaginary men" were not allowed to occupy bases. Say, for example, Bill—the youngest and smallest—comes to bat while I'm pitching and flares a base hit to short right field. Bill streaks for first base. Danny on defense, who was shaded toward left-center, busts his ass to get to the ball. Meanwhile, I charge from the pitcher's box to second base. If Danny and I can relay the ball quickly and prevent Bill from taking second base, Bobby—who bats next—has to literally cream a home run or else he'll strand Bill somewhere short of home plate. With no imaginary men in the game, any runner left on base—when it's time for him to bat again—is automatically out. In four-kid ball, singles are the kiss of death.

For the best weeks of that summer, the four of us claimed the Miller School sandlots every evening from just after suppertime (the Official National Suppertime of Wisconsin is 5:30) until dark—

usually about sixteen innings. If there was even the ghost of a moon, we kept playing. Once, in the dark, Bobby hit a line drive through the box that I never saw. But I stopped it with my ear and pounced on the ball before Bobby reached first.

"Hah! You're out!"

Then we all agreed it was too dark to keep playing.

Because four-kid ball was such hard work, and because it was all in the family, we played with ruthless rancor. Winning or losing decided each kid's mood for the next twenty-four hours. Nonetheless, I can't remember a single final score (mostly, we scored thirty or forty runs per side), nor can I remember whether one team won more often than the other. Bobby was the best player—and he was a good enough hitter that I was allowed to pitch him fastballs. Bill was the easiest out, which made him the key player in the game. Like all kid baseball, the main goal in those four-player family feuds was the out.

In kid baseball, runs pile up in dozens. We used to lose count regularly, scream at one another for ten minutes, then abandon the problem and start all over at 0–0. We lost track of the score so often because, in kid baseball, getting a run usually just involves hitting a fair ball. It hardly matters whether the ball comes to earth where the fielders are, or where they ain't. Every game is a clinic in corralling a crazy round ball that has rocketed or spiraled or blooped, with unpredictable topspin, off a round bat, usually toward a little kid with a huge glove whose natural inclination is to duck and cover. In kid baseball, before grownups took it over, we didn't allow fastballs because there were no catchers, and no umpires. We grew quickly impatient with a kid who passed up too many pitches because they were "too high" or "too low" or "too hard." And we'd yank a pitcher who couldn't deliver the ball consistently into a batter's swinging zone. Our objective was perpetual motion. Without fastballs, catchers or umps, there were no walks and precious few strikeouts. Of course, it was possible for a kid to whiff despite getting cans-of-corn tossed into his wheelhouse one after the other, but he had to be legally blind, hopelessly uncoordinated or wearing a cast.

I struck out pretty often, mainly because (everybody could see this, but no one ever bothered to point it out to me) I tended to close my eyes when I swung the bat. I've always wanted to repeat my childhood with my eyes open all the time.

When we played baseball, we didn't keep count of many things, except kids. Danny, Bobby, Bill and I represented a really important number, because you couldn't play any sort of game at all without at least four bodies. Most other numbers were barely significant. In kid baseball, hits were good, runs were great, but final scores were fleeting phenomena, and statistics did not exist. The things that we treasured most, because they were so hard to do and three of them got you up to bat, were outs. This philosophy was embodied in the basic baseball game that every kid played for countless hours when I was a kid, which was called workup. Kids played workup when there wasn't enough manpower for two whole teams (about three quarters of the time). Workup involved seven, eight or nine kids. (If you had ten, you had enough to choose up sides, so forget workup!) In workup, three kids would bat, the rest would spread around the field. Workup was always "pitcher's hands," with no catcher, no first baseman, no ump, no fair pitching hard, no imaginary men. If a batter made an out, he had to go to right-center field and start working his way back up to bat, one out at a time. The last fielding position before a kid got to bat was pitcher. Since there were no teams, there was no score—except sometimes the kid who batted the longest, scored the most runs and made the fewest outs declared himself the "winner"—a meaningless designation that pegged the kid as a twink.

Because outs were our yardstick and our grail, the most coveted team members were the kids who had a knack for outs. When our grade at St. Mary's played challenge battles against the public school kids from the Miller School, the hitting star was always a Public named Stitch, who could crush the ball like Ted Kluszewski and run like a Sherman tank. But the hands-down best player was our guy, Fin. Fin fashioned outs.

*   *   *

All the games between the Catholics and the Publics started
with Fin. Fin made diplomatic contact across Monroe Street with
Stitch, and they negotiated a day for each game. Fin recruited our
team. When we played, Fin was the shortstop, the most prestigious
position. No one ever questioned why Fin got to be shortstop.
Shortstop was where most of the outs started. Fin was born a shortstop.

Fin was not only the best athlete in our class. He got As and he
was immune to the stigma, among boys, of scholastic excellence.
(The most respect I ever got for being "smart" was when Overacker
paid me a dollar to take his Iowa Test of Basic Skills for him.) Fin
was so brilliant that he had even skipped a grade. This astounded
me. Even Beatrice Dwyer, my academic nemesis and spelling bee
rival, who was not only sickeningly bright but saintly in her demeanor, had never been nominated for grade skipping. And why
not me? I got As, too. And I was a veritable angel!

Fin was my first experience, although I perceived it dimly then, of
noblesse oblige. In fifth grade, when Fin leapfrogged—by ecclesiasti-
cal decree—into my class, a year younger than every other kid, I resolved to conspire with my classmates in giving the rookie a cool
reception. Technically, Fin was a "little kid," even though he stood
bigger than everyone in my class except Gunderson, Overacker and
a tongue-tied beanpole named Gladstone. However, to my dismay,
Fin's celebrity preceded him. While I stood aloof from him, everyone else was busy killing and roasting the fatted calf. Feeney, our
rat-faced class emcee, set the tone for Fin's welcome by awarding
him the desk on his right hand, in the front row. Kiegel, Overacker
and Gunderson, the alpha males, treated Fin immediately as a
peer. Soon, Fin surpassed peerhood. Feeney, Kiegel, Overacker,
Gunderson—even Sister Claveria—began deferring to him. At recess, I couldn't help but share the general homage toward Fin's
precocity. He was strong; he was fleet; he was deft; he was pic-
turesque. He was obviously a god of the playground. But inside
school I still thought something was fishy. Kids didn't grade-skip,

especially under the iron regime of principal Sister Terence, simply because they had a velvety jump shot or because they could hit a softball all the way to Hollister Avenue on the fly. Kids skipped because their grades were stratospheric! Was Fin *that* smart? To me, he didn't seem even as smart as Beatrice Dwyer—who, admittedly, was a whiz. She was stuck in the old treadmill with me and Koscal and the idiot Kamperschroer brothers, Kippy and Kenny. What else was going on here?

One day, I sidled up to Beatrice Dwyer. Besides being a brain, Beatrice was plugged into the grapevine. I posed the issue of how a kid like Fin gets skipped, while other kids with equal—or even better—grades slog along station to station.

"Well," said Beatrice with a knowing curl in her lip, "it's s'posed to be cuz you're more mature [she pronounced the "t" as a "ch"] than everybody else. But that's not why."

"No?"

"No."

"Well, then, why?"

"It's cuz he's rich."

I recoiled. Rich? Well, yes, Fin was from a prosperous and patrician family. His father was one of the foremost physicians at the Tomah Clinic, where every kid in town got his strep throat cultures and got his chicken pox diagnosed and got shots for diphtheria and measles and whooping cough and . . .

"He lives on Lake Street," said Beatrice.

"Yeah. I know."

Lake Street was our Bellevue Avenue. Lake Street, one long block that rose gently above all the proletarian enclaves that surrounded it, and overlooked the blue expanse of Lake Tomah, had the biggest houses in town. They had flagstone walkways, two-car garages and statues of deer on the lawn. One of them—Fin's, in fact—had tall white columns and an actual pediment. Lake Street's denizens were our most successful and esteemed citizens, our doctors, our attorneys, our oilmen, our Ford dealers. If privilege could be presumed in Tomah, it would be presumed by the Lake Street swells. But I doubted Beatrice. In the secular realm, over at the public school, I averred, a kid like Fin, son of Hippocrates the healer, might indeed benefit from his status. But this was St. Mary's, where the Gospel of Jesus was our guide. And everybody knew what Jesus had said about a rich man entering into the Kingdom of God.

"What?" said Beatrice.

"You know, how it would be easier to stick a sewing needle all the way through a camel."

"That doesn't sound right."

"Well, that's what it says," I growled. "Look it up."

"Well, you're wrong anyway," said Beatrice. "Fin skipped cuz he's rich."

Beatrice's assurance disturbed me, but I clung to my faith in the Church's incorruptibility. A week later, Beatrice buttonholed me on the way to recess.

"I found out," she said, smirking.

"Found out what?"

"My mother told me, and she found out from our neighbor, who works at Shutter's at the cash register, who talked to Mrs. Schober."

Mrs. Schober was the third-grade teacher.

"Mrs. Schober told her," said Beatrice Dwyer.

"Told who?"

"Our neighbor, while she was buyin' groceries [she pronounced the "c" as "sh"] at Shutter's."

"About what?"

"About Fin's mother, dummy."

"What about Fin's mother?"

"About Fin's mother jist walkin' straight into Father Mulligan's house and sayin', 'I want you to skip my son up a grade.' And Father Mulligan jist sat there and said, 'Okay.'"

"That's stupid," I said. Father Mulligan was a huge, affectionate St. Bernard of a man, the softhearted godfather of every kid at St. Mary's. He was also the personal delegate of Jesus for all of Tomah, and he would never compromise the spirit of the Gospel, especially if it meant helping some rich mother shove a needle through a helpless camel. "Why would Father Mulligan do that?"

"Dummy," snapped Beatrice. "Cuz they give a lot of money to the Church! They got their own window!"

It was true. Fin's family had contributed so much to St. Mary's that their name was etched permanently into one of the stained glass windows that lined the neo-Gothic walls of St. Mary's Church.

"Because of a window?" I muttered, crestfallen.

"You have no idea," replied Beatrice in that permanent annoying superior tone that only faltered when I kicked her butt in a spelling bee, "how much one of those windows costs."

Eventually, I forgave Father Mulligan his small concession to Caesar. He was, after all, no match for Fin's mother, who was ahead of her time. Father Mulligan had been ambushed. People in the Midwest in those days tended to be stoic and long-suffering, instilled with a belief that you got whatever you deserved if you worked hard enough for it—and if you didn't get what you wanted you probably didn't deserve it. You shut your trap and went back to work. Or went downtown to the Crow Bar and cried in your beer. Fin's mother didn't subscribe. She was rich. She was married to the Doctor. She believed in entitlement long before entitlement became a middle-class pathology. I tried to picture my mother doing what Fin's mother had done. I couldn't. Even armed with my report cards (with better grades than Fin's) and my record of exemplary conduct, Mom would never dare to barge into the presence of the prelate of God and demand indulgences for me. And even if she asked, her humility would have defeated her. Father Mulligan would have chuckled affectionately, put an arm on her shoulder and gently guided her out his door, back into the Real World. We were easy people to reject. We had no window.

I hated several kids in my class. Feeney, for instance, and my best friend, Koscal. But I couldn't bring myself to hate Fin, even though his very presence offended my sense of fairness. He was condescending toward me, but never cruel. His genteel restraint had a positive effect on the other bullies in my class. After Fin's arrival, I got pounded less.

Before Fin, our games against the kids over at the Miller School were irregular and spontaneous. They just sort of broke out among kids who happened to be lingering around the Miller School sandlots after school. One year, there were no Catholics vs. Publics games at all. After Fin arrived, the games were prearranged and orderly. We even played a few games against kids from St. Paul's, the Lutheran school.

But Lutherans were cannon fodder. The main games, the real games, the passionate, screaming, cursing games with shredded elbows, slandered mothers, collisions at home plate and promises of revenge, were against the Publics. We hated the Publics. They hated us. They called us "catlickers" and "mackerel-snappers." We knew no expletives that applied to attendance at a public school, so we just said, "Shut up!" or called them "dipshits." This was actually more effective. "Catlicker" is a pretty lame pun, and we all knew it. Besides, there was no genuine religious hostility in our rivalry. The Publics were a theological hodgepodge, including a few Catholics. For our part, we weren't exactly rosary-chanting zealots. We went to St. Mary's because our parents sent us there. We wanted to beat the Publics because they went to the other school, across the street. Monroe Street was our border, and borders define enemies.

When Catholics played Publics, we played regulation games, complete with catchers and first basemen. This meant each grade had to muster up a complete batting order of nine kids—at least to start the game. This wasn't easy. There were never more than sixteen boys in my class at St. Mary's. Numerous factors reduced the available manpower for baseball. Farming was one. Two kids in our class had to catch a public school bus out to "the country" to put in four or five hours of chores on the family homestead. Paper routes and music lessons reduced the pool further. And there were several kids who were simply too abject and leprous to even invite. These included a sweet feebleminded kid with incredibly bad breath, named Mikey, whom nobody ever hassled because it was a mortal sin to pick on retards, a fat kid we called Butterball, a catatonic dwarf named Gertz, Nordling the nerd and, finally, Bissell—who cringed and quaked in the presence of danger, which included almost everyone and everything because Bissell lived in mortal terror of his own shadow.

One of the great misconceptions of our time is the belief that the last kid picked for any team is the rock-bottom worst athlete in the talent pool. In fact, the last kid picked—which I usually was—is simply the worst among the ablebodied and willing. Every class of kids has a small pod of untouchables—like Gertz, Nordling, Bissell, Butterball and Mikey (not to mention all the girls)—whose afflictions are so profound that to allow them onto a playing field is both a threat to their well-being and a hindrance to the game. Now and then, early in a school year, some meddling nun would scoldingly shoehorn Gertz and Nordling into a game of playground softball only to watch in horror as Gertz stood frozen with a bat, trembling violently as twelve or thirteen perfect pitches floated through his strike zone, or as Nordling, exiled to right field, responded to a fly-ball sliced in his direction by rolling into a fetal ball on the asphalt and honking rhythmically, like an unspeakably ugly duckling in distress.

Gertz and Nordling were grateful not to be picked. For them, sports were a relentless storm of ignominy and vituperation. They had discovered no consolation in their own unappreciated skills, because they had none. They saw no salvation in their own martyrdom, no grace in their sufferings. They feared, abhorred and fled sports. I understood Gertz and Nordling better than most of the other kids and I sometimes wished I could join them, as they skulked off to separate corners of the playground and waited out the ordeal of recess. But I possessed just enough secret skills to keep me trying to play the games until I reached a certain crucial point of development, beyond which I couldn't help playing. Sports, like gambling, suck you in by rationing your triumphs, larding them with failure. Catch one pass in five hundred attempts, and suddenly football takes hold of you. Run one swinging bunt into a single, after a thousand strikeouts, and baseball has you under its spell. Also, I was—although I would have denied the aspersion if anyone had ever cast it—stubborn. Somehow, I regarded playing with other kids—who didn't particularly want me playing with them—as a right guaranteed by the Constitution and the Holy See. Mutely, I declined exclusion. I clustered with everybody else at choose-up time and I saw no stigma in being the last loaf on the shelf. My sideline-stalking obstinacy was rewarded each spring when Fin would canvass the boys in our class about a game with the Publics. Fin would work his way methodically down the roster, adjusting the game day to one kid's piano lesson, cajoling another kid to bag his 4-H meeting for the sake of the team. Eventually, decimated by paper routes, parental punishments and cows that couldn't wait to be milked, Fin would get around to me. I was always surprised. The other kids would never tell me there was going to be a game, for fear I might show up and volunteer. By the time Fin vetted me, the team was out of options. It was either Benjamin or forfeit.

"Lookit, uh," Fin would say, "howdja like to be in our game, against the Publics. Prob'ly Thursday."

"Thursday?"

I didn't say I would have to check my schedule. I said, "Me? Gee! Okay! I'll be there!" I never played hard-to-get. I'd never been hard-to-get. I had no concept of hard-to-get.

Sometime every spring, usually mid-May, the weather would break. By then, the major league season had been running for five weeks, and the baseball fever was upon all of us. There was still a tenacious crust of filthy ice along the edge of our playground. In the morning, when we filed into church for eight o'clock Mass, the hawk wind from Canada still raked our hilltop and aggravated our chilblains. But, if you didn't mind the bat stinging when you fouled the ball, or running in place in the outfield to keep your feet from going numb, you played baseball in wintry May. One by one, each grade scheduled a Catholics vs. Publics showdown over at the Miller School backstops. Eighth grade got first dibs. Fin would have to work our games around the older grades' schedule. His best-laid plans were regularly foiled by snow squalls and manpower crises. But persistence is the name of the game in the upper Midwest. Sooner or later, the sun comes out, the mud dries up, the flu holds off and the eighth graders don't have the diamond.

If we were lucky with weather, we played the Publics maybe twice in May before school let out. Sometimes, there was only one game, a schedule so brief that each battle was all the more momentous. Battle was our metaphor. We had all grown up not playing cowboys and Indians in the neighborhood, but World War II. Our enemies were always krauts or Japs (occasionally Koreans) and our battlefields were always one of two beaches—Normandy or Iwo Jima. In Catholics vs. Publics, the other team were always the Japs and the Miller School fields were Iwo Jima.

They looked like Iwo Jima—after the battle.

The Miller School fields were actual sandlots. Like most of the fields where I ever played baseball as a kid, the Miller School fields sloped uphill. Their chicken wire backstops were arrayed at the bottom of the hill, at opposite ends of the block on Hollister Avenue. Each infield was mostly flat, ankle-deep with white sand and, by late spring, ringed with two generations of sandburs. These sinister seeds would lie in wait, attaching to your socks, clinging to your jeans and forcing the occasional batter to step out of the box and pick stickers off his shoelaces. The outfield climbed gently upward, in a sere wasteland of kid-trampled gravel, shallow rain gullies, tufts of weeds and swirling dust. Atop the hill stood two Miller Schools—in far-off center field the majestic red-brick pile where Tomah kids, in pioneer times, had attended high school, and in left, the low-slung brand-new annex, made of white brick, glass and space-age aluminum. The schools were rimmed by asphalt, where girls played hopscotch and four-square and other candy-ass pastimes. If you hit the ball all the way uphill to the asphalt, you were a superman. Once, Stitch, our grade's public school Goliath, hit a drive that bounced once before reaching the side of the new Miller School. This was a shot similar to the time Henry Aaron landed a drive on the roof of the building across Waveland Avenue at Wrigley

Field. We all just stood transfixed—even Stitch, who forgot to run—watching the ball bounce around the Miller School pavement three hundred feet uphill.

The most challenging spot to play defense at the Miller School was a patch of spindly oak trees halfway up the hill in right-center field. The oaks had been climbed, engraved, stripped, gouged, peed on and tortured by tens of thousands of barbaric public school pupils for fifty years. The ground beneath, eroded by weather and dug into by claw-fingered children at every recess since the McKinley administration, was a jagged webwork of exposed oak roots, dead branches and fist-sized rocks where every unguarded step was a twisted ankle. Backpedaling for a flyball was an invitation to permanent spinal damage. Because no one could safely function under the oaks, center field at the Miller School sandlot was an unpopular position to play. This is where I usually ended up.

I also hit last in the batting order. This was a clue for Aston that I was not highly regarded as a batsman. Aston could count. Not that he needed to. Aston wasn't big, tall, strong or especially bright. But he was anthropologically precocious. He figured out which kids were feared or favored and he eagerly, deviously, ingratiated himself with them. He also discovered that social stratification among kids tends to be haphazard. A kid who intervenes to apply a little order to this messy process has a huge advantage. He gets to decide between winners and losers, between the kids who get picked and those who get picked on. Aston never rested in his vocation as social director, nor did Feeney, his Catholic counterpart. In order to retain their status, which they held by guile rather than might, they were always better informed than anyone else.

So when I stepped up to bat the first time, Aston was prepared. I barely knew him—except as a pest—but he knew me intimately, and he knew that I commanded no loyalty among my fellow Catholics. He knew he could abuse me at will. Fin, our unofficial captain, would defend—with fist and claw, if necessary—almost any kid on our team, even Erdmann (commonly known as Turd Man), who only bathed once a month. But Fin had never stood up for me.

Aston could use any device to distract me, say anything to demean me, badger me until my face went red and my eyes filled up and I couldn't see straight, but I had to swing the bat, as hard as I could, in anger, hoping ridiculously to smash the ball into his face. He made fun of my raggedy clothes and my lousy baseball skills, my scrawny frame, my teensy dick and my divorced mother. All of it worked. First time up, I struck out swinging. Aston brayed triumphantly, flinging handfuls of sand toward me as I slunk back to the fence and picked sandburs off my cuffs. After the third out, in an act of extraordinary charity, Fin spoke to me as we trudged onto the field.

"You shouldn't listen, Benjamin," said Fin. "He's a jerk."

In that game, Fin had decided to try me at third base. It was an audacious experiment. Despite the fact that I was still afraid of the baseball, Fin installed me in the position where the hardest line drives tend to go. On the other hand, Fin was at shortstop, just to my left, and his range was octopoid. With Fin covering almost every inch of space between second and third base, I had very little defensive responsibility.

Infield play on the Miller School fields was a unique challenge, which Fin had mastered. Any ball hit on the ground to the left side of the infield tended to die immediately in the sand. Fin would charge unerringly at the crack of the bat and plunge into the dunes like a seagull after a frankfurter. In a half-second, Fin exploded in a whirlwind of flying, stinging sand and inside this tornado of grit, an arm would arc and the ball emerge, humming toward Gunderson at first base, who snicked it from the air just as the Public batter stretched, too late, for the bag (actually, a side-slat from a peach crate). Fin at shortstop was one of the prettiest sights of my childhood. He waited for nothing. He attacked everything. He seemed incapable of misjudging, dropping, booting or fumbling one of the most elusive objects in every other kid's arduous experience—a baseball. His hands were like magnets, and the ball, to Fin, was steel wool. I envied Fin—not because I wished for his skills. I knew they were beyond my potential. I envied him because I knew he was a natural. He had never failed. He had found, in life, so far, no jolts, no blows, no knots, no terrors. He dove blithely into the sand because he could not possibly picture the monsters who lived underneath. I envied Fin his purity.

Of course, I resented the hell out of him, too, especially after chasing a pop foul near third base, twisting the wrong way and lunging at the sinking ball, only to see it tick off my new baseball glove (a present from my dad) and bounce into the sandburs.

"Shit," I said.

"It's okay," said Fin, graciously implying that I would make my first successful defensive play at the exact moment hell froze over.

The next pop fly, an inning later, was easier. It was straight up, right over third base. Nervous, trembling, huge-eyed but determined, clenching my teeth, shuffling in the sand, squinting to fight off the sun, I circled under the ball. There it was, in my sights. I opened my glove. I remembered—don't snap at the ball. Just let it drop, nestle it into the pocket and squeeze. And I would have. Honest to God! But suddenly a shadow swept over, a bigger glove filled the sky, blocked off the sinking baseball and snatched it from the sky an inch from my mitt.

Fin.

He had come over to help. He'd stolen my out. And he'd shown everyone—especially Aston—that I was useless. You couldn't trust Benjamin with a simple, goddamned pop fly.

Well, maybe he was right.

Maybe I couldn't hit either. Under Aston's derision, I had stepped from the batter's box after two strikes, and this was unheard of. Maybe Henry Aaron did this against Don Drysdale, but kids didn't pull this kind of stunt. Kids stayed up to bat.

"Whaddya doin'?" shouted the Publics' pitcher.

To justify my behavior, I rubbed at my eye.

"Whaddya? Bawlin'?" yelled the pitcher.

"Get in there!" shouted another Public.

"What the hell ya doin'?" said one of my teammates.

"Hey, pussy!" crowed Aston. "Ya quittin'?"

I stepped back in, ignored Aston at short and sneered—as best I could sneer (it looked like a smile)—at the pitcher. He threw a good pitch and I passed on it.

"Aw, come on!" said the pitcher. "What was wrong with that?"

"Pussseeee!"

Taking a pitch calmed my jangled ganglia and moved Aston from my immediate consciousness. I studied the pitcher, a homely kid with an unruly shock of black hair and the face of a thirty-year-old convict. His teachers must have been shaken the first time this kid stepped into class. He wound up elaborately and served a new pitch, right down the middle of the plate.

For Fin's sake, more than mine, I didn't want to strike out again. In any given school year, notwithstanding the holy cards I got for perfect catechism recitation, or the gold stars I lined up on the bulletin board for reading twice as many books as any other kid on the face of the earth—and with the possible exception of my altar-boy promotion from six o'clock Mass with groggy Father Rourke to eight o'clock Mass with jolly Father Mulligan—no honor I attained was more exalting than Fin's invitation to the game against the Publics on the Miller School sandlot. For a long time, I thought there was no human parallel to this experience. Then, I saw my first telecast, on WKBT, of the major league All-Star Game. That game was virtually the same as ours, except for the fact that the All-Stars had spectators, bats that weren't chipped, cracked and taped, and a place where they could pee in private, rather than up against the oak trees in center field. Actually, that was another difference: major league outfields never had trees.

But the feel of the All-Star Game was the same as us against the Publics. Each was a game where you couldn't just walk on. You had to have a specific invitation, from either Stitch (if you were a Public) or Fin (if you were a Catholic). Each team—the National League All-Stars, the American League All-Stars and us—was a patchwork of everyday foes, rivals, strangers, pals and acquaintances bonded for the moment by baseball, by a ravening hunger for the game, and by a common opponent. We were teams for a day but our mission galvanized us into unnatural brotherhood. We were like the food chain observing a truce, wolves and bobcats side by side with bunnies and chipmunks. If I were to look down the bench (if we'd had a bench) at our team, at Gunderson, Feeney, Fin, Kiegel, Overacker, Turd Man, Four-Eyes Fuchs and all the rest, the only teammate among them whom I might even remotely regard as friend was Koscal, an association that was more an embarrassment than a boon. But Koscal had the advantage here, because he was strong and agile, with a cannon arm and power at the plate that rivaled Gunderson and Fin. I was only present by default—a last-minute fill-in like Don Schwall, incongruous among the All-Stars with a 6–4 record and an ERA over 4.00, replacing Warren Spahn, who had a touch of tendinitis. I was invited only because Lagerbloom had a *Milwaukee Journal* paper route he wasn't able to escape, Laufenberg was home with his second week of the mumps he got from his little sister, and Fiedler had orders from his old man to weed and hoe three acres of strawberry fields by Friday or surrender his bike for the entire summer.

Only by looking across the diamond could I see a group of contemporaries more alien to me than my own teammates. Among them, the only Publics I knew by name were the legendary Stitch, a gangling stick named Drinkwater (universally known as Stinkwater), Aston the Asswipe and a boy named Neitzel, who lived on the same block as my grandparents.

Like the All-Star Game, there were opponents on the Miller School field—mostly the serious jocks among us—who were closer and friendlier with each other than they were with their own teammates. Fin and Stitch, of course, were thick as thieves. Feeney and Aston—each one a conniver enforcing the pecking order in his grade, each cuddly, malevolent and glib—sparred like scorpions in a Mason jar. Stinkwater and Gunderson agreed to share Stinkwater's new MacGregor first baseman's mitt. I watched all this manly camaraderie with voyeuristic absorption. Here was a frat house where

I wasn't normally allowed to darken the door, so I studied raptly its rituals and gestures, its gibes and its affectations.

As closely as I watched, I usually forgot almost everything in the year that elapsed between games. I had to be constantly alert for signs, nuances and indirect commands. I dared not ask questions. To do so would have flouted the Code. I spoke to no one unless spoken to, and no one ever spoke to me, except to tell me when to bat, or where to go when our team took the field. I never thought about the social peril I faced every time I gripped the bat or squinted into the sun at a sinking flyball that I could not possibly catch. I was just glad to play, willing to do anything for the team, endure any abuse, stand exposed to my own incompetence at any position on the field. I expected to screw up, but I knew that if I accomplished anything positive—slipped one good moment into my customary bouquet of screwups—that these kids, my nominal teammates, my daily tormentors, might become, would become—yes, they would—my friends, my pals, my personal cheering section for God knows how long. Maybe even overnight!

Besides, I had my new glove.

I had gotten it the previous June, for my birthday, from Dad. It was some Japanese brand that nobody'd ever heard of, but it was lovely nonetheless, a fragrant shell of sienna cowhide, etched with the signature of some *gaijin*—unknown to his native America—who had made a career for himself as the token foreigner among the Hiroshima Carp or Nippon Ham Fighters. My new glove, which I had kept carefully away from sun and moisture in the back of my sock drawer, was five times bigger than my hand, a giant maw from which, seemingly, no pop fly or frozen rope could escape. Its pocket was "Sure-Grip," its webbing cunningly braided, its immense thumbhole equipped with a little strap around which I could curl my thumb—so that I could never drop my glove inadvertently. I loved my glove. It had served me well in battles against Bill and Bobby. This was its debut appearance on Broadway.

Just before the game started that day, there had been a hasty conference between Fin and Kiegel over "what to do with Benjamin." We only had nine players, so they had to put me somewhere in the field. I had brandished my new glove flagrantly while they conferred, trying to convey the message that this was a new Benjamin they were dealing with, properly equipped at long last and ready to flag down everything that came my way. The decision, during which no one even looked my way or noticed that I had a glove at all, was to put me where Fin could baby-sit me. I went where I was told. I was a team guy all the way.

My glove had, somehow, missed one pop-up, but that—I decided—was a moment of stage fright. I would've caught the second pop—it was in my sights and virtually nestled in my Sure-Grip pocket—if Fin hadn't horned in and snatched it away. That had been my out, probably my only chance in the whole game to do something right and vindicate my invitation. Fin had stolen my out, but I quelled my outrage. Fin, after all, had no proof that I could catch a cold.

I was up first that inning. I already had one strikeout. Aston quickly goaded me into two more strikes. The payoff pitch was on the way—straight, fat, slow, a little high.

"Swing, you stinkin' pussy! Swing!"

I did what Aston commanded. I channeled my hatred into the bat and chopped viciously at the ball. Clunk.

Contact.

It took me a moment to open my eyes, look toward the diamond and locate the ball. I had hit it solidly, a sharp liner that skipped on the gravel behind Aston and two feet to his left. I saw Aston, his sneering face a mask of concentration, on his hands and knees, scrambling to his feet, turning toward the ball. The sand and gravel was killing the ball's momentum. If Aston moved quickly, he had time to dash into short left field, grab the ball and gun me out at first.

Fat chance.

I had only one known athletic talent. I had legs. No one in my grade, except this kid Vandermeer on a good day after a complete breakfast, could catch me. One of the games we played at recess, during sneaker season in the fall and late spring, was pom-pom poll-away, which was idiotic in its simplicity. One kid was "it." All the other kids were not. On the command "Pom-pom!" (yes, there was more to it than that, but it was too silly for any self-respecting kid over the age of six to recite the rhyme in full), everyone had to run across the playground. The "it" kid would pursue and tag as many other kids as he could before they reached safety across the playground. The tagged kids would join "it" in picking off more kids every time they crossed. The winner was the kid who lasted longest without being tagged.

Normally, a kid didn't want to be "it" at the start of a pom-pom game, because it was hard work. Despite the numbers of kids crossing, you could go through three or four gasping pom-poms before you tagged anyone who could actually help you seriously reduce the number of runners. Fat kids and slow kids were easy to tag, but they couldn't catch anyone else. They were dead weight.

I preferred to be "it," because I had legs. In pom-pom, I let the fatsos and sluggards go by. I spotted the jocks, Gunderson, Kiegel, Fin, and ran them down. Above all, I looked for Vandermeer. If I could get Vandermeer—or if he could get me—we'd end the game in four or five pom-poms. No one ever acknowledged that I was fast—it would have been bad form—but none of the jocks or alphas ever challenged me to race. They raced each other; not me.

So, when I hit the ball past Aston, it didn't matter how quickly he moved or how strong his arm. I was two steps past first base by the time Aston's throw smacked into Stinkwater's new first baseman's mitt.

"He's out! The pussy's out," roared Aston.

Someone else said, "Shut up, Asswipe."

I took first base. Stinkwater ignored me. Aston started ragging the next batter. I didn't smile. I knew every small triumph is prelude to a fresh screwup.

Next up was a kid named Kronek, dumb and burly. He swung on

the very first pitch from the neanderthal pitcher and sent a towering flyball toward left field, where Stitch patrolled. Seeing the ball leave the bat on its majestic course into the sky, I took off blazing around the bases. Voices rang in my ears as my dazzling speed carried me around second (actually a twelve-inch square of asphalt siding) and close to third before the ball could come to earth. I was on my way home before the shouts of my teammates became comprehensible.

"Jesus Christ!"

"Go back! Go back!"

"Huh?" I mouthed, stopping between third base and home.

"Back to first, stupid!"

Back to first. But why? Kronek had hit the ball.

"Go back! You dipshit! Back!"

Well, okay. Fine. But I don't see why.

As I sprinted back across third base and toward second, just avoiding being tripped by Aston, I saw Stitch's throw preceding me, across the diamond, to Stinkwater, who snatched the ball from the air, stomped on first base and yelled, "Yer out!"

"Yer out," repeated Asswipe. "Ya stupid pussy! Jesus, what a total dipshit!"

Why? What did I do?

I obeyed the unanimous demand, from both sides, that I get the hell off the field. As I approached my team, the general sentiment I managed to derive from a hail of exasperated invective was "You didn't tag up, ya dumb stupid shit! What the hell's wrong with you? Don't you know one goddamn thing?"

Tag up?

I knew the term. In endless nights of listening to Earl Gillespie, the mellifluous voice of the Milwaukee Braves, I had heard of runners "tagging up" a thousand times, just before they took an extra base or tried to score from third on a deep fly with less than two outs. Sometimes, they "tagged up" just to "draw a throw." So I knew about tagging up. But I had never studied it in the flesh, nor had Earl Gillespie ever told me what "tagging up" was for, exactly. I figured it was one of those baseball enigmas, like the balk, the hit-

and-run, the phantom tag, whose abstrusity had no effect on the enjoyment of the game. Besides, learning baseball on the radio was nothing like live combat on the sands of the Miller School.

Fin prevented Kiegel from slugging me. Then, momentarily suspending Paladin's Code of enigmatic silence, he conducted a brief tutorial on the practice of tagging up—which turned out to be less mysterious than I had come to believe.

"Sorry," I said to Fin.

"No big deal," said Fin. "Listen, whyncha go to center field next inning?"

Maybe Fin was being nice by forgiving me. Maybe he wasn't forgiving me at all. Maybe center field was my penance.

I survived a whole inning in the center field forest without a ball being hit in my direction. In our following at bat, we forged a three-run lead, no thanks to me. I popped out to the pitcher. Next ups, a one-out looper and two infield errors loaded the bases with Publics. Fin speared a line drive for the second out. A kid named Schermerhorn, beetle-browed and prematurely pimply, bestrode the batter's box, swung late on the first pitch and creamed the ball—straight at me.

Normally, I couldn't judge a flyball to save my mother's life. The job was a little easier if the ball was a little off to my left or right. I could do some mental geometry and get myself close enough to the descent of the ball to wave at it convincingly or even bounce it off the webbing of my glove, after which I could pounce on it and fire it back to the infield before the batter made it all the way around for a home run. Your earnest near-miss was all anyone really expected of me.

But a ball hit straight at me was my worst baseball nightmare. There were no angles, no perspective, no helpful horizon. A tiny sphere, straight up, grew quickly, frighteningly larger, directly before my eyes, and I had to decide, in two or three seconds, when that sphere would enlarge to exactly the size of the Sure-Grip pocket in my Japanese baseball glove, so I could be there, on the spot, to intercept its progress. I gazed, mystified, at my dilemma. Seventeen other kids, expecting failure, glared at me. A few shouted. The Publics on base didn't hold their bases and tag up. They all headed home, knowing I'd never catch the ball.

I refused to give up hope. Someday, I knew, I would catch a fly. Maybe today. I responded to the impending ball by stumbling three steps forward. The voice of Fin rang clear in my ears.

"Noooooo!"

I backpedaled desperately, raising my gloved left hand symbolically—to represent the way a fielder would catch a fly if he knew what he was doing. This movement knocked my cap—a five-year-old Brooklyn Dodgers Roy Campanella replica cap—off my head. I continued scrambling backwards, pitching as my feet slid off rocks, yawing as my heels caught in tree roots.

The ball was in range now, but twelve feet above my outstretched glove and headed for the imaginary bleachers. If I had moved backwards at the crack of the bat, instead of forward . . .

I hit a huge root and lost my footing, landing on my tailbone just as the ball encountered its own difficulties with the center field oak trees. It clattered through a cluster of new leaves, clacked into a forked branch and arrested in mid-flight. Ten feet above me, six feet in front of me, Schermerhorn's drive hung for a second in the foliage and then dropped straight down toward the gullied dirt. Biting my lip with tailbone pain, I scrambled to a crouch and threw myself forward, reaching out to catch the ball as it descended from the battered oak.

My glove stretched. The ball plummeted. I sensed, way off on the diamond, that the runners had frozen in place.

I missed.

Two inches beyond my glove, the ball landed.

"Aw, shit."

I looked for it, ready to grab it and fling it with all my strength somewhere toward home, maybe to hold Schermerhorn to a triple. But I stopped before touching the ball.

"Huh."

The ball wasn't on the ground. As I watched, it spun to rest in the crown of my faded blue Brooklyn Dodgers Roy Campanella replica cap. I gazed perplexed at this, the oddest baseball problem I had ever encountered. I would have probably gone ahead and thrown the ball to the infield anyway, except for Earl Gillespie, who often had to fill up long, dull stretches of a Braves game with gentle memories and amusing anecdotes about the olden days of baseball. Among these hoary tales was the story of the outfielder, hopelessly chasing a bleacher-bound flyball—beyond the stretch of his glove. In desperation, the player yanked his cap from his head with his right hand, leapt, stretched and—at the last instant—snagged the drive in his cap. The umpire, scurrying into the outfield, saw the ball hit the cap, saw the fielder tumble and somersault in the grass, saw him bounce back to his feet, fumble in his cap and pull out, like a rabbit from Houdini's top hat, the ball. And the umpire, still galloping, thrust out his thumb and roared, "YERRROUT!"

Well, there was the ball in my cap. It hadn't touched the ground. Was Schermerhorn out or wasn't he?

"Hey!"

"What the hell ya doin'?" came screams from the diamond.

"Throw it! Throw it!"

I couldn't. I didn't dare move the ball. I looked to my team and opened my arms in the international symbol of befuddlement.

In a moment, questions had mingled into the expletives and curses. The entire complement of Catholics and Publics were trooping out toward me in center field, as I guarded the ball in my cap like a prairie chicken hovering over her egg, to begin one of the most prolonged and virulent arguments ever conducted on the Miller School sandlots. Lincoln had Douglas. Mozart had Salieri. Hemingway had Morley Callaghan. Earl Warren had *Brown v. Board of Education*. Fin and Stitch had Schermerhorn's home run in Benjamin's stupid Brooklyn Dodgers cap. The stupid Dodgers weren't even in Brooklyn anymore!

"Hey, way to go, Benjamin! He's out!" said Fin, when he reached the scene and assessed the situation.

"Bull*shit* he's out!" wailed Stitch.

"Bullshit he ain't!"

"Bullshit he is!"

"Bull*shit*! The ball's on the ground! That pussy didn't catch it!"

"Did, too! He caught it in his cap."

"He didn't catch it! It *fell*!"

"So?"

"So? He's out!"

"Nah. The ball never touched the ground!"

"The ball never touched the ground? Look! The ball's *on* the ground!"

"It's not on the ground. It's in the cap!"

"And the cap's on the ground!"

"But the cap's a cap. It ain't the ground!"

"What?"

"The ground is *under* the cap. The ball's in the cap. The ball is NOT on the ground."

"Oh, Jesus, Fin! But the cap was ON the goddamn ground when the ball landed in it."

"Yeah, so?"

"So he's not out!"

"Bull*shit*. He's out."

"How? How? How!"

"Hey, Benjamin!"

"Huh?"

I didn't really want to get involved. After all, I'd missed the ball. I had nothing to be proud of. Plus, as indicated by Stitch's casual adoption of Aston's coinage, I was probably going to spend the rest of my kid career in Tomah being referred to by everybody in both the parochial and the public school system as The Pussy. I suspected that this designation—although still undefined—was worse than Asswipe and Turd Man.

Fin pressed. "Where was your hat?"

"Where do you wear your damn hat?" added Stitch, testily.

"Uh. My head."

Fin turned to Stitch. "There," he said, with finality.

"There *what?*"

"There you have it."

"Have *what?*"

"Hey, Benjamin."

Why me?

"Huh?"

"You leave your hat on the ground a lot?"

"No."

"You wear it?"

"Yeah."

"On your head?"

"Uh huh."

"There you go!" said Fin to Stitch.

Stitch was turning beet-livid. "What the *hell* you talkin' about?"

Everyone was gathered round now, intent on the argument, muttering gutturally with each riposte. A few Publics glowered at me like I had started this whole mess. I supposed I had, unless you wanted to blame the tree.

"Okay," said Fin, "if Benjamin kept his hat on the ground all the time, then the hat is part of the ground. But if he keeps his hat on his head, it's part of him. It ain't the ground. The ball lands on Benjamin—anywhere—that means your guy's out."

"Bullshit!"

"Hey, you can catch the ball with your cap, can't ya?"

Stitch conceded this point, but bellowed back, "But only if you're holding your cap!"

"Bullshit. Who says?"

"I say!"

"Who the hell are you?"

"Well, it's my field!"

"Bullshit it's your field. You don't own this field."

"Neither d'you, catlicker!"

The argument continued, wandering thus extemporaneously, with ritualized but colorful ejaculations, for another twenty minutes. After the first ten, the debate broke up spontaneously into small group discussions, with Catholics and Publics vehemently exploring the labyrinthine channels of one of baseball's deepest metaphysical riddles. Where does the individual self end and the ground begin? Eventually, each kid had flung his glove on the ground at least twice. Several shoving incidents had almost broken into fisticuffs, and Aston had taken the opportunity to call me a pussy to my face roughly 425 times. I was ready to break into bitter tears and go home when Stinkwater interjected a fresh issue.

"Shit. It's gittin' late," he said.

"It's gonna git dark," said someone else.

"Goddamn Benjamin," added Aston.

Suddenly, spurred by expediency, Fin and Stitch joined hands and leapt the epistemological chasm. They devised a hasty compromise, determining that a drive that lands in a baseball cap lying on the ground can be regarded as a "ground-rule double." Schermerhorn, who was way past second base when the ball hit the oak tree, bleated in protest. But this was mere theatrics. He was tired of the argument, too. He sighed, trotted to the infield, took his base and, in a dizzying minute, the game was restored. As the Publics headed toward the backstop, I overheard Aston arguing with Stitch that a ball landing in a cap should only be a ground-rule double if the cap belonged to "somebody who can catch the ball, not some pussy who's scared shitless of the ball and falls on his ass every time the goddamn ball comes in his direction—Jesus! What a gyp!" Based on my history, I couldn't help seeing the merit in this point.

We managed to squeeze in two more innings before darkness fell and the spring chill swept down the hill on a twenty-mile-an-hour north wind. Schermerhorn's ground-rule double ended up sparking a five-run rally that put us several runs down. Around the backstop, feeling responsible for the downturn in our fortunes, I kept a low profile among my fellow Catholics. Notwithstanding the daily example of Jesus' love for the diseased, disgusting, downtrodden, drummed into all of us by the dread Sister Mary Ann, no one offered me solace. I was shunned. On the other hand, no one tossed me to the sand and started kicking my head. I counted my blessings.

The tension around the backstop got a little worse in the inning after the cap incident, when I got to bat for the duration of a single swing. I hit a weak one-hopper to second base that turned out to be the third out. In the last inning, with Overacker, Gunderson, Fin and Kiegel batting in succession, and the Publics' left fielder losing a routine fly in the twilight, we scratched back miraculously to a one-run lead. But in these games, runs came easy, and one run up was as good as six runs down, especially when Kiegel, who roamed left field like an ambulatory Electrolux, had to leave. If he wasn't home by dark, to bed down a half-dozen horses, lock up the chicken coop and do his homework, his old man would strap him 'til he couldn't sit down. Since Turd Man had been summoned home to supper by his sister just after the cap incident, we were down to seven players. We abandoned right field and, with a fatalistic sigh, Fin sent the third baseman, Four-Eyes Fuchs, to Kiegel's post in left field. Fuchs and I constituted the entire outfield defense—a recipe for disaster. Fuchs could catch the ball, but he was slow and couldn't see much of anything six feet out from his nose. I was a gazelle with eyes like a falcon, but my hands were concrete and my glove was a sieve.

Luckily, the descending darkness was as hard on batters as it was on fielders. The Publics managed to load the bases on a swinging bunt and two errors. But Overacker, who was pitching now, struck out the weakest Public hitter and Fin saved the tying run by some-how stabbing a looper hit straight over third base.

None of this defensive heroism mattered, however, because the next hitter was Stitch, with the bases loaded. Stitch, besides having the physique of a grown man, including armpit hair and the begin-nings of a mustache, could see in the dark. He strode to the plate twisting the bat handle, spitting in the sand and smirking at Over-acker. I could see this happening; Four-Eyes Fuchs had no clue. I looked over. Fuchs was adjusting his glasses. I looked at Stitch. He brandished his bat and took Overacker's first pitch.

"Too stinkin' low, rag-arm," said Stitch. "Get it up."

Overacker nodded. Like all of us, he knew we wouldn't survive

Stitch's ups. Stitch hadn't made an out for the whole game. None of us could remember the last time Stitch made an out. We all just slouched in the field, crestfallen—even Fin—awaiting the inevitable and hoping Stitch's game-winning rocket wouldn't kill one of us. Overacker had stalled as much as possible, even starting Stitch with that clearly unsatisfactory pitch, hoping for the air to become so black that even Stitch's owl vision couldn't penetrate it. But nightfall had settled into a translucent gloom. Everybody could still see Stitch, looming over home plate, brandishing his bat—and Stitch could see the ball. Winding up in a slight hunch, ready to duck, Overacker delivered Stitch's pitch.

Stitch's shoulders tightened. His hips shifted forward, one beat early. A hesitation in his swing hinted that, for a second, he hadn't seen the ball coming off Overacker's hand. Still, he connected, resoundingly. Stationed just to the left of the leftmost oak tree in center field, I saw the ball jump off Stitch's bat. It wasn't one of his moon shots, just a long, humpbacked line drive toward left field. At the crack of the bat, I started running toward the ball—mainly as a demonstration to everyone else of my sincerity. Fortunately, this was Fuchs's play, if he could possibly catch it, which no one expected. If ever there was a decisive hit, here it was, rising up the Miller School hill, trailing smoke, hooking ever so slightly toward center. As I dashed ostentatiously into left-center field, I cast a glance at Fuchs, pushing his glasses up on his nose and shuffling irresolutely to his right. His body was bent, as though hunkering would help his cloudy eyes see through the dusk. Fuchs was out of the play, a reality enforced by the cries that suddenly exploded from the infield.

"Fuchs! Get it!"

"Fuchs! To your right!"

"Fuchs! Run! Fuchs!"

"Fuchs! You four-eyed fuck!" This last from Feeney, the only kid in our class with the temerity to shout the f-word in the presence of St. Mary's Church.

With Fuchs feckless in the corner of my eye, I followed the flight of the ball, which seemed to glow in the dark. It was curving more toward center. It was moving, fatedly, across my path. Unless tripped by a boulder, foiled by a gully, hobbled by an oakroot, I could reach this ball.

In my whole baseball career, I had caught perhaps ten flyballs— out of several hundred hit my way—each a drifting butterfly hit gently to where I stood. I had never made a difficult catch of any kind, and this drive, off the bat of Stitch, the Mickey Mantle of seventh-grade Tomah, was the toughest I had ever addressed. This was the sort of hit to which I had always—wisely—responded by ducking and waving a pantomime glove as the ball whistled past. A baseball could put you in an iron lung.

Nonetheless, I ran, devouring the distance with fluid grace, the fastest kid in my class (except maybe for Vandermeer). I ran because a conviction was forming in my brain, an unprecedented notion. Somewhere between the crack of Stitch's bat and the moment I un-seeingly, instinctively leapt a leg-crippling six-inch ditch between center field and left, bringing me within ten yards of Stitch's ball, it occurred to me that I had nothing to fear.

The ball was not going to kill me. A baseball, after all, was less dangerous than a Schwinn. The only part of me it was likely even to touch—if I could reach it—was my hand, which was safely engulfed in my beloved Japanese fielder's mitt. I was chasing this ball with the only talent in my barren arsenal of athletic weapons. Speed.

As I ran to the ball, I was swept over by a sensation I had never before felt on a playground or ballfield among kids my own age. Suddenly, inexplicably, I was confident.

Fear is every kid's co-pilot. Every kid starts out life small, vul-nerable, ignorant and incompetent. If he survives the reckless oblivion of infancy, his first sentient response to reality is an over-whelming desire to find the nearest available womb and crawl inside with a comic book and a bottle of Yoo-Hoo. Other kids, if they're normal, exacerbate this private terror, by demanding that a kid per-form athletic tasks he has never learned—to do it immediately, to do it well and to do it with a swaggering display of self-assurance alien to the fear throbbing in his bosom. And if he falters, either in performance or bravado, or simply obeys his fear and declines to take the test, fear wins out. The other kids seize the advantage. They sublimate their own fear by tormenting the coward.

Meanwhile, back at the Miller School sandlot, my latest test was imminent. To everyone, in an instant, it became clear that I was the only kid on the field who could reach Stitch's ball. Aston's cry emerged above all the others, piercing and profane.

"Fall, pussy!"

I would not fall. My feet were quick, my ankles strong. My eyes cut through the evening gloom and saw the ball. For a moment, for the first time, I felt fearless. The ball was inches away, spinning into a blur and humming like a Red Chinese mortar shell. I stretched, almost overrunning the ball. I flicked open my glove, and heard Stitch's game-winning drive snap into the pocket of my glove, sharply, an echoing impact that silenced every stunned kid on the Miller School sandlot—except Fin, who shouted:

"L'kOUT!"

Fuchs had never seen the ball. But he could see me, and as he spied me flying toward left field, he broke into a loping run—straight at me—guilty for his astigmatism, desperate to pitch in, hopeful of finding the ball somewhere in my vicinity.

He crashed into me, at full gallop, as the ball met my glove. Fuchs's impact jarred us both to our heels, but I held on, held tight, held maniacally to the ball—for one second, two seconds. Then I saw Fuchs's glasses, floating before my eyes, falling toward the rocks, certain to break, leaving Fuchs sightless and ridiculous. Fuchs, whose life since kindergarten had been a purgatory of cracked lenses, taped bridges, lost nosepads, bent frames, mangled earpieces, bat jokes, Helen Keller references and exasperated parents, uttered a bleat of painful portent that began with, "My gl—" Empathy seized me. With my bare hand, I reached out to grab Fuchs's precious glasses, snatching them, saving them, holding them aloft as I tumbled to the ground. And I forgot, just long enough, the ball, which trickled from my glove as I slammed to the gravel, tore my pants and ripped a flap of skin off my knee.

By the time Stitch and all the other runners had rounded the bases, and everyone else had poured uphill to sort out the collision, there was no question that I had failed to hold the ball long enough for the out. My previous record convicted me. Fuchs was unanimously awarded an "E" for effort. He didn't thank me for saving his glasses. Aston took the opportunity to declare me a pussy one last time before everyone dispersed, disappearing quickly and convivially into the night. I limped into nightfall by myself.

> . . . *Paladin, Paladin,*
> *Far, far from home.*

Next day at St. Mary's, our grade coped silently with defeat, except for an obligatory undertone of grumbling about how Benjamin had blown a routine fly and booted the game. Even this conversation had dissipated by the afternoon recess, when we played a little listless softball and then crept back into school at the toll of the bell.

I noticed Fin beside me. Expecting another round of recrimination, I started to shear off to the edge of the crowd. Fin stopped me with a hand on my shoulder. "Hey."

I bent him a sullen ear.

"Yesterday," said Fin.

"Whut?"

"Nice catch."

Fin paused, and let me pass through the doorway first.

PART V

"Tackle"

Grass's last gasp is a burst of vibrant denial. While trees obey autumn's warning, quietly shed their calico leaves and withdraw from life, the grass explodes in desperate greenery. At the end of Waunona Way, where I played football in eighth grade, the field was juicy with rain and rank with stubborn verdure. When I ran, I went high-legged and springy, else the Triffid grass would tangle my sneakers and cramp my style. When I crashed to earth in a tackler's embrace, we both bounced harmlessly and came up smeared with meadow.

We played there—me and Blomeier and Giles Hamilton, fat Timmy and huge Herbert—'til frost had scourged the weeds and winter had edged them in brown. Next fall, the grass was back but we were gone, all of us in high school.

But I still had football—mostly underneath the mercury vapor light in front of Scott's house on Lakeview Avenue. There wasn't any grass to break our falls, but we didn't fall that often. It wasn't tackle; it was touch.

Scott and his brother Jake had invented a game suited to that stretch of brightly lit street, called two-hand-touch passball. Because passball was half-basketball—with give-and-go's, post-ups and fast breaks—it thrived on a narrow field with small teams. Depending on the available bodies, we went two-on-two or three-on-three: Scott and Jake, Dick, Keener, Schuster, Blumreich, Barry Chase and sometimes the Morton brothers from up the block.

We only played at night, usually after the game. On a Friday night, we'd pile into Dick's Chevy and go off to historic Breese Stevens Field, to watch our high school team get bludgeoned by East or Beloit, and then we went to McDonald's, parked there with the heater on and the windows frosting over. Burgers and fries and Beatles on the radio. After, we'd go to Scott's and start a game of passball, just when the neighbors were turning off Carson and going to sleep.

It was football in a minefield. If you didn't remember the sewer grate next to Scott's driveway, you could mangle a knee. There was a flagstone wall on one sideline that could scrape your flesh right down to the bone. The mercury vapor bulb, outglowing every light on Lakeview and turning your skin a sickly lavender, was at mid-field, leaving both end zones in purple gloom under drooping trees that clawed at passes and blinded receivers. You had to catch the ball by ear and feel, with Schuster's finger in your mouth.

And you had to stay alert. The neighbors didn't like our noise. 'Round midnight, one would call the cops, who'd creep up on us sirenless and stealthy—then never lay a finger on us. Keener or Blumreich would shout "Cheezit!" and we would bolt, plunging through gardens, whanging into woodsheds, tripping over tricycles and waking up a square mile of dogs. And laughing like criminals.

By the time I was a senior, we were outgrowing passball. At most, we played a game or two, without reverence for the tradition, and thoughtless to what came next in life. It didn't occur to me that this was my last gasp of freelance play.

The last gasp for all of us.

Blomeier's Last Choke

Football is a Catholic thing.

This intimation dawned on me—though faintly—in seventh grade, when Overacker, the handsomest of the thugs in my class at St. Mary's, somehow requisitioned one afternoon's use of the high school football field, down at the Monroe County Fairgrounds. His plan was a showdown between us and the Publics. With a Maryknoll zeal that belied his phlegmatic norm, Overacker immediately began recruiting gridders. Unlike Fin, Feeney or any of our other more socially astute alpha males, Overacker was blithely indiscriminate. He buttonholed kids who, normally, never got picked to play any game, who cringed and fled at the mere sight of a ball—kids like Nordling, Gertz, Butterball. He even considered Mikey the retard and Bissell, who was terrified of his own shadow.

Overacker's egalitarianism, however, was both appropriately catholic, and Catholic. Football wasn't finicky, fastidious and elitist, like basketball. It wasn't cerebral, sophisticated and selective, like baseball. Football, like the Vatican, wanted everybody. Without scruple, it craved bodies, the healthy and halt, the mighty and the lame, sinners, pariahs, runts, creeps and cretins. Only after it had rounded up and baptized everybody would it sit back, sift through and hand out assignments. One kid would be ordained quarterback.

Others would be altar boys, the runners and receivers. The lesser souls—the linemen—would sing in the choir, or shuffle humbly in and out of the Mass bearing cruets and patens and candle-snuffers. And everyone, like Crusaders battling heresy and iniquity, played defense. Even the benchwarming congregation, banished from the field, couldn't just go home and watch Sergeant Bilko. They knelt, in the rain and wind, uttering the ritual responses— "Hold that line!" *"Kyrie eleison!"* "Block that kick!" *"Et cum spiritu tuo!"*—shivering, waiting. Injury and pain, anathema in other sports, were sacraments in football. Pain exalted the game. Suffering and sacrifice, crucifixion and gore, were equally sacred at Notre Dame de Paris and Notre Dame de South Bend. When one player went down, clutching his leg, a bone protruding hideously from his flesh, another soul was called. And he must be present in body and soul, must be ready to rise from the pew, crash the transept and stand in for his martyred teammate.

St. Mary's School conditioned me for football. In endless rounds of drill and memorization, it taught me to be selfless, submissive and redundant. Planted every morning for six years in front of a life-size crucifix—the dead Jesus nailed on planks, crowned with thorns and gushing blood—I learned the beauty of violence and the virtue of suffering. I exulted in agony. Once, playing in the enormous yard in front of my grandfather T.J.'s house, I was trying to tackle a twice-my-size neighborhood kid named Senzie as he galloped toward a touchdown. I clung to his hips, delaying his progress while awaiting the arrival of other defenders. With each step he took, his heels swung upward and cracked into my chin, clattering my teeth and rattling my brain inside my head like loose seeds in a dry gourd—and I couldn't remember feeling anything quite so blissful and worthy. I knew I was burning every twig of my pitiful strength for the sake of my fellow man, doing the right thing and—for my efforts—getting kicked in the face at a rate of 120 times a minute. It was as though, in that moment, I had found the meaning of life. I was rewarded in my rapture when my hands lost their grip on Senzie's hips and I slid down his legs, pinioning his knees and bringing him, with a twist and a curse, to earth just as my teammates arrived at last and piled on top of me.

I loved this game.

Overacker's Catholics vs. Publics Super Bowl at the fairgrounds was my first chance to play real football—with grass and dirt and tackling and pain—among my classmates at St. Mary's. Until then, all we ever did at school was recess football. The playground was paved, so we played two-hand touch.

The difference between tackle football and touch football is the difference between kick-boxing and pattycake. In touch, rather than a pell-mell plunge toward the narcotic catharsis of aggravated assault, pass rushing was a halfwitted nursery rhyme.

"One-apple, two-apple, three-apple, four-apple . . ."

There was no running the ball in two-hand touch. Three out of four passes fell incomplete. Blocking was desultory—a simian facsimile of ballroom dancing, between kids who couldn't foxtrot and never tried very hard, for fear of falling down, ripping their good school clothes, bloodying their knees and facing retribution when they got home. In touch football at recess, the pecking order prevailed rigidly. On each team, only two or three players mattered. The quarterback was always Fin or Overacker. The receivers, regardless of whether they could catch the ball or not, were always Kiegel and Gunderson, plus Turd Man Erdmann and sometimes—even though everybody hated him—Koscal, because he was too good to suppress. Four or five guys ended up playing pitch-and-catch up and down the playground. The rest of us milled. If you asked Fin or Overacker for some job to do other than shadow blocking and mock rushing, they'd say, "Go long." Then, if you went long, six or seven other superfluous kids, eager for a break in the routine, would join you. You'd all lumber along in a sort of ragged herd, zigging and jostling downfield, as inseparable as a blackbird flock, each kid waving an arm and lying through his teeth.

"I'm open! I'm open!"

Football was a change of season, inevitable and imperceptible, like leaf abscission or snow flurries. In August, when school started,

I passed by front yards where kids were still playing Wiffleball, still bouncing a rubber-coated baseball off the stoop, empty lots where kids were still brandishing Louisville Sluggers and announcing their alter egos on the Milwaukee Braves.

"I'm Henry Aaron!"

"I'm Eddie Mathews!"

"I'm Adcock!"

The Braves were a fading power then, all hitting and not much pitching, and every September, they fell out of the running in the National League, allowing our devotion to wander. There was harvest in the country and drizzle in the air. Suddenly, Woodruff's Store had more football cards than baseball cards next to the cash register. Bill Wade. Hugh McElhenny. Chuck Bednarik. I'd see a couple kids tossing a football on my way home from school. A few days later, among the rocks and burrs at the Miller School baseball diamond, twenty kids would be mauling one another over a frayed pigskin.

By October, every store window downtown would be elaborately painted with a tempera cartoon, predicting and depicting the victory of the Tomah High School football Indians over the weakest possible Homecoming opponent in the South Central Conference, usually Mauston or Nekoosa. On a Saturday before that big game, I would walk downtown to see the student artwork in the windows. Summer's brief desperate month of humidity was a memory. The sky was a turquoise scrim splashed with dabs of white and framed in garish edges of maple red, elm yellow and oak umber. The air was still sharp from a morning frost. At my feet, harlequin leaves fluttered and crunched. Over radios that crackled from porches or car windows while husbands cleaned eaves troughs, hung storm windows, raked leaves and flushed radiators, snatches of the broadcast from Madison—the Badgers vs. Michigan or Illinois or Indiana—accompanied my excursion.

When I finally began my kid football career the way God and Bronko Nagurski intended, on grass, in dungarees and sneakers and a food-stained sweatshirt, without a pad, a helmet, a mouthguard or a cup, I was transported. Here was a game where you could be a human sonnet, leaping, flying, snatching victory from the sky, or you could be a bulldozer in a ditch, spewing mud, strewing grubs and crushing vegetation. You could step on kids, paint yourself in green stains, tear off people's clothes and ruin your own. You could carry the ball or steal it. You could kick the ball, catch the ball, drop the ball or just knock the ball around. You could be frustrated by slipping on the grass or fumbling a lateral, only to exorcise your failure on the very next play by driving your shoulder, full-speed, into another kid's gut and planting him on his bony ass.

One year after my parents broke up, we were living in T.J.'s big house way out on the end of Superior Avenue where the street turned back into Highway 12 and headed to La Crosse. Despite his tendency toward tyranny, T.J. never objected to kids using his yard for football. It was a spectacular yard, as big as a regular football field, edged by elm trees but otherwise uncluttered. If I wanted a game, I simply had to take my place on T.J.'s epic lawn and start punting a football back and forth. By and by, some kid from a nearby house, Hinkley, who lived across Superior Avenue, or one of the Crams, whose house on T.J.'s newly subdivided back pasture was still barely half finished, or one of the Klapp brothers down the street, or Senzie, a natural athlete, lean and wiry, would join me, followed by all the others, followed by choose-ups and wholesale mayhem. The only fixed rule we ever observed was no equipment. Every now and then, a kid would proudly sport a set of shoulder pads his big brother had worn for high school football or a plastic helmet his idiot father had bought him for Christmas from Montgomery Ward's. We'd tell the kid he either dumps the equipment or he doesn't play. This prejudice against gear wasn't because we were chicken. We expected to get torn up, bashed or bruised when we played football, because the honor of the game required that each kid's only weapon was his flesh. All the paraphernalia of organized football—the pads, the helmets, the cleats and gloves—were not, to us, protective. They were the tools of cowardice. One kid with pads and helmet was like a drunk driver in a school zone. He could break

your arm, bust open your skull—kill someone—and come away un-
scathed. No fair.

In seventh grade, when Overacker announced the big game of
tackle at the fairgrounds, I was ready. For two or three autumns, I
had bled all over T.J.'s lawn. I was eager for the big time. My forte
was defense. This was mostly because the other players tended to be
bigger than me, and they wouldn't give me the ball. But in tackle,
you don't need the ball. Football is the only sport with balls where
you can end up in the Hall of Fame without ever handling the ball,
except by accident. Vince Lombardi never got the ball at Fordham.
Big Daddy Lipscomb hated the ball. If somebody had given Dick
Butkus the ball, he would've broken it. I was the seventy-five-pound
version of Lombardi, Lipscomb and Butkus. I didn't want the ball.
I wanted release. I was also, usually, the fastest midget on the field.
Even better, I was annoyingly stupid. After the big kid with the ball
had knocked over, stepped on, stiff-armed or outrun every other kid
in his way, I was still on my feet, ducking and scooting until I could
glom on to the runner, cling to his clothes, ignore his forearm
whacking my skull, tangle his feet, and drag him to the grass.

"You little cocksucker!"

That's all he could do. Call me a cocksucker. I didn't even know
what a cocksucker was. If this had been a normal kid interchange,
this lead-footed clod would have beaten me senseless for laying even
a finger on his inviolate form. In football, I got to jump him, trip
him, claw grooves into his skin and stretch his shirt until it looked
like Kate Smith's nightgown, and then knock him off his feet. In
football, I charged headlong into bullies, took their churning knees
in my chops, hung on for dear life, and brought them down like
cardboard skyscrapers in a Godzilla flick. Sometimes, I even made
crashing noises as the monsters bit the sod. They couldn't retaliate
because tackling wasn't just allowed in football. It was required. It
was heroic.

Tackling was payback for my whole childhood.

Alas, when Overacker's big game rolled around early in my
seventh-grade autumn, on a perfectly manicured emerald field not

yet trampled by the varsity wars of Tomah High School, the whole exercise was largely a letdown. There wasn't terribly much tackling, by me or anybody else. This was probably because baseball determined both teams' roster choices. The best baseball player on each team, Fin for us, Stitch for the Publics, got to be quarterback. In Fin's case, this was a felicitous perquisite. Fin was an able passer blessed with a primary receiver, Overacker, who had several natural gifts. Overacker could catch the ball consistently even though he was missing one finger, and he tended to be wide open all the time, mainly because he would summarily flatten any kid who tried to follow him downfield. Fin and Overacker, sensing the Publics' reluctance to impede Overacker's pass patterns, connected repeatedly on long touchdowns. Stitch, although the scariest slugger in either school, could not translate his baseball dominance to the position of quarterback. Passing the ball constantly, in a personal effort to keep pace with his archrival, Fin, Stitch launched an endless rain of wobbly ducks into the sky. They fell to earth we never knew where. They rarely reached a Public receiver. Our side steadily built up a seven-touchdown lead and the running game, on both sides, was forgotten. With this development, I had few opportunities to tackle brutes, rip my clothes and win my stripes for school and Savior. In the entire two hours before we all gave up and straggled home, I experienced only one moment of distinction, in a play that was both unexpected and perplexing.

At the very beginning of the game, the opening kickoff bounced to my feet. I gazed at it with my usual air of detachment. The ball and I were veritable strangers to each other. After three or four years of the other kids never throwing me the ball, never handing me the ball, never letting me touch the ball, I had naturally begun to treat it like the Sacred Host, which could only be handled by a priest or—in the case of a fire in the Tabernacle—the oldest nun available (and only then with a whole lot of praying, genuflecting and self-effacement). So, here I was, standing on the ten-yard line at the fairgrounds, as football's Body of Christ rolled sideways and bumped into the toes of my Keds.

The Publics, having kicked the ball, were charging downfield *en masse*. I waited for some priestly teammate, Fin, Overacker, Kiegel, Gunderson—someone!—to grab the ball and plunge into the stampede of Publics.

Nothing.

I caught a glimpse of the fast-encroaching Publics, who were led by Aston, the cherubic sadist who gleefully exploited every chance he had to torment me. I felt glad that I wasn't responsible for the ball. I waited.

Still, no one seized the moment.

Worse, I sensed no movement, by one of our customary leaders, toward the now inert ball. It just lay there, on the grass, at my feet. "Wilson," it read. I felt a vague temptation, a sinful tingle in my fingers, to pick up the ball myself. I stifled this.

I peeked at the Publics. They had crossed our forty-yard line. They stretched from sideline to sideline like a John Ford Indian charge, puffing, grunting and squalling homicidally. Somebody, it occurred to me, better do *something*—fast!

"Jesus, Benjamin! Run it!"

Who said that?

I looked.

Five yards away, Overacker was glaring at me. "Come ON!" he shouted.

Me?

Some new sensation, like a two-hundred-volt shock or a wet sock across the eyes, slapped me. I had permission. It was First Holy Communion, only with a football. I didn't check again with Overacker, who might have already repented his impetuosity. I didn't look to Fin, whom I expected to be pale with alarm and crying out, "No, no, no! Not him!" I couldn't wait any longer. The footsteps of the Publics were thumping in my ears.

I snatched up the football, tucked it under my arm and looked downfield. Aston was five yards away, charging, smirking.

"G'na kill you, dickface!"

While Aston swelled before my eyes, I could almost feel every drop of my blood evacuating from my brain, my face, my heart, my kidneys, and rushing, panic-stricken, to my legs. My trusty legs— the fastest (or maybe the second fastest) in the seventh grade. Acting on instincts I had never previously employed, I eluded Aston—effortlessly. I sidestepped his charge and fended him off with a hand to his face. He left a smear of surprised spit on my hand as I slid to my left and headed upfield. Another Public, florid and freckled, flew at me, but I shifted right, made him miss, and left him tumbling to the grass with arms full of air. This was getting weird. Another Public thundered toward me, large and confident. But my feet danced, as though possessed of a power unconnected with mind or body, and the Public fell aside, having barely touched me. Stitch loomed in my path. I foresaw doom. My left hip swiveled left, my feet swerved right, Stitch believed my hip. Suddenly, Stitch was gone.

Where?

I'd gotten past Stitch. How?

Curiouser and curiouser.

I dared not ponder miracles. More Publics were encroaching. One by one, they fell behind me, inexplicably. I zigged, I zagged, they stumbled, they tumbled. I made it past the fifty-yard line and only two or three Publics remained. What had I done?

Something new.

I outshuffled the last remaining Publics, almost easily by now, surefootedly—and I had only the end zone in view. No more shifting and shucking. I was on my way. A touchdown! Wow! My legs, still operating independent of my brain, turned on the juice—too late. Stitch had recovered and lumbered up behind me. He caught me at the Publics' twenty-five and pinned my legs. I went down. Several Publics jumped on top of me.

"Hey. Nice goin'," said Overacker, as I emerged from the pile.

Of course, I never carried the ball again that game. After that day, a year went by before anyone let me touch a football in serious combat. By then, I was out of St. Mary's and I never saw Overacker again. We had finally fled Tomah for the greener pastures of Madison.

I was an eighth grader at the Franklin School, on the unfashionable south side, and my best friend—who lived upstairs from us on Simpson Street—was a kid named Blomeier.

Almost as soon as he spotted me, one day in July, Blomeier had adopted me as his sidekick. I was amazed and flattered by Blomeier's attention. A stocky kid with a buzzcut, Blomeier was a major social force in our neighborhood. Blomeier represented, to me, a novel concept in human relations. He cultivated people and arranged them rationally on a scale of significance.

Blomeier was also the first intentionally charming kid I'd ever encountered. The first time we met, he questioned me like a personnel manager at a job interview. He seemed captivated by the story of my life. I told him about Tomah, my grandparents, St. Mary's. I confessed, bashfully, that I got pretty good grades in school and he approved of this. He told me about his favorite authors and lent me several books. I treated them like required reading. I told him my favorite book was *20,000 Leagues Under the Sea,* and he nodded enigmatically. Blomeier showed me his collection of plastic model World War II airplanes, brightly and weirdly painted. He never followed the conservative painting instructions specified by Aurora or Revell. His British Spitfire was a striped masterpiece in gold and red. His P-38 Lightning was a poem in metallic blue and matte green with silver highlights. I emulated Blomeier, adopting his hobby and trying out ever more daring variations on his painting style. Blomeier introduced me to the best kid sites in the neighborhood. There was a house on the end of our block, abandoned by the American Legion, with all its windows intact, and a kid could sneak inside through a loose basement window. Before it was finally razed and replaced by another cookie-cutter fourplex, we had roamed every inch of the empty house and salvaged any objects inside that seemed to have even the remotest value. Blomeier hid two stolen copies of *Cavalier* magazine in a cubbyhole on the second floor, but only let me see them once. On our bikes, we rode up and down Waunona Way, and all the side streets. He knew where every significant kid lived and he told me their names, but I forgot most of them. Blomeier, although barely thirteen years old, was interested in rich people. He knew about all the important plutocrats on Waunona Way, how they made their money, what cars they drove, what size engines they had on their cabin cruisers and where they went on vacation. In Tomah, I didn't know many people who went beyond their own backyard for vacation, much less anyone who ventured so far they needed an airplane to get there. But Waunona Way was full of people who routinely spent two weeks, or even three, at Mount Rushmore, or Yosemite, or even in Mexico.

On one trip down Waunona Way, almost two miles from Simpson Street, Blomeier stopped and assumed an attitude of reverence beside a mailbox that read "Hamilton." The Hamiltons always went to their summer home in Door County, so they weren't around now, explained Blomeier. Otherwise, Blomeier pointed out, he would probably be hanging out all summer with Giles Hamilton, the younger of the two scions of the Hamilton fortune—which had been earned through the manufacture of luggage racks for automobiles. "The most extensive line of luggage racks in the whole industry," recited Blomeier.

"Gee," I said. "No foolin'?" I had no idea anyone could possibly make a fortune from luggage racks. But now I knew, and I was impressed.

Suggesting a stroke of fortune that was outright providential, Blomeier noted that Giles Hamilton was our age. Moreover, he was in our grade—at the Franklin School. "He could have gone to prep school," said Blomeier.

"Wow," I said. I had never heard of prep school, but I figured it was like military school, where my mother kept threatening to ship me. I didn't ask Blomeier for a clarification. He had awed me with his worldly wherewithal, and I had been struggling since I met him to conceal my rural ignorance, while learning from his example.

Blomeier's family and mine, plus Grady the landlord and a young couple with a new baby upstairs in Apartment 4, occupied one in a string of fourplex apartment buildings that had filled the weedy flats between the Beltline highway and the shade-dappled lakeside affluence of Waunona Way. One street closer to Waunona Way lived the Kratzenberg twins, Mark and Gary. The Kratzenberg twins were also Blomeier followers.

Mark and Gary, also in our grade at Franklin, seemed to spend most of their time sitting around their yard, waiting for Blomeier to come by. If Mark and Gary weren't waiting for Blomeier, it seemed to me, they were waiting on him. If we'd be hanging out in one of the neighborhood orchards, eating green apples and reading comic books, Blomeier might ask Mark or Gary to bike over to Four Lane, the local variety store, to buy a quart of Coke. Not only did the appointed Kratzenberg immediately hustle off to Four Lane, he'd use his own money to buy the Coke. And Blomeier would drink most of it. This kind of deference was degrading, I thought, but it was Mark and Gary's own doing. Too eager for his approval, the Kratzenberg twins had lost Blomeier's respect.

Not like me.

When school started at the end of August, I finally laid eyes on Giles Hamilton. I waited at the corner of Simpson Street and Hoboken Road for the school bus and climbed aboard with Blomeier. Without comment, he left me to sit beside Giles Hamilton. Blomeier didn't introduce us, but I sensed it was too soon for such formalities. I rode to school that morning beside some strange kid with an oversized head and an air of menace. I later found out I had taken the seat almost never occupied on our school bus, next to Rudy Martin. No kid at Franklin School ever ventured that close to Rudy Martin except by accident. No kid ever assigned a school locker on either side of Rudy's school locker ever actually used the locker, for fear of encountering Rudy. If your locker was next to Rudy's, you just spent the whole year shlepping all your books from class to class to class. Rudy was one of those kids whose only purpose in going to school every day was to choose a victim at random in the school hallway, shove him in the chest with both hands and say, "Who you lookin' at?"

"Huh? Looking?"

Another shove, this time with sound effects, a human body crashing into steel lockers.

"You lookin' at *me*, fucker?"

This was before Travis Bickle entered the above line into the public domain.

"No, Rudy. I'm not looking at you."

Thump. Crash. A crowd gathering at a safe distance.

"You fuckin' liar. I'm gonna fuckin' kill you!"

"Rudy, look—"

Thump. Crash. Sympathy from the crowd, but no volunteers to help the victim. The Code was in effect, and each man was an island.

"What the fuck were you *sayin'* about me?"

"Saying? Me?"

Thump. Crash!

"Okay, fucker! You wanna fight?"

"What? Fight?"

Rudy was no bigger than any other kid in class, but he was a solid knot of permanently clenched muscle. He had the intellect of a pit bull on PCP and a death wish that made him invincible. His only possible future lay in violent crime. The thought of fighting Rudy Martin would have troubled Jake LaMotta.

"No, Rudy, I don't wanna f—"

At this point, Rudy would often switch from chest shoving to ear slapping. The victim's universe would begin to hum in falsetto.

"You chicken? You're fuckin' chicken, aren't ya?"

In order to deflect Rudy's attention, several kids had previously tried admitting they were chicken. There was no shame in this. However, this confession tended to strike Rudy as a license to kill. There were kids who had survived their beating after saying, "Yeah, Rudy, I guess I'm chicken," but then they spent the rest of their schooldays in a state of incontinent terror, dreading gym class and unwilling to set foot outside the school grounds in a group smaller than ten.

"Come on, Rudy. Whaddya doin'? You know I'm your friend."

Nobody was Rudy's friend. Hitler would have crossed the street if he had seen Rudy coming his way. But humoring Rudy was the only possible escape.

"What the fuck you talkin' about. You ain't my friend!"

Whack! Ow! Hmmmmmmmm.

"Hey, Rudy, just the other day, people were sayin' you're a bully. And I said to 'em, hey, Rudy ain't no bully. He's just—"

Whack! Ouch! Hmmmmmmmm.

"Who? Who said?"

"Um." You couldn't actually name someone. Rudy would hunt them down like a wolverine after a wounded bunny, and the death would haunt you for the rest of your life. Here, another diversionary tactic was necessary. Fortunately, Rudy was stupider than library paste.

"Girls. A coupla girls were sayin'—"

"Shit! Fuckin' girls! What the fuck do *they* know?"

These interchanges took place before the death of chivalry. Paladin always treated women like ladies, even whores. Especially whores! So when someone invoked girls as his critics, Rudy was stumped. While he festered with this quandary, there was a moment for the cornered kid to slip beneath Rudy's gaze and hightail it to science class. Whew.

For some reason, when I sat down beside Rudy that first day on the bus, he was in his dormant phase, grinding his molars, kneading his crotch, oblivious to society. Several weeks later, after two or three close calls, I won immunity from Rudy's malice. I accomplished this by accidentally bonding with the only person on earth Rudy feared—his brother, Rocky. Rocky was old enough to be a junior in high school, but various setbacks had slowed his matriculation. The latest, during the previous school year, happened while Rocky was showing off for a girl who purported to be a freshman at the University of Wisconsin. Rocky had totaled his motorcycle while drag-racing an eighteen-wheeler on an ice-covered highway. He had broken every bone in his body. The girl, who turned out to be a physically precocious sophomore at Central High School, had not survived. The accident made Rocky a living legend, the only human being in the world who was certifiably tougher than Rudy.

I had known hoods in Tomah, but they had claimed this designation largely through fashion. Their jackets were leather, their shoes pointy, their hair rigid and glistening with pomade. Rocky was the genuine article. The first time I had ever seen him, in my first moments in Mr. Barnett's home room, Rocky had strode up to the girl seated beside me, a lanky wisecracking black girl named Charmaine, and he had kissed her—a long, wet, noisy, interracial tongue-wrestle that had sent the classroom into an awestruck moment of pin-drop silence. By the time it ended, Charmaine's skirt was somehow bunched around her waist and Rocky was saying, "You still love me, Char?"

"Boy," said Charmaine, "you want to keep that hand, you best take it out of my pants."

I looked at the hand in Charmaine's panties, which were chartreuse. I knew somehow, without evidence, that the girls at St. Mary's had never worn chartreuse lingerie. As Rocky slid his hand from danger, slowly, down Charmaine's thin, ebony thigh, I noticed that the hand was disfigured. One finger was bent at an odd angle from the knuckle; a ridge of scar tissue ran from thumb to wrist. Later, I noticed small scars around his eyes and, when I saw him in the shower in gym class, I joined the other boys in admiring the surgical repairs on his knees, his cervical spine and down the middle of his chest. Rocky had spent more than half the previous year in the hospital, and he showed not one sign of injury or fear. He had killed a young girl in a flaming wreck, desolated her family, split open his own skull like a kicked cantaloupe and come out of it all with a song in his heart, a glint in his eye and a hand on Charmaine's ass. No wonder Rudy was scared of him.

On one of my first days at Franklin School, before I was evaluated and moved up to the "eight-one" group, I was sitting in class among the yahoos and malingerers in "eight-two." Alphabetical order had seated me next to Rocky. Mrs. Nissalke was running a grammar drill. Rocky—put on the spot by Mrs. Nissalke and in danger of losing his epic dignity—was struggling to identify the verb in a sentence. Without thinking about consequences, I whispered the verb, just loud enough for Rocky's ear. In the past, mainly to relieve the suspense, I had frequently done Overacker the same favor. Overacker had never thanked me. Rocky was different. With Rocky, an unsolicited helping hand was like Androcles yanking the thorn. Rocky got the answer right, and a smile from Mrs. Nissalke—a gesture of vital importance to Rocky, not because Mrs. Nissalke was the teacher, but because she was young, blonde, and yummy, and Rocky could readily, even realistically, picture himself mounting her in the supply closet. Rocky was the first kid I ever knew who thought about sex all the time—accurately.

After that verb, I enjoyed Rocky's protection. Rudy never messed with me, nor did anyone. My career as a grade school outcast dwindled into bittersweet memory—even before the kids at Franklin had decided what to do with me. In fact, for a while, I felt almost like an object of juvenile courtship. I had spent the summer being groomed, although obliviously, as a Blomeier protégé. Within a few weeks of the start of the school year, I had fallen into Rocky's seductive sphere. Rocky offered me the flattering attentions that an older man of the world bestows upon a promising youngster. One of his first gestures was to share with me some of the favorite volumes in his private library, a dog-eared collection of mildly pornographic pulp paperbacks—which were the only books Rocky ever allowed in his school locker. One day, between classes, he opened a Grace Metalious novel to the page on which a vixen named Doris hiked her skirt, dropped her drawers and presented herself rearward to her lusty male companion. Until this object lesson in kinetic anatomy, I had been perplexed by the seemingly impractical disparity between male and female in this region of the body. Why, I wondered, were girls plagued with all this superfluous tissue and wasted motion? Under the deft command of Grace Metalious, however, Doris's derriere assumed a vibrant and playful life of its own. Doris's lyrical buttocks wiggled, winked, mamboed and moued mischievously, demonstrating to me, more clearly than any previous example, not only the utility but the veritable superiority of the female bottom, over the male, for almost any purpose other than—perhaps—the hundred-yard dash. Forever after, thanks to Rocky (and Grace), I came to watch the departure of any girl, that fine rhythmic flow toward the horizon, as a silent song of the body electric. I suspect it was not Rocky's intent to arouse in me such artsy perceptions, but I nonetheless remained beholden to him.

For a while, despite the blandishments of Blomeier—who gradually acquainted me with what he regarded as the Franklin School elite, which included the princely Giles Hamilton—Rocky proved a far more alluring companion. He belonged clearly to an older set of kids, who circulated in a demimonde unlike anything I had ever imagined in Tomah—even during my Fat Vinny period. Unlike Blomeier, but a lot like me, Rocky lived in single-parent chaos, dependent on an overworked, underemployed mother for his food and board, and dimly conscious of the threat of sporadic violence from an absentee dad who could show up drunk, jealous or both, at any odd moment. We both knew how that felt. Although Rocky lived on Waunona Way, by the lake, it was in a ramshackle Victorian eyesore that had long preceded the neighborhood's ascension to fashionability. Rocky's room, where he invited me several times, was a musty grotto too close to the water table, wherein his cache of forbidden treasure included a half-consumed flask of Jack Daniel's, an entire case of Lucky Strikes somehow bootlegged from the PX at Truax Field, the mangled handlebar from his totaled motorcycle, a pile of titty magazines, a shoplifted RCA Victor phonograph that played a steady stream of 45 rpm records by an obviously non–Top 40 group called Hank Ballard and the Midnighters, a .22-caliber revolver (with three chambers loaded) and several blackmail-quality Polaroids of Rocky's past girlfriends, including one—from math class—whom I recognized. Under Rocky's pedagogy, I might have eventually become a hood—started smoking, drinking, getting laid. At the very least, I stood to get unlimited motorcycle rides and a new hairstyle.

This all changed the day Mrs. Reichstag, who doubled as a math teacher and assistant principal, cornered me in the hallway just after my first month at Franklin. I labored not to look at Mrs. Reichstag's bust, which was the largest on the faculty.

"David," she said (grownups always called me David; kids treated me as though my parents had neglected to give me a first name), "we're moving you from the eight-twos to the eight-one group."

One of the things that surprised me about Franklin was the strange prestige that smart kids seemed to command because they got good grades. In Tomah, the only truly acceptable pretext for boys to go to school at all was to play sports. At Franklin, kids like Giles Hamilton, Blomeier and Danny Crawford got good grades and suffered not even a hint of ridicule. When Mrs. Reichstag abruptly bumped me onto the college-bound track, I was greeted with congratulations, even by a few kids who had been left behind in the eight-twos.

Rocky said, "Nice goin', punk. Make me proud of you."

"Huh?"

Becoming an eight-one brought Blomeier back into my life. For a while, I'd barely seen him, except on the bus. Occasionally, I'd notice him in the corridors at school, where Rudy Martin seemed to prey upon him with particular focus. Rudy responded to any hint of superiority the way a muskellunge responds to a crippled minnow. Blomeier, besides being an academic star in the eight-one group, struck a habitual attitude of grave hauteur that rankled Rudy to a fever pitch. Rudy literally prowled the halls for a sighting of Blomeier, and Blomeier, despite his every effort to placate Rudy, could only manage a wheedling condescension that further aggravated his antagonist. A day hardly passed without Blomeier absorbing a half-dozen chest-blows and locker-clangs at Rudy's mercy. I could only sympathize. No one ever interfered with one of Rudy's cross-examinations.

Once I'd cracked the eight-ones, Blomeier rediscovered me, not only owing to my improvement in status but also for the possibility that my immunity from Rudy's evil eye might rub off on him.

Rocky, no longer in class with me, would still pause in the halls to chuck me on the arm and offer an obscene remark that I usually didn't fathom until I'd passed it by the encyclopedic Charmaine for interpretation. Rocky continued to protect me—but not Blomeier—from his psychotic brother. But Rocky was gravitating away from formal education, skipping school for as much as a week at a stretch. By the end of the semester, he only came by school to harvest the occasional girl, sell black-market cigarettes or brag about the income from his various enterprises—which ranged from legitimate motorcycle maintenance to bookmaking, burglary and pandering. Rocky was a Renaissance man.

One Wednesday, with a labored offhandedness, Blomeier turned to me at the bus stop and invited me to the game.

"What game?"

"Every Wednesday, we play, down at the end of Waunona Way."

"Play what?"

"Tackle."

Something tingled in my loins.

"Okay."

That first Wednesday, on a gray day in October, Blomeier showed me to the field, down Waunona Way on our bikes, to where houses ended and vacant fields, rimmed in scrubby woods, bordered on railroad tracks and marshlands. The field, partly concealed behind a row of weed-sprung gravel piles, was a grassy bowl on a cul-de-sac. The flat playable center of the field was almost a hundred yards long and at least thirty yards wide. The grass was deep, rank, and soft. Here was T.J.'s lawn all over again.

For this Wednesday afternoon football game—like Catholics vs. Publics—admission was by invitation only. Blomeier and I arrived late, just in time for choose-ups. I recognized the players, although not entirely by name, most of them eighth graders, a few husky seventh graders—all of them among the most vigorous athletes in the neighborhood. Giles Hamilton towered above them all. Also present was a thick slogger named Sternweiss, and Wayne Westwick, who fancied himself already a ladykiller at the age of thirteen. He'd actually had a date once, with a girl. There were other kids from the bus—Stamm, Thielke, Merkle, Brusbussen, fat Timmy Tollefson, Joey Imhoff, Tony DeMarco, Huge Herbert Roth, Kunkel, Sparrow and several whose names I didn't know. The Kratzenberg twins, who operated almost entirely at Blomeier's behest, had not been included.

No one complained to see me show up. No one said, "What the hell's *he* doing here?"

This was a fresh wrinkle.

Two or three kids actually grunted out a sort of welcome. Giles Hamilton caught me for a moment in a hooded stare, appraising me from head to knees as though he'd never before seen me. I shuffled penitently. Choose-ups started, with Giles Hamilton and Sternweiss as captains. Joey Imhoff, Huge Herbert Roth, Tony DeMarco and Wayne Westwick got snatched up early. Despite the fact that I was a completely unknown factor, I was picked only third to last—probably on the theory that no matter how bad I was, I couldn't be worse than fat Timmy Tollefson and the terminally uncoordinated Brusbussen. Or, perhaps, they remembered the Danny Crawford gym class incident.

Coming to public school Franklin from parochial St. Mary's, both gym class and Danny Crawford were worlds of mystery for me. Catholic schools didn't have gym class. So the whole experience of dressing up in shorts and undershirt three times a week for adult-supervised recess, followed by every kid getting naked and taking a shower together—this was mind-boggling. Perhaps most surprising to me was that, once I was naked, other kids didn't come up to me, ridicule my penis and beat me senseless. I knew that if these kids had been Catholic, they would have tried to kill me as soon as I was naked. I knew Catholic kids. The kids in *Lord of the Flies*, I figured, were all Catholic. When I discovered, in the Franklin School locker room, the remarkable Christian restraint of public school kids naked together without ripping each other limb from limb—as I knew Catholic school kids must do if they were to retain even a shred of their self-respect—my religious faith trembled imperceptibly. I had taken my first step on the road to apostasy.

Danny Crawford was a comparable shock to my system. Like Rocky, Danny Crawford was off schedule for graduation—but for altruistic rather than criminal or recuperative reasons. Through the grapevine, I learned that Danny Crawford had been born in a middle-sized city in Georgia, and had reached school age at a time of mortal strife. Central High School in Little Rock was recently integrated in Arkansas, Martin Luther King, Jr., was beginning to make a name for himself in Alabama, and Thurgood Marshall was challenging the educational orthodoxy of the entire Jim Crow South. In this atmosphere, a little black boy walking several miles to school all alone was a target for sudden, unexplained, permanent disappearance. The only thing Danny Crawford's parents could think of to protect their two sons was to hold Danny out of first grade until his little brother, Henderson, was old enough to attend kindergarten. Walking to school together, the two boys would enjoy some small measure of safety in numbers—or, in the worst case, one little boy might escape to report the lynching of his brother. Hence, thanks to the Ku Klux Klan, Danny Crawford at Franklin was fifteen years old in the eighth grade, with the body of a boy perhaps two years older than that. In the shower after gym class, all the other kids did their best not to stare openly at Danny's nude beauty, which resembled, in ebony, one of those marble Adonises that are strewn all over the Greek landscape and the British Museum. He had the sort of natural sculpted muscle that comes only from genetic good fortune and a very hardworking childhood.

Until my first gym class, I hadn't consciously noticed Danny Crawford, who blended quietly among the other black kids in my class. Danny came by his subtlety studiously. He dressed always in sensible shoes, pressed slacks, a spotless plaid shirt and white underwear. He spoke to adults with the formulaic courtesy customarily instilled in children by nuns, priests and those petty tyrants in Dickens novels who distinguish themselves by beating little boys and kicking dogs. Danny Crawford had suffered serious educational deprivation when he was younger, but he hung academically among the eight-ones by sheer tenacity, excelling at the courses in which he had an aptitude and fighting, tooth and nail, the subjects that bewildered him. In gym, of course, he was transcendent. Even among kids his own age, Danny Crawford would have been superlative. In eighth-grade gym class at the Franklin School, he was a horse among hamsters. His team always won; the other team rarely scored. Usually, Danny Crawford's opponents, try as they might, quickly, respectfully succumbed. There was a certain pride in being on Danny's team, or in losing to him, or in just sharing the same playground. After a game, we had an inevitable ritual—of kids approaching Danny in a mixture of false camaraderie and supplicant meekness to say, "Nice game, Danny."

To which Danny always replied, "Thank you. You, too."

It was like being blessed by Father Willie Mays.

Anyone forced to take gym class three times a week in public school in those days remembers the President's Physical Fitness Tests. Under some sort of government decree, gym teachers everywhere had to subject their pupils to a seemingly endless series of athletic travails, all of which were duly recorded on official scorecards by the gym teacher and, when they were finally completed, mailed off to Washington to become some massive database that politicians would eventually use to trumpet the fact that America's young people had become flabbier, weaker, lazier and slower than any generation in history, and we'd damn well better start shaping them up before the Communists win every event in the Olympics and march on Yankee Stadium. The President's Physical Fitness Tests were a godsend to gym teachers. Since they went on interminably, Mr. Thompson, my gym teacher, was spared week upon week of lesson planning. He simply had to supervise the tests and scrawl results on forms provided by the President's Council on Physical Fitness, which I think (but I wouldn't bet on it) had some connection to either the Reverend Bob Richards or Jack LaLanne.

The beauty part of the President's Physical Fitness Tests was that, although every kid (except Danny Crawford) bombed out on several categories, there was at least one test that was right up each kid's alley. I was barely average when it came to push-ups, pull-ups and rope climbing, but I was so thin and wiry that I could do sit-ups until Mr. Thompson laid a hand on my head and said, "That's fine, son. We don't have all day." My fifty-yard dash was among the best in the class, although a full second slower than Danny Crawford, and my shuttle run—thanks to quick feet—was a veritable blur.

The President's Physical Fitness Tests were an obligation and we grumbled over them appropriately. But secretly, we all loved this stuff, partly because the tests were such a showcase for the magnificence of Danny Crawford. We enjoyed the President's Physical Fitness Tests even more because they were the rarest of competitions among boys. Without threat, boasting, challenge or violence—the usual accompaniment to kid-on-kid showdowns—we measured ourselves. It was scientific! It was democracy! Every kid had to do every test, and no kid could fudge the results by cheating, pounding another kid, bullying the test-taker, skipping a test or two or whining that the sun got in his eyes. Mr. Thompson was an impeccable umpire. In every reasonable case—perhaps once every test, if a kid skidded on a puddle of sweat or collapsed in an asthma attack—Mr. Thompson allowed do-overs. Usually, they didn't help. There were pleasant shocks—always a few reputedly tough kids who couldn't even climb all the way up the rope, who tripped over their own feet and blew their time in the shuttle run, or ended up walking, gasping and blue-faced, the last hundred yards of the 440, lapped gleefully by droves of kids they had trampled and intimidated for half a dozen grades.

Among the last of the tests, after the standing broad jump, the free throw competition and the softball toss, was the high jump. Mr. Thompson set up the standards, crossbar and mat in the middle of the gym, with his customary dispatch, ordering kids crisply around and thanking them for their help. Mr. Thompson was my first gym teacher, and a good introduction to his type. He was an imperturbable sixty-year-old man with a shiny dome, a potbelly, a whistle he never blew and a white T-shirt his wife had laundered at least a thousand times. He knew his role in life, to make kids run around and play games all day for forty-five minutes at a time without breaking into fistfights. He did this efficiently and amiably. He seemed to understand, serenely, that his was not a calling that would alter in any way the fate of humanity, but it would provide him a living wage and an endless flow of small gratifications. He would walk the halls between classes, rather than stay in his office in the gym, just for the pleasure of hearing kids shout at him, "Hi, Mr. Thompson!" to which he would always reply with equal enthusiasm, remembering every kid faultlessly by name—even in the first week of school. Kids didn't exactly get close to Mr. Thompson, but we felt comfortable with him almost immediately. As grownups go, he was almost a kid.

The cool thing about the President's official high jump test was that you got more than one chance. Mr. Thompson started the bar around thirty-six inches, which most kids, except fat Timmy Tollefson and Huge Herbert Roth, cleared with ease. Mr. Thompson offered fat Timmy a second crack, but fat Timmy—knowing his limitations—demurred and found a soft gym mat from which he could watch the rest of the competitors in comfort. Moving up in six-inch increments, Mr. Thompson swiftly reduced the field. By four feet even, survivors were down to a half-dozen. Curiously, I was among them.

Of course, I wasn't a technically sound high-jumper. None of us were, not even Danny Crawford. We had all seen the Olympic high jump and we knew that the proper form for clearing the bar was a technique called the Western roll, in which the jumper—at the peak of his leap—turned his torso parallel to the bar and "rolled" over it, keeping his hands clear and trying not to clip the bar with his trailing leg. Most of us eighth graders taking the President's Physical Fitness Tests, however, were doing the first formal high-jumping (as opposed to hedge-, fence-, dog-, flower-patch- and garbage-can-jumping) of our lives. None of us had either the practice or the coordination to even attempt the Western roll. What we did was hurdle the bar. Despite the absurdity of this method, Mr. Thompson didn't criticize or offer advice. His job was to record our results, not groom the next John Thomas.

Two more kids pooped out at fifty-four inches. Raoul McFadden jiggled the bamboo but cleared the height. A beanpole named Waldrop got over, too—just barely, by sucking in his butt at the last instant before it pulled down the bar. I, fifty-eight inches tall at the time, leapt, leaned sideways, cleared the height and landed on the mat to a shout of surprise from twenty-eight kids. Danny Crawford followed by soaring three inches above the bar.

Mr. Thompson switched to two-inch increments. At fifty-six inches, Raoul and Waldrop crashed the bar. I expected to also. I walked up to it. It touched my forehead. Irresistibly, a girl named Debbie popped into my head. Debbie had been my first crush, in fourth grade. She lived on Elizabeth Street, near T.J.'s house. Every day, I walked Debbie home from school and, to show my love for her—rather than holding hands or writing poems about her limpid eyes and rosebud lips—I jumped over stuff. Anything that stuck up more than a foot off the ground, I jumped over it for Debbie. I jumped over stone walls, rail fences, birdbaths and arborvitae. Debbie's walks home from school became a sort of one-kid, no-horse equestrian show. Rosebushes, for me, were easy. Lawn jockeys were a cinch. There wasn't a trash can in Tomah I couldn't clear with inches to spare. Once, I even got over a mailbox mounted in a whitewashed milk can.

But that had been four grades before. My mother had moved from T.J.'s upstairs to our run-down apartment on Superior Avenue, and I had ceased to walk Debbie home. Beautiful, freckled and redheaded, Debbie had discovered boys—which left me out of the picture. After losing Debbie, I didn't keep up, consistently, with my shrub-jumping. And even when I was in practice, my tallest shrub had never been fifty-six inches!

On the other hand— No! There was no other hand. Fifty-six inches was way too high. I backed away from the high jump pit, took a deep breath, shrugged philosophically and charged. The bar rushed at me. Inches from it, I clenched my teeth, flung up my arms, pushed off the gym floor with all my scrawny strength, tucked my knees into my chin and took flight, waiting to hear the clatter of the bar against my sneakers.

There was no sound, save for the rush of air in my ears, and then a thump, as my Keds hit the mat. I staggered and turned to the bar. A roar went up from the class. The bar hadn't moved. I looked at Mr. Thompson, who was shaking his head, writing on his clipboard and suppressing a leathery smile.

I walked off the mat dumbstruck. Kids started thumping on me. It took a while for me to understand why. In the entire history of this grade, going back for years—before I came to the Franklin School—no kid had ever been *ahead* of Danny Crawford, in any sport. When I realized this, I looked sheepishly toward Danny Crawford. Danny was smiling at me.

He took his jump, coolly, smoothly, and cleared the bar with only a tiny tremble at the end. We were tied again. The earth resumed its normal rotation.

It would have been nice to stop there. There were only two kids left in the President's high jump competition. On the one hand, you had Danny Crawford, who could have walked into the Green Bay Packers locker room and passed for Willie Wood. And there was me, who looked like the tubercular little brother of the ninety-seven-pound weakling in the Charles Atlas ad. This didn't make sense. Not only that, Danny was talking to me, telling me I'd made a terrific jump and encouraging me, as Mr. Thompson inexorably lifted the bar to fifty-eight inches.

I was fifty-eight inches!

Kids were shouting and laughing. "Go, Benjamin!" someone said.

Blomeier was in my gym class. He had hit the bar early, at forty-two inches. I glanced at him. He looked irritable.

"Let's go," said Mr. Thompson. "The bell's going to ring."

I went first, of course. Deep breath. Hard run. I could feel veins bulging in my head. Hey, looka this, Debbie! My head snapped back. My torso bent. My feet cleared the bar. I twisted in the air and succumbed to gravity, dropping straight toward the bar and sucking in my ass. I felt the bar, a brush against my bottom. A pause. A wobble. The click of bamboo as it touched the floor.

All together now:

"Aaw!"

I didn't mind, after all. I had actually cleared fifty-eight inches, just brushing the bar on my way down. And Danny Crawford, after making it over fifty-eight, missed at sixty. I'd ended up within two inches of Danny Crawford, where no man had ever gone before.

"That was really close," he said to me as we trooped to the locker room. He'd almost been defeated—by a pencil-necked shrimp—but he seemed happy about it. I looked for Blomeier in the locker room, hoping for a comment, but couldn't find him. He left without taking a shower.

My first appearance at the football game at the end of Waunona Way was only a week or so later. In choose-ups, Blomeier landed on the opposing team from me, selected by Giles Hamilton. This combination rarely altered over the ensuing weeks. Normally, we played a game up to five touchdowns and then started a new game. We'd play until dark, usually ten or twelve games. If one team strung together three or four lopsided wins, we'd break up and rechoose.

I assumed my customary Catholic role of quiet sacrifice and kamikaze defense. I neither asked for the football nor was it given to me. Sternweiss, my team captain—who later went on to a modest career as a high school fullback—played the dual role of tailback and quarterback. Giles Hamilton did the same for the opposing team (which, always, for some reason, in my mind, was called the Phillies). This was a familiar situation to me, like Overacker and Fin—two egomaniac jocks hogging the ball—and it made my responsibilities blissfully simple. When my team had the ball, I would simply stand at the line of scrimmage, impeding a Phillie. After a few plays, I noticed that this particular Phillie tended to be Blomeier. He made it his habit to line up opposite me. When play started, he would pounce, usually grabbing me by the neck and trying to twist me to the ground. In the interests of my team, I would play along with Blomeier, dancing and writhing with his abuse until I sensed that Sternweiss had either turned the corner or thrown his pass. After a while on offense, my neck was sore and raw and I welcomed the chance to play defense.

On defense, I simply homed in on Giles Hamilton, who was large and athletic, but way slower than me. Also, I discovered something about him that I had difficulty reconciling. Being small and reputedly weak, I imputed to the bigger, better-looking, more popular and arrogant kids in my sphere an *übermensch* invincibility. They moved about inside a sort of force field. Mere mortals bounced off them like flies off a screen door. Only fellow demigods could pierce the shield and bring them down. This wasn't a rational belief, of course, and I knew it wasn't true. Yet, indoctrinated by Blomeier, I looked across the line of scrimmage in my first game against Giles Hamilton and was swept over by a familiar awe. At Franklin School, Giles Hamilton was the white Danny Crawford. Tackling Giles Hamilton, certainly, would be like wrestling with a biblical angel.

Early that first day, the angel had the ball. Giles Hamilton rounded his right end and turned the corner, nothing but me between him and a touchdown. I had a good angle and I lowered my shoulder, expecting to tumble like a tenpin as soon as I made contact. I hit him in the thighs, wrapped his knees and Giles Hamilton hit the grass like a sack of spuds. He had barely gained five yards. I walked back to my huddle, slapped repeatedly on the back by teammates, confused. Giles Hamilton was easy to bring down. Giles Hamilton was soft?

None of my teammates knew this. They were impressed by my tackle. I didn't tell them about Giles Hamilton. It was one of those things you didn't say out loud. It would be like snorking up a loogie at the Communion rail. But as the games wore on, I tackled Giles Hamilton frequently, so often that Blomeier began stalking me, trying to block me before I could get to Giles Hamilton. Blomeier succeeded infrequently, as I made another discovery. Blomeier wasn't a football player.

All in all, the afternoon was shaping up quite strangely. It only got stranger when—with the score tied at four TDs each—Sternweiss prevented a Phillies touchdown by intercepting a Giles Hamilton pass close to our end zone. Giles Hamilton converged on Sternweiss and started pulling him to the ground. Sternweiss turned, saw me nearby and flipped me the ball.

"Go!" he said.

Go?

Who? Me?

Already, three Phillies were almost on top of me, dismemberment in their eyes. On the other hand, the ball felt good nestled in my arm. And my instincts were marvelously in tune with the situation. Faced with large, hostile kids who outnumbered me, my instincts had always flowed straight to my feet. I didn't have to ponder my options.

I ran.

First, I scooted left, fleeing the three Phillies, who constituted a nameless blur in the corner of my eye. As I saw them shift toward me, I noticed, looming darkly in the corner of my other eye, the sideline, which consisted of trees. Again, I reversed my direction. As things turned out, I was able to accomplish this maneuver much more deftly than my pursuers, two of whom bumped into each other. The third simply kept going, into the trees. Suddenly, I was running downfield and there were only two Phillies visible. Giles Hamilton was still tangled with Sternweiss on the grass. Tony De-Marco, thick and nimble with breath like truck exhaust, was closing in on me. Depending again on some sixth sense I had never before deployed, I bore right back at him, until he was close enough to reach out and rip off my lips. Then, I shifted two inches, ducked down beneath Tony's flailing hand and slipped past him.

"*Shit!*"

Blomeier was the last Phillie, but he was easy. I simply ran, right past him. Blomeier did a matador and then followed me, losing ground, eighty yards. I pulled up in the Phillies end zone, near the gravel piles. I was breathing hard, exhilarated, stunned. My cheeks were pink and stinging with the rush of autumn air. I turned to look upfield, toward my teammates, when Blomeier finally caught up, lunging at my head, grabbing my neck and wrenching at it until, to end his struggle, I crumpled to the ground, went fetal and waited for him to let go. This didn't happen.

"Get off him, Blomeier," I heard Sternweiss say, a moment later.

Blomeier stayed attached to me, like a lamprey.

"Yeah," came the voice of Giles Hamilton. "Get up."

Blomeier let go.

I got up. My teammates surrounded me, whacking and tousling me.

"That was great!"

"Faked those suckers right outa their *jocks!*"

None of us, of course, were wearing jocks.

I regarded this whole touchdown episode as a fluke. After all, Giles Hamilton was out of the play and his teammates had simply relaxed when they saw me with the ball. Blomeier's choke hold expressed eloquently his teammates' dismay at giving up a touchdown to a bit-part newcomer. It was an act of natural frustration that I immediately dismissed. Blomeier was, after all, my best friend.

Darkness was encroaching. We started the last game of the day by kicking off to the Phillies. They stalled at midfield and punted. On offense, Sternweiss tried running once and passing once, for a gain of several yards. In the huddle, he said, "What's your name."

"He's Benjamin," said Wayne Westwick.

"Whyncha trying running it once?" said Sternweiss.

"Me?" I said.

"Yeah. You did pretty good last time."

"Yeah," said Wayne Westwick. "He's pretty fast."

Two other kids nodded approvingly.

"Well . . ."

It was getting dark. Sternweiss was getting tired. It was a good time of the afternoon for wild-ass experiments. So we broke the huddle. Fat Timmy Tollefson hiked the ball to Sternweiss, who flipped it to me just as Giles Hamilton tipped over fat Timmy and loomed above me. I did the only thing I could do—planted my feet, clutched the ball and shoved a shoulder into Giles Hamilton. And then I fled, tearing away from his hands and churning like a Mixmaster. Somehow, I was free of Giles Hamilton and pointed upfield. I eluded Tony DeMarco, knocked over the feckless Brusbussen, juked Blomeier and then just tore ass the rest of the way, Phillies gasping in my wake. Just like that, I had another touchdown.

"Jesus *Christ!*" shouted Tony DeMarco. "Son of a *bitch!*"

Before I could turn, again, Blomeier landed, clinging to my neck with one arm while hammering the growth plates in my skull with his free elbow. Eventually, two of my guys arrived and piled atop Blomeier and we all fell in a heap.

The next time we had the ball, just before it got too dark to play, Sternweiss didn't bother to draw up a play, delay or try to deceive anybody. He took fat Timmy's spot at center and hiked the ball straight to me. While he blocked Giles Hamilton, I bobbed my way through the other six Phillies and ran the length of the field, again, for the touchdown. Blomeier, hot on my heels, pounced in the end zone and tried to yank my head off my neck. This became our little tradition.

The next Wednesday, Blomeier didn't invite me to play. Sternweiss did. And Tony DeMarco, Joey Imhoff and Kunkel. Wayne Westwick wouldn't play unless I was on his team. The next week, Sternweiss picked me first for his team. And then he gave me the ball almost every play.

In less than a week, while I rode the bus and went to class, did my homework in front of the television and subsisted largely on cheese sandwiches, word got around Waunona Way that I was the best football player in the neighborhood, a sort of football idiot savant with hips like Crazy Legs Hirsch. It took me a month to adjust to this. Every time Sternweiss huddled up and told me to run the ball, I'd say, "Jeez, Greg. Y'know, the other guys—"

And the other guys would break in, saying, "No, Benjamin. Run the goddamn ball!"

So I ran the goddamn ball. For a long time, I had no idea what

was going on or why I was such a success. Mrs. Ducklow, Mrs.
Schober and the nuns at St. Mary's, whenever faced with a kid who
was an abject failure at virtually everything he attempted, would
spout that old chestnut about how every last person on earth has a
special gift, one little niche of human endeavor wherein he can excel
above all others and express the loving grace of Christ our Lord. Of
course, like all intelligent Catholic schoolboys, I made the Sign of
the Cross and quietly regarded this whole argument as patent bullshit.

All through grade school, I had seen the tall, the strong, the swift,
the handsome, the bright and the affluent among my peers reap notice, praise and reward, while the rest of us gleaned consolation
from the crumbs at their feet. We lived by the motto "Nice try."
Most kids sense, without ever putting the point into words, that it
isn't just the victory that goes to the anointed; the chances to win at
all are carefully portioned out only to the chosen few—to the kids
who get picked first and placed at the head of the line. This was a
rule of life as strict as Paladin's stoic Code, and I didn't resent it. But
suddenly, down at the end of Waunona Way, my orderly universe
trembled on its foundations. Getting the football every play wasn't
like striking it rich on Wall Street, or going to Harvard on a full
scholarship. It was just a game, after all. But, among the kids in the
game, neither Wall Street nor Harvard had much meaning. Getting
picked first, getting the football, scoring touchdowns, these were
the coin of our realm. For that moment, throughout that damp and
colored autumn, I was the kid I had always stood by and watched. I
was Fin. I was Gunderson. I would've been Overacker if I could've
worked up the attitude—which was the only hard part. I was surprised every time I got picked ahead of bigger, stronger, handsomer
kids like Giles Hamilton, Tony DeMarco, Joey Imhoff and even
Blomeier. I was embarrassed every time my teammates insisted I
take the ball and run. I was shocked to elude the rangy romeos and
lumbering brutes on the other team. Every touchdown seemed a
fluke, especially when—invariably—my penance for success was
Blomeier, wrapped around my neck and pummeling my head.

The other kids dealt more equably with my talent. The only kids unenthusiastic about my emergence as the neighborhood football star were Blomeier and Giles Hamilton. Not that I caught on. I still hung out on Simpson Street with Blomeier, talked with him at the bus stop, and thought of him as my best friend. Giles Hamilton's approval really didn't apply. He occupied a plane beyond my ken; he associated with me only on Wednesdays, for football. His station in life had made him cool, unapproachable, inscrutable—and better than me, except for the only flaw I had ever perceived in Giles Hamilton. He was, I thought, soft.

I changed my mind one day, during a game.

I had jigged and ducked through several Phillies and outrun two more. I was sprinting down the sidelines, and the final obstacle was Giles Hamilton, who had been playing deep. He chose an angle to intercept me and turned on the jets. I saw him in the corner of my eye and realized I couldn't cut back toward the middle of the field. I was committed to a straight line. I ran as fast as I could but Giles Hamilton's angle was inescapable. He had me. At full bore, he closed in, left his feet and speared me, head-first, head-on and keening deep in his throat like a puma felling a wapiti. From me—I was barely ninety pounds and both my feet were in the air during impact—he didn't encounter much friction. We stayed airborne for about thirty feet until we hit a copse of maple saplings in the woods. Spindly trunks snapped like jackstraws. We crashed, bounced, tumbled and skidded another three yards before the underbrush got a grip. I found myself propped up against the trunk of an aspen. Within seconds, both teams were in the woods, half rushing toward Giles Hamilton and me to count broken bones, the other half looking for the football. Rubbery, young and unpadded, neither of us was hurt—or even seriously bruised. We both rose a little wobbly. I said, "Woo! Nice tackle, Giles."

Giles Hamilton almost smiled. "You okay?" he said.

"Yeah," I replied as it occurred to me that all along, this kid hadn't been soft at all. He had simply been rich. Watching me streak down the sideline on the way to my fiftieth touchdown in the last

month or so—every one of them scored against his team—Giles
Hamilton had ditched a lifetime of well-schooled, dignified reserve
and lowered himself right down to my level.

In the end, Giles Hamilton's flying tackle felt better for me than
it did for him. I sure remembered it longer.

Besides, I got the touchdown the next play.

And Blomeier grabbed me by the neck.

We knew the season was almost over when kids started wearing
gloves for the whole game and the pockets of snow along the edge
of the field went all week without melting. Some of us began to
sense we'd never do this again. Next year was high school. Half
these kids would be trying out for varsity sports, or other after-
school activities. Some of us wouldn't even go to the same high
school. Sternweiss, in fact, made first string on the freshman football team. Giles Hamilton developed into an all-conference hockey
player. Tony DeMarco was a basketball star at Edgewood, the
Catholic high school. Blomeier's family moved the following summer, and he ended up at Monona Grove High.

Our swan song came in the icy gloaming a week before Thanksgiving. My team was up 4–3, and we were close to the winning
score, on what would have been the Phillies' twenty-yard line—if
we'd had yard lines. But it was fourth down, and all seven Phillies
across the line of scrimmage knew I was going to run the ball. This
inspired, in Sternweiss, a bit of trickery.

"Wayne," he said in the huddle. "You be the quarterback, okay?"

"Me?" said Wayne Westwick.

"Yeah," said Sternweiss, "but you're not gonna get the ball."

"I'm not?"

"Benjamin," said Sternweiss.

"Yeah?"

"You stand behind Wayne, okay? And sort of over to the side."

"Okay."

"Timmy," said Sternweiss.

"Yeah?"

"Make like you're gonna hike to Wayne. Only don't. Hike it over to Benjamin. Okay?"

"Like crooked," said fat Timmy Tollefson.

"Right."

"So I don't get the ball?" said Wayne Westwick.

"Right," said Sternweiss.

"Benjamin gets it."

"Yeah."

"Past me."

"Yeah."

"Only I'm at quarterback," said Wayne Westwick.

"You just stand there, okay? Like you're gonna get the ball."

"But I don't."

"Right."

"Got it," said Wayne Westwick.

"You sure?" asked Sternweiss.

"What am I? Stupid?" said Wayne.

"Yeah," said Imhoff. Everyone snickered. Wayne slugged Imhoff in the arm. Imhoff slugged back. Wayne retaliated. Et cetera.

Sternweiss went to the line of scrimmage, muttering instructions to fat Timmy. Clearly, this setup wasn't much of a trick, but Sternweiss wasn't exactly Weeb Ewbank in the strategy department. Besides, all he wanted was to cause a little hesitation among a few Phillies—which was all I usually needed for a mere twenty-yard touchdown trot.

We lined up. Everybody was breathing a little hard, visible puffs of air curling past our ears. The cold had made our noses red and our cheeks rosy, except for Mike Merkle, who was too swarthy to ever show much color but his own. By the end of the game, our shirts and sweaters had all been yanked out of shape, torn in places, and they hung off us like draperies in a gutted house. Our pants were pulled down to half-mast, our knees baggy and shiny with chlorophyll. Our hands stung with cold weather, scraped knuckles and hairline cuts. I noticed that fat Timmy Tollefson, his great moon of a face pointed at Wayne Westwick, his eyes trained on me, was bleeding from the chin. We all felt good.

"Hike!" shouted Wayne Westwick.

Timmy Tollefson hiked the ball, angling it neatly in my direction. It was a perfect hike, except for Wayne Westwick, who—probably because he completely forgot what he was supposed to do—lurched to his left, stuck out an arm and knocked the ball into the air. It soared over my head, bounced ten yards behind and kept going, the wrong way. I turned and chased the ball, way past midfield.

By the time I had picked up the ball and turned to check out how bad the situation was, I faced a phalanx of Phillies. My teammates, as kids are prone to do when their best-laid plans gang aft a-gley, were still standing where I had left them. Far downfield, at the line of scrimmage, Sternweiss was whacking Wayne Westwick in the chest and shouting something at him. Good, I thought.

Meanwhile, Tony DeMarco was descending on me. None of my teammates were blocking for me. A few were arguing. The rest just stood stock-still, staring. Great.

> . . . *Paladin, Paladin,*
> *Far, far from home.*

To stall the DeMarco disaster, I shifted right and starting running laterally, looking for a crack in the Phillies. There wasn't much there, so I said to myself what the hell and steered upfield. Tony DeMarco was now behind me, closing in, breathing hard enough that I could smell him. With Tony on my heels, I couldn't slow down when Giles Hamilton planted in my path and spread. I ran straight ahead and he caught me in his arms. This collision should have ended the play, but—as a last resort—I made a little juke to my left and hit Giles Hamilton clean in the temple with my hipbone. He grunted, let me go and went down like a clay pigeon.

Next up were Huge Herbert Roth and Ricky Sparrow, closing in from two sides. I slipped between them with a little burst, but then found myself nose-to-nose with Mike Merkle, who would drag you down by your nuts and your shoelaces if he could catch hold. I did a little jig, left-right-left, and somehow eluded Merkle's implacable talons.

For a few seconds, I had some space. But there were still more Phillies to go and Tony DeMarco in gasping pursuit. That was when everything slowed down and cleared up.

Beyond its sheer pleasure, I rarely thought how I felt when I ran with the football. But if I could have named the sensation, I would have said that the way running with the ball made me feel was *bigger*. The football was like one of Alice's cakes. I cradled the ball, spotted the holes in the defense, took my first step and grew. In one step, I was the same size as everybody, even Huge Herbert Roth. One step more and I was bigger. I was greased Goliath. I sometimes wonder if the great small guys in football, Tommy McDonald, Mel Gray, Barry Sanders, ever felt that same sudden, inexplicable rush of bigness.

Whenever I got big, things brightened in front of me and slowed to a crawl. I saw where everybody was, I measured distances and did geometry, I could feel movement behind my back. As I faked out Mike Merkle that day, I did my calculations and saw the only real remaining problem, which was Blomeier. He hadn't chased me. He was parked at the goal line, patrolling, waiting, seething. Blomeier wasn't fast, strong or agile, and he had never been able to bring me down. But this was his last play of the whole season. He had scores to settle with me. I had spurned Blomeier's patronage and ruffled Blomeier's ego. I had tampered with the proper balance of society. Blomeier tensed and glowered and waited for me.

A few weeks before, finally, I had given up the fantasy of Blomeier as my best friend. He thereafter abandoned all efforts to mold me in his image, and—save for the occasional burst of brief violence and the inevitable end zone choke holds—we had ceased all intercourse. My Blomeier void was filled by other kids, who had come to believe a backyard football game was incomplete unless I was invited. I was feeling at home at Franklin School, where not one kid cared if my mother was a fallen-away Catholic divorcée on welfare. Half the student body was in the same boat, plus they were black, or white trash, or their old man was in jail, or their parents couldn't afford to pay the heating bill. The south side was the tough part of Madison, but gentler than Tomah. I got good grades at Franklin, and this seemed fine with everybody there, even the eight-twos, who still said hi in the hall. Thanks to Rocky, Rudy still left me alone, and made up for it by ragging on Blomeier. This was another ax for Blomeier to grind.

I dipped and spun once, eluding two more Phillies and catching a backwards glimpse of Tony DeMarco, who was giving up the chase. My teammates were the only players close to me now, except for Blomeier, who slid menacingly toward my angle of approach. He poised himself to block me from the end zone at all costs.

It wasn't as if I wasn't going to score. Even if Blomeier tackled me, my momentum would carry me to the touchdown. But that wasn't the point. Blomeier didn't care about one more damn touch-down. He didn't care about football. He wanted my head. He was going to rip it right off my neck, or dislocate his elbows in the effort.

I churned toward Blomeier, girding myself for the pain. At least this would be Blomeier's last choke.

I was maybe ten yards short of Blomeier when Danny Crawford flashed unsummoned into my mind. Danny Crawford smiling at me, slapping my shoulder and saying, "Nice jump, Benjamin."

Jump?

Why hadn't I thought of this before? I wasn't just a runner. I was also a jumper. Blomeier was barely taller than me—sixty inches if he was an inch. But there on the goal line, Blomeier was crouched. He stood maybe fifty-four inches, from shoetops to buzzcut. I could do fifty-four inches.

My teammates' footsteps pounding in my ears, I squeezed the ball, speeded up and aimed myself at Blomeier.

Right in Blomeier's face—which was suffused with a hatred I never came to fathom—right toward Blomeier's hands—which were reaching out to tear open my trachea—I planted a Ked and reprised my President's Physical Fitness high jump.

Blomeier's hands grabbed at air. His eyes tracked upward, following my sneaker soles—which cleared the top of his head by six inches. I landed on my feet in the end zone, bumping butts with Blomeier. I had barely turned before my team, shoving Blomeier aside, engulfed me—laughing at the football season's most improbable play. Sternweiss, Wayne Westwick, Joey Imhoff and all the others covered me with thumps of praise and then both teams ended the season with one last, celebratory pigpile. Fat Timmy Tollefson was the last to pile on, and he almost killed all of us.

We headed back to Waunona Way together, pushing our bikes and talking loud. The exceptions were Giles Hamilton and Blomeier, who had skipped the pigpile. They were gone already, before we noticed.

Happy ending.

DAVID BENJAMIN was born in Sparta, Wisconsin, in 1949 and lived in nearby Tomah until he was thirteen. He began his first novel, *The Adventures of Stanley and Peggy, the Sniderman Twins,* in the fourth grade. It remains unfinished. A contributor to the *Chicago Tribune, The Philadelphia Inquirer,* the *San Francisco Chronicle,* and the *Wisconsin State Journal,* Benjamin is also the author of *The Joy of Sumo: A Fan's Notes.* He now lives with his wife in San Francisco and Paris.

A B O U T   T H E   T Y P E

This book was set in Galliard, a typeface designed by Matthew Carter for the Mergenthaler Linotype Company in 1978. Galliard is based on the sixteenth-century typefaces of Robert Granjon.

3/02

A16
3/3